T0373475

List of Tables and Figures

Acknowledgments

This book is the culmination of years of learning, during which I have benefitted from the knowledge and help of countless people. My foremost thanks must go to my "adoptive" families who opened their homes and hearts to me during my stays in Costa Rica. *Muchísimas grácias a doña Lila Falcon Calera, y a Abilio Mora Mora, Amable Godínez Guzmán, Ritxy Mora Godínez, y Xiani Mora Godínez por haberme hecho parte de sus familias.* I must also thank the hundreds of other families of Santa Cruz and Palomas who answered my queries not just with information but with their hospitality and friendship as well. Times have been tough for coffee-producing households in Costa Rica, and tremendous strains have been put on families who grapple with difficult decisions about coffee production and migration. One might suspect that such stress would harden people to the world, but the Costa Rican families who opened their hearts and hearths to me in the early 1990s remained wonderfully open, generous, and giving during my research visit in 2006.

Much of the research for this study concerned the operations of Coopeagri, R.L. In San Isidro, I am grateful to the managers, directors, and employees of Coopeagri who talked with me for hours on end about coffee and cooperatives in Costa Rica, gave me tours of their facilities, and allowed me access to their records. I would also like to extend my thanks to the managers of the La Meseta, El Aguila, and El General *beneficios* for telling me about their factories and explaining the technical aspects of coffee processing. In San José, historian Elizabeth Fonseca kindly took time to help me become oriented, the Universidad de Costa Rica allowed me use of their library, and the employees at ICAFE helped me sort through their stacks of archival materials. Many thanks, as well, to the cooperative leaders, factory workers, and farmers of Coope Montes de Oro, and CoopeSarapiqui for all their time and assistance during my 2006 visit.

Writing is a solitary endeavor but certainly one that builds on the insight of others. I received many useful comments on earlier drafts of this book, especially from Laurel Bossen. Donald Von Eschen, Hal Benenson, and Robyn Eversol also provided useful advice. Later versions benefitted in particular from the wisdom of Richard Wilk and anonymous reviewers of the manuscript. Brian Thom made my map presentable. Gaby Vargas-Cetina helped with Spanish translations—all errors, of course, are mine. I have enjoyed working with the staff of Northern Illinois University Press, who have all done a marvelous job. Monique Lefebvre was my wonderfully efficient and cheerful research assistant in Costa Rica in 2006.

Financial support for this research was provided in part by an Alexander Laidlaw Fellowship for Cooperative Studies; from McGill University I received a Graduate Faculty Research Grant, Friends of McGill Fellowship, Max Bell Fellowship, and a summer bursary from the Department of Anthropology. Throughout the research and writing of this book, the Department of Anthropology and the center for Society, Technology, and Development (STANDD) at McGill University provided me with the use of their facilities. Follow-up research in 1993 was funded in part by a STANDD research stipend. Follow-up research in 2006 was funded by a New Initiatives research grant from the University of Ottawa.

I could not have written this book without the support of my family. My parents set me on this path by instilling in me a wonder of the world and a love of learning. My daughter, Rose, has lifted spirits with singing and dancing. My greatest debt is to my husband, Donald Attwood, who throughout has been a sounding board, a comfort, and a friend.

Preface

I descended from the Talamanca Mountains into Costa Rica's Valle del General for the first time during the *veranillo* (little summer) of June 1990. While I had spent a month in 1988 in the *Meseta Central* (central plateau region around San José) conducting an evaluation of a USAID-sponsored tourism and development program, this was my first venture south. From the hairpin turns of the Pan American highway, I searched for signs that Pérez Zeledón was the "rapidly developing" canton my friends in San José (the capital city) had described. As the cloud forest thinned and the valley came into view, small homesteads and *cafetales* (coffee fields) appeared, much like those I had seen in the Meseta Central surrounding San José.

The dynamic character of Pérez Zeledón I had heard so much about was not apparent at first. Shops in the municipal center of San Isidro were sparsely stocked; its streets were unpaved and pot-holed; and apart from four coffee-processing factories, there was little industry. Muddy, rutted roads crawled through the canton's eleven districts. Yet, new homes and businesses—primarily agricultural supply stores and service sector enterprises—were springing up everywhere. During the next year, hundreds of women and men opened their lives to me, and I discovered that hopes for opportunities of a good life ran high.

As in much of Costa Rica, the economic bustle of Pérez Zeledón has its foundations in coffee. Following the completion of the Pan American highway in the late 1940s, thousands were drawn from the crowded Central Valley to this new frontier with hopes that *el grano de oro*—the golden bean, as coffee is called in Costa Rica—would bring them a better life. And on the whole, it has. Nevertheless, supporting a family by growing an export commodity crop for volatile world markets is a risky and frequently frustrating task.

Family farmers in Costa Rica have much in common with household enterprises throughout the world. Like smallholder sugarcane farmers in Maharashtra (Attwood 1992), cocoa farmers in Nigeria (Berry 1975), or Kekchi Maya farmers in Belize (Wilk 1991), their farms are relatively small, and the "family household is the major corporate social unit for mobilizing agricultural labor, managing productive resources, and organizing consumption" (Netting 1993: 2). Like their counterparts in Colombia (Ortiz 1973) and Venezuela (Roseberry 1983), coffee-producing households in Costa Rica have long had to shape their economic strategies to deal with limited resources, household dynamics, local elites, state policies regulating the domestic economy, and the risks and uncertainties of both crops and markets.

To the outsider, family farmers in Pérez Zeledón may not appear sophisticated. They use no tractors, no mechanical harvesters, no fancy machinery to tend their coffee trees. Like Colombia's fictional Juan Valdez, they hand-pick their coffee, which they then deliver to collection stations any way they can—by truck, mule, oxcart, wheelbarrow, or even by shoulder. Despite the small scale and seeming simplicity of their operations, they are not naive. Farmers are aware that an increase in import tariffs on agricultural inputs (such as fertilizers and pesticides), a severe frost in Brazil, or a war halfway around the world can dramatically alter their lives. On any given day they have at their fingertips news of world events and local and international coffee prices.

As small and relatively independent producers who control much of the production process, these domestic enterprises are often more flexible than larger producers, but they are nonetheless subordinated to larger economic and political units. Although by Central American standards small-scale farmers in Costa Rica have fared relatively well, the country since the beginning of the 1980s has been facing the results of a severe debt crisis that "crippled the economy, eroded financial security, and aggravated social tensions" (Brockett 1990: 94; see also Castillo 1988; Rodriguez 1988; Villasuso Etomba 1989). By the late 1980s the situation had improved, but the crisis was not over. The failure in 1989 of the International Coffee Organization (ICO) to renew its agreement regulating the international coffee trade resulted, yet again, in a glutted, unstable, and ever-more competitive global market. Since then, revenues for the Costa Rican state and its farmers have fallen sharply.

The booms and busts of the world coffee market are not new to Costa Rican coffee farmers; as prices plummeted in 1990, the problems of making ends meet were constant topics of conversation among the cowboy-hatted farmers and their families who crowded San Isidro on market day. They are not the only people in this predicament. As rising aspirations, standards of living, and expanding trade agreements, such as GATT and NAFTA, draw millions of smallholders throughout the world into international markets, family farmers worldwide face a number of challenges, both old and new.

Consumers in the industrialized world do not always recognize the ways in which their lives are entwined with those of family farmers in the non-industrialized world. As I began my work in Costa Rica, I wondered about the links in the complicated chain that connected me and my morning cup to the *cafeteros* (coffee farmers) of Costa Rica. How have they coped in this complex economic environment? Could they continue to do so?

Coffee production and marketing are daily concerns for the people among whom I lived. They depend on the yields of their coffee trees and the price of the crop to provide their families with food, clothing, and a secure home. Hence, this book focuses on coffee as a commercial crop.

But coffee production is also entwined in people's larger efforts to build better lives. Most of the men and women I met want more than mere survival: they want to improve their standard of living and build better communities for themselves and their children. They want clean water and good health, fine schools, better roads, and playgrounds and community centers where they can enjoy their leisure time with friends and family. This book, therefore, is also about the struggle of ordinary people to build better communities, at times in conjunction with—though often despite—development projects planned and promoted through national and international agencies. It is about how farming families, acting together and alone, cope with their realities and their dreams in a rapidly changing, unpredictable, and often hostile world.

WHEN I FIRST WENT to Pérez Zeledón in 1990, I found that coffee producing families in the villages of Santa Cruz and Palomas (not their actual names) were overall fairly optimistic concerning coffee production and their futures in general. For the most part, the Costa Rican government had been fairly supportive of small farmers. Most families had devised strategies both within the household and collectively, through regional processing cooperatives and community development associations within their communities, that allowed them to weather the periodic crises that appeared. Coopcagri, then the region's only coffee-processing cooperative, was instrumental in providing competition to the private processing companies in the canton and therefore in ultimately helping farmers obtain the highest prices possible for their coffee.

When I returned to Costa Rica in the summer of 2006 to study the impacts of the prolonged coffee crisis and of Fair Trade on coffee farming families, I found a country strikingly different, yet at heart very much the same. Though the North-American-style shopping malls of San José have yet to reach Pérez Zeledón, the canton has seen enormous changes, as well. Once muddy, dirt roads are now paved; cars are no longer the possessions of a few; communication is facilitated by cellphones and home telephones. Coopeagri has flourished and now operates several large supermarkets and gas stations throughout the canton.

For farming families, though, times have not been altogether good. In the thirteen years between my visits, the coffee crisis has grown worse, and many farmers had torn up their coffee crop and brought in dairy cattle—or more commonly, left their farms in search of wage labor jobs elsewhere. In the years since my initial research, the Fair Trade movement gained tremendous ground. This movement is part of a growing trend in "ethical" consumption: Northern consumers are buying coffee that is grown in socially and environmentally sustainable ways. Thus, when I returned to Costa Rica, I was curious whether production for Fair Trade might provide farming families with a way to cope with this on-going crisis. My research efforts in 2006 brought me to speak again with farmers in Pérez Zeledón and to speak also with farmers in two cantons in the provinces of Herédia and Puntarenas; these farmers have a much longer history with Fair Trade production than do those in Pérez Zeledón. At the moment, Fair Trade and other markets for "sustainable coffee" provide farming families with new markets and at times higher prices than the conventional coffee market, but these new markets are small, unreliable, and place certification demands on farmers that many find burdensome.

About the Research

I conducted ethnographic fieldwork in Costa Rica for one year in 1990-91, for an additional month in the summer of 1993, with migrant workers in Connecticut in the summer of 1995, and in the cantons of Pérez Zeledón, Herédia, and Puntarenas in July 2006. Like all anthropological research, this work was part of a long process shaped by both interests and opportunities. My own interests in the mundane aspects of farming households began early. Though mine was not a farming family, I have spent much of my life observing farmers. I have vivid childhood memories of German farmers tilling their tidy fields in the Rhine Valley; as I grew in rural Maryland, fields of corn and sorghum dominated the landscape, and my classmates at school talked often of harvesting crops and slaughtering livestock. Later, during four years spent working and traveling in Europe and Morocco, I enjoyed the charms of Amsterdam, Paris, Barcelona, and Fez, but it was the sight of bent backs laboring in open fields that intrigued me the most. Another year traveling through Africa showed me worlds where household production was the norm, yet geopolitics, commodity markets, and tourism were clearly powerful forces of change. When I returned to my native New Mexico to study anthropology, I saw similar forces at work among the family farmers of the Rio Grande Valley. The survival of such household producers in contemporary societies intrigued me.

I was led to Costa Rica as much by opportunity and chance, as by interest. After completing my master's degree on San Juan Paiute women and their basket-weaving cooperative, I worked briefly as a consultant on a USAID project that brought a small group of rural Costa Ricans to New Mexico for training in tourism and sustainable development. Many in this group were small small coffee farmers, and several were members of a coffee cooperative. I spent many hours discussing coffee production and coffee cooperatives with them.

When I was sent to Costa Rica in 1988 to evaluate the USAID project, I was further intrigued by the overwhelming presence of coffee in Costa Rican life and the large number of smallholder cooperatives. Later that same year I decided to continue my research in anthropology; and my interests in household producers and cooperatives, my Spanish language skills, and my contacts in Costa Rica led me back to that country.

My initial intent in 1990 was to evaluate the effectiveness of cooperatives in helping small-scale coffee farmers cope with the risks of export commodity production. A principle aim of my research was to compare household economic strategies among these farmers, focusing, for example, on the criteria they used in choosing to sell their crop to cooperative or private coffee-processing factories. Because of the dominant role that coffee played in the lives of these farmers, it made sense to use a commodity approach, or what Marcus calls a "follow the thing" research strategy (1995). By focusing on historical and contemporary linkages between coffee farmers, processors, and marketers, I hoped to better understand the world system as an integral part of the local context, "rather than something monolithic or external" (1995: 102).

Following the advice of Costa Rican acquaintances, I decided to conduct my research in Pérez Zeledón, rather than with the farmers I already knew in Turrialba. Pérez Zeledón was noted as one of the fastest-growing coffee regions in the country. It also had a large coffee-processing cooperative and four private factories, which would give me the opportunity to compare the performance of private and cooperative factories from the point of view of the small farmer.

After several weeks of talking to farmers and agricultural extension agents and visiting communities throughout Pérez Zeledón, I decided to focus on the farming communities of Palomas and Santa Cruz in part because they were comparable in terms of size, infrastructure, and resources. An equally important reason for choosing these two communities was that I wanted to contrast farmers who sell coffee to a cooperative with those who sell to private factories. Agricultural extension agents and cooperative officials reported that Santa Cruz had a high proportion of co-op members and was *muy coopertavista*, whereas Palomas was known for having very few co-op members. Thus, during the initial stages of field research, I had hopes that community-level factors would help explain why some farming households use the cooperative while others do not. I soon realized that the reported contrasts were exaggerated and that households in both communities presented a more complex pattern of production and marketing strategies. Nevertheless, the study of two villages did broaden the scope of the research and allowed for comparisons in unanticipated ways.

As my research progressed, I also became aware that the cooperative was only part of the lives of farming families in Pérez Zeledón—and for many a very small part—so I expanded my research beyond merely trying to evaluate the effectiveness of the cooperative as an intermediary between small farmers and the world market. I began to focus on the myriad problems that coffee-producing households face and the variety of ways in which they try to cope.

During my stay in each community, I lived with local families. In Santa Cruz, I boarded with a family who lived about two kilometers from the village center. In Palomas, I rented a room from a single, elderly woman in the center of the community. In order to observe work patterns throughout the entire agricultural season in both communities, during the year of my research I stayed alternately two or three weeks in each community. These living arrangements enabled me to observe at close range a variety of activities and interpersonal relationships in the communities. My "adopted" families were warm-hearted and extremely supportive. My incorporation into their households as a temporary family member not only provided me with companionship and moral support but also allowed me to gain a better understanding of household and family dynamics.

I was, of course, a curiosity in Palomas and Santa Cruz, and residents were concerned about my objectives. People were intrigued that I was an American by birth, a Canadian by choice; curious about my status as a wife away from her husband and as a daughter away from her family; suspicious because I was a stranger—perhaps working for the government to increase their taxes, possibly even working for the CIA.

I was gradually able to reassure people that I was essentially a naive student wanting to learn about coffee farmers and their problems. Most people soon felt confident that I was not working undercover for either the Costa Rican government or the CIA and that I would preserve their anonymity in my writings. (Except for public figures, acting in public contexts, pseudonyms are used here.) Some suspicions may have lingered, but as I became better known as *buena gente* (good people), all but a few soon became my teachers, not only answering the questions I posed but offering personal information and insight into their lives.

In addition to conducting informal inquiries and participant observation, during this first year of research I systematically collected data in three stages, beginning with a general census of all households in each community to determine the size and composition of each village and to identify the coffee-producing households. Next, I selected a stratified sample of seventy-six coffee-producing households (see Chapter 3) and did two follow-up interviews of each. In the first, I collected detailed information on landholdings, crop production, and processing-factories used, including reasons for their selection. I also probed for people's general attitudes and responses to changes in the Costa Rican economy and the international coffee market. Because I had already met these families during the initial census and had come to know some of them quite well, the interviews were generally relaxed, often characterized by friendly joking and lively banter. Stereotypes of generous Costa Rican hospitality are well deserved. I was frequently treated to coffee or sodas and something to eat (tamales, cakes, and rice pudding were frequent treats). More often than not I was sent home with a backpack full of fresh oranges, mangoes, or other goodies.

Because the first follow-up interview focused on agricultural production, I interviewed mainly senior male members of the household. Though most men did not hesitate to provide information concerning production, marketing strategies, and yields, I had some difficulty obtaining detailed information concerning incomes. Of the women interviewed, about ten in each community (roughly one-quarter of sample households) eagerly answered any question I posed, but most were reluctant to discuss coffee production aside from their participation in the harvest. For particulars concerning production I was consistently told that I must speak with their husbands. Usually these same women were present during the the second follow-up interviews with their husbands, participating to various degrees in the discussion. Women were more enthusiastic in talking about their other income-earning activities, particularly the few who were engaged in entrepreneurial activities in their homes.

The second follow-up interviews were conducted between three and six months later, so that I could confirm data gathered during the first session and collect additional information on political activities, community involvement, and non-agricultural sources of income. While men and women were often both present for the discussions on agriculteral activities, on the latter topics, I interviewed men and women separately. All my interviews went very smoothly, though with busy lives, the families did not always find it easy to schedule time to talk to the *gringa* anthropologist. (The term *"gringa"* is not used pejoratively in this area—is simply a descriptive term. Attitudes toward North Americans are generally not hostile.)

In all my work, I sought both quantitative and qualitative data. Fine qualitative data are the trademark of the anthropologist and provide the crucial ethnographic context within which quantitative data need to be analyzed. Though I offer no elaborate statistical analyses here, quantitative data provided an invaluable double check on assumptions and hypotheses that I formed daily through less structured methods. Often, assumptions made on the basis of information obtained through interviews and casual conversations proved erroneous when I carefully added up the number of cases. Thus, throughout my research and the writing of this book, I have tried to strike a balance between these equally important types of data.

In addition to formal interviews, I also learned about household production activities, labor use, and social activities by attending bi-weekly community meetings and monthly meetings of the cooperative's Women's Group, by picking coffee and helping with other farm chores, and through the all-important afternoon gossip sessions on neighbors' front porches. The eagerness of neighbors to befriend me and, in their turn, extract information from me, provided me with many opportunities to learn not just about their lives but about their perceptions of me and my work, as well. I had little trouble communicating in Spanish and collected much of my data through informal conversations. To gain additional background information, a local research assistant in each community helped by gathering genealogical data on sample families.

To understand the operations of the coffee-processing factories and the working of the international coffee market, I interviewed factory managers and employees and gathered information from primary and secondary sources provided by the factories and by the Costa Rican Coffee Institute (ICAFE). Managers at Coopeagri, the coffee-processing cooperative in Pérez Zeledón, were particularly open and helpful, taking time from their busy schedules to talk with me and giving me access to reports, archived materials, and data from their computer databases.

In 2006, my follow-up research on the continuing coffee crisis and farmers' perspectives on Fair Trade led me back to the villages of Palomas and Santa Cruz in Pérez Zeledón, as well as to Herédia and northern Puntarenas provinces. In order to understand the role of Fair Trade in the Costa Rican coffee sector, I conducted semiformal and informal interviews with officials at ICAFE and cooperative leaders and *beneficio* employees at CoopeSarapiqui (Herédia), Coope Montes de Oro (Puntarenas), and Coopeagri (Pérez Zeledón). Farmers' perspectives and responses to the current crisis, and their understandings and perceptions of Fair Trade, were obtained through multiple informal interviews with six coffee farmers and members of their families in these three regions.

This book rests on comparative research and analysis at several levels: between two rural communities; among households within those communities; between cooperative and private coffee processors; among coffee-producing nations in Latin America; and between Fair Trade and free trade markets. This approach allows us to understand better how people's responses to global challenges are mediated by cultural, social, economic, and political factors at the household, community, and regional levels. Household strategies incorporate a mixture of accommodation, resistance, and reshaping of internal and external influences. But, as we shall see, the ease with which family farmers can adapt to an increasingly globalized economy depends also on national visions of the family farmer and on state policies that affect their futures.

In writing this book, I did not want to present a travelogue of me and my journey of discovery. Instead I try to present what that journey led me to understand about the lives of family farmers working to support themselves in an increasingly complex world. The enthusiastic responses I received when I asked people to describe and explain the events in their lives lead me to believe that what is written here reflects their real concerns, too. I hope this book does justice to what they taught me.

Abbreviations

ACPC	Association of Coffee Producing Countries
ADC	*asociacióne de desarrollo comunal* (community development associations)
BNCR	*Banco Nacional de Costa Rica*
CACM	Central American Common Market
CEPN	*Centro para el estudio de los problemas nacionales* (Costa Rican Center for the Study of National Problems)
Coopeagri	*Cooperativa agro-industrial de Pérez Zeledón* (Agro-Industrial Cooperative of Pérez Zeledón)
DINADECO	*direction nacional de desarrollo comunal* (National Institute for Community Development)
Fedecoop	Federacion de Cooperativas (Federation of Cooperatives)
GATT	General Agreement on Tariffs and Trade
ICA	International Coffee Agreement
ICAFE	Instituto de Cafe (Costa Rica Coffee Institute)
ICO	International Coffee Organization
IDA	*Instituto de desarrollo agraria* (Institute for Agrarian Development)
ITCO	Instituto de Tierras y Colonización (Land and Colonization Institute)
NAFTA	North American Free Trade Agreement
NGO	Non-governmental Organization
UPIAV	*union de productores independientes de agroproductos various* (Union of Independent Producers of Various Agricultural Products)

Farmers of the
Golden
Bean

Part One

Coffee and the Family Farmer

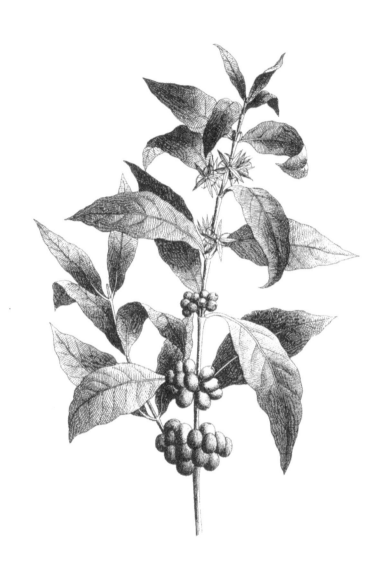

1

The Fate of the Family Farmer

For seven months, Flavio Valentes and his seventeen-year-old daughter Rocío have watched the sun rise and set over the concrete boulevards and tidy suburban houses of Connecticut, a strange sight for a Costa Rican coffee farmer. But tomorrow he and his daughter will return to Costa Rica and their much-missed family. The savings from their minimum-wage jobs as landscape gardener and chambermaid will cover most of the debts left behind when fate and the world coffee market conspired against them.

Flavio is no stranger to the ups and downs of coffee farming. Raised on a small coffee farm in the Central Valley surrounding San José, he learned young how to coax coffee to give its best. Looking for better opportunities in the expanding frontier of Pérez Zeledón, his father sold their farm in Terrazú and moved south. There he was able to buy twice as much land, but he soon defaulted on his loan from an agrochemical company, and the farm was confiscated. There was to be no inheritance for Flavio and his twelve brothers and sisters.

But in Pérez Zeledón, Flavio met and married his wife, Hannia. They had two daughters and supported themselves on the coffee farm Hannia inherited from her father. During the 1970s and early 1980s, coffee was good to them. They built a concrete house, bought a truck, invested in new land, and banked their savings in a few head of cattle. When coffee prices dropped dramatically in the early 1990s, the Valentes family worried but were confident that they could ride out the bust. But prices continued to drop and costs continued to increase.

When they heard that credit was available for pig production and that a slaughterhouse in San José was predicting a market boom, they, like thousands of other desperate coffee farmers, quickly invested in pigs—hoping to recover their losses from coffee. Before long, pig production nationwide exceeded demand; prices did not even cover the cost of transport to slaughter. As a final blow, a pig disease swept the country, and the Valentes lost half their herd.

By early 1995, many of their neighbors had been forced to sell their lands, and they themselves were heavily in debt. One evening the family decided that, rather than sell any land to pay their debts, Flavio and Rocío would go to the United States.

After seven months of hard, lonely work, they are ecstatic about returning home. "Diós nos bendijo" (God blessed us), they say. The farm, for now, is safe, and a new grandchild is waiting. The coffee harvest is a good one, and prices have recovered somewhat. But the future remains uncertain.

The household enterprise, the oldest and most widespread production unit in the world, is also the least understood. And not surprisingly. Households are complex and variable systems: open, dynamic, fluid, and adaptable. Social scientists, politicians, and policymakers long have debated the fate of family farmers like the Valentes, as they become immersed in world markets. Theorists, from Marxists to neoclassical economists, typically have characterized household producers in nonindustrial societies as "traditional" people who differ significantly from "modern" capitalists by their use of a distinct mode of production or a peculiar "moral economy."[1] Smallholders have variously been portrayed as subsistence-oriented "communalists," *unwilling* to embrace capitalism; as helpless victims *overpowered* by the capitalist system; or as backward, inefficient, and "tradition-bound" producers, *unable* to move successfully into that system. Scholars and policymakers from both the left and right have predicted (and even encouraged) their demise—particularly in regions where agro-export development policies have promoted the spread of lucrative cash crops, such as coffee.

The Promises and Perils of Agricultural Exports

Policies promoting the production of agricultural exports in the developing world have sparked a great deal of controversy concerning their long-term impact on national economies and family farmers alike. Neoclassical economists and institutions such as the World

Bank and the International Monetary Fund tend to favor policies promoting agricultural exports, arguing that they allow developing nations to specialize according to their "comparative advantage" and thus maximize their international trading potential, creating export earnings that can be invested in domestic development (see Balassa 1989).

But the promises of agricultural exports are tempered by economic and social perils. Critics argue that the notion of comparative advantage frequently leads to overdependence on one or two crops. Agricultural exports are notably vulnerable to erratic world markets, and dependence on only one or two commodities is extremely risky (see Booth and Walker 1989; Evans 1979).

This type of "classic dependency" has been found throughout Latin America, Brazil being a notable example. In the latter half of the nineteenth century, per capita income in Brazil increased tremendously because of booms in world coffee and rubber markets (Furtado 1965:163–64, cited in Evans 1979:57). But with an economy almost entirely dependent on those two exports, Brazil was devastated in the 1930s when coffee prices dropped by 60 percent. With a limited industrial base and a dramatic decrease in export earnings, Brazil was unable to pay for necessary imports of manufactured products or even food (Evans 1979:55–60).

In the early twentieth century, Central American nations supporting themselves primarily with coffee and banana exports found themselves in a similar position. At times, economic returns from those crops were good. From 1870 to 1920, economies throughout Central America showed steady growth. But dependence on only two export commodities left the countries of this region vulnerable to "an international economic system over which they had only the most minimal influence"—particularly in the Great Depression of the 1930s (Brockett 1990:36–37). By the 1950s, it had become clear that uncontrollable fluctuations in international market prices were wreaking havoc throughout the region. The combination of falling export prices and rising import costs created an unfavorable balance of payments for Central American economies that had focused on export agriculture rather than building an industrial base.

Central American nations attempted to deal with this problem in several ways. In the late 1940s and early 1950s, they sought to reduce dependence on coffee by promoting diversification, but high coffee prices in the 1950s tempted further support of the coffee sector. During the late 1950s and early 1960s, Costa Rica joined its Central American neighbors in a number of attempts at regional integration, designed to limit their reliance on export agriculture and to promote industrialization for a regional common market. Following numerous less comprehensive bilateral and regional trade agreements in the early 1960s, Guatemala, Nicaragua, Honduras, El Salvador, and Costa Rica formed the Central American Common Market (CACM). The plan was to create a market large enough to support new industries, reducing dependency on unstable agricultural exports and on expensive manufactured imports.

Despite impressive growth rates in Central America during the 1960s, the contributions of the CACM to this "golden age" were relatively minor (Bulmer-Thomas 1987:176). The regional alliance faced a number of problems in weaning Central American economies from their reliance on agricultural exports. First, there was no framework for equitable distribution of net benefits among the five republics, and the CACM was plagued by internal conflict and disputes. Second, by focusing primarily on the production of consumer goods, industry still had to rely on imported machinery and raw materials. In addition, the capital-intensive nature of the new CACM industries meant that relatively few jobs were created; highly unequal income distributions throughout most of the region resulted in limited markets for consumer goods (176; see also Irvin 1988).

Throughout this shaky period of industrialization, export agriculture continued to attract local investors. CACM industries were therefore dependent on external finance, and multinational enterprises entrenched themselves in the region. The decline of the CACM came in the early 1970s when oil prices skyrocketed, making industrial investment even less attractive. Meanwhile, other commodity prices rose (coffee, in particular), and new hybrid plants and technologies made agriculture all the more attractive.

As with earlier attempts in the nineteenth century, this regional, geographically based alliance failed to improve the fragile economies of export-dependent Central America. Export agriculture continued to expand and remains to this day a mainstay of countries desperate for foreign exchange.

Coffee as Commodity

Consumption

Coffee has become a daily ritual, even a necessity, for millions of aficionados worldwide; it is a means of living for the millions of farmers who toil in their fields to produce it. The exchange linking producer and consumer, what Appadurai calls a good's "commodity situation" (1986), is what makes coffee valuable or not for farmers. Coffee has little direct use value to farmers: it is a luxury beverage with little nutritive value for either farmers or their livestock. Its primary value to farmers stems from the historically, culturally, socially (and perhaps politically) shaped desires of other people. It is the changing nature of this value (shifting with supply and demand) that makes commodities such as coffee so volatile and the lives of coffee farmers so potentially precarious.

The use of coffee as a beverage was first recorded in Ethiopia in 575 A.D. From there consumption spread. Though it is difficult to determine a precise date when coffee was introduced into Arab-Islamic cultures, in that milieu coffee was prized as a "non-alcoholic, non-intoxicating, sobering, and mentally stimulating drink" (Schivelbusch 1992:17). In 1640, the first commercial shipment of coffee was sent from Yemen to Amsterdam (Mwandha, Nicholls, and Sargent 1985:2). By 1700, coffee was "firmly established as a beverage . . . among the trend-setting strata" of European society (Schivelbusch 1992:18–19). As well as being an exotic novelty, coffee became noted for its purported medicinal qualities, but it was the spread of Puritan ideology and a bourgeois work ethic that paved the way for coffee in Europe. As sobriety became more valued, coffee began to replace alcohol as a common drink; the social context of the coffeehouse as an intellectual gathering place and a center of business also contributed to its rising demand.[2] Coffee consumption rose with the increase in real income across European societies (Goodman 1995:133). From the male-dominated, business-oriented coffeehouse, the beverage moved into middle-class homes to become a breakfast and afternoon drink and a social drink for women (63).

Coffee's stimulant qualities and the social rituals attached to coffee drinking continue to spur consumption throughout the world today. Despite a slight decline in world consumption in the early 1980s (Mwandha, Nicholls, and Sargent 1985:14),[3] the late 1980s and early 1990s have seen a renaissance in coffee consumption in North America. The North American coffee market of today is becoming like that of nineteenth-century Europe: tastes are more refined, and gourmet and estate coffees are prized.

New modes and networks of distribution available to small-scale regional roasters allow today's consumer to buy a mind-boggling assortment of specialty coffees from around the world in coffee shops, supermarkets, and even corner stores (Roseberry 1996). In airports, on university campuses, and along city streets, Starbucks, Second

Cup, and Van Houte coffeehouses serve lattes, cappuccinos, and espressos to eager customers. Roseberry characterizes today's market this way: "New coffees, more choices, more diversity, less concentration, new capitalism: the beverage of postmodernism" (763).

Production

Mintz's observations about the historical growth of sugar production can be applied equally to the world of coffee: "Had there been no ready consumers for it elsewhere, such huge quantities of land, labor and capital would never have been funneled into this one curious crop" (1985:xviii–xix). As European tastes for the beverage grew, so did their determination to control production. As early as 1707, the Dutch East India Company began planting coffee in Java; the French followed suit and by the mid–eighteenth century had successfully established coffee in their colonial territories (Goodman 1995:130). In the early 1840s, Costa Rica was the first country in Central America to establish regular coffee exports. By 1850, after disease destroyed coffee plantations in Ceylon and the Dutch Indies, the center of world production shifted to Latin America, where Brazil, Venezuela, and Costa Rica were already major producers (Palacios 1980:15). By the 1880s, coffee had become a major crop throughout Central America and Colombia.[4] Today, among primary commodities, coffee ranks second only to petroleum as an export, providing more than 25 percent of the foreign exchange earnings of sixteen countries in Latin America and Africa and employment for at least 20 million people (Mwandha, Nicholls, and Sargent 1985:xii).[5]

Coffee has several qualities that make it an attractive crop for small farmers and nonindustrialized nations eager for export earnings:

- it is easy to store and handle
- its value, by weight, is high for an agricultural product
- it can be grown on steep slopes (often unusable for other crops)
- it is precocious for a tree crop
- it is labor-intensive, rather than capital-intensive
- once neglected, coffee can be fairly easily rejuvenated.
  (Mwandha, Nicholls, and Sargent 1985:104)

In addition, coffee can be processed with relatively simple technology and, once processed, can be stored for long periods of time. Finally, coffee does not grow in Europe and North America, where the markets are largest, but thrives in tropical and semitropical environments.

On world markets today, the two most important coffee varieties are *Coffea arabica* L. and *Coffea canephora* L.[6] *Arabicas* are grown in most of Central America, Colombia, Brazil, Kenya, and Tanzania; the heartier *robusta,* as the *canephora* is called, is grown at lower altitudes, primarily in Uganda, Tanzania, and Indonesia. From these two species, three main categories of commercial beans are recognized in the marketplace: *milds, Brazils,* and *robustas.* Climate, altitude, soil quality, and harvesting procedures contribute to the overall quality, but the marketplace distinguishes coffees primarily by variety and method of processing.

The international coffee trade deals in unroasted, "green" coffee, the clean, dried beans that have been extracted from the center of each cherry (the pulpy fruit surrounding the beans). There are two main methods of processing: dry and wet. Mild arabicas are processed by the wet method; Brazils (unwashed arabicas) and robustas are processed by the dry method, though wet processing is becoming increasingly common everywhere.

With the simpler dry method, farmers dry their cherries either in the sun or by mechanical driers. The dried cherries are then hulled in machines that remove the shell, dried pulp, husk, and an inner skin called the parchment; the coffee is then bagged and sold. An increasing number of small farmers now own hand hulling machines, but most take their dried cherries either to central "hulleries" or to local *maquinistas* (as the hullers are called in Venezuela) who hull on commission.

The wet method is more complicated and expensive but produces a better quality bean. The cherries are first washed in large tanks, where dirt, leaves, and unripe or rotten cherries float to the top and are skimmed off. Next the washed cherries are put through pulping machines, which remove the outer shell and most of the pulp. The beans are then soaked in tanks, washed again to remove any remaining pulp, and dried. Finally, the beans are milled to remove the parchment, leaving "green" coffee, or *café en oro,* as it is called in Costa Rica.

To prevent the cherries from fermenting, wet processing must start within twenty-four hours after harvesting. Although a longer delay will not render the beans totally useless, fermentation lowers quality because it affects the taste of the beans. For this reason, timely harvesting is important. Old cherries fallen from the trees and collected days later from the ground have already begun to ferment; on the other hand, the beans from green cherries are immature and bitter when processed. Both yield an inferior product.

Booms, Busts, and Commodity Agreements

The periodic booms and busts (see fig. 1) that plague the world coffee market are due to a number of factors affecting consumption, production, and distribution.[7] Events and trends in large consumer markets (such as the United States) and producing nations (such as Brazil) particularly come to mind. But the technical nature of coffee as a crop and international geopolitical relations also affect supply and demand in important ways. Those who depend heavily on coffee production have been constantly concerned with alleviating the dramatic price fluctuations that have plagued the coffee industry since the mid-1800s.

As the world's largest coffee producer, Brazil has played a key role in the rise and fall of world prices. Its overproduction has led to frequent decreases in world market price, but Brazil was also the first in 1906 to stockpile supplies at home in order to raise world prices (Mwandha, Nicholls, and Sargent 1985:84–85). Nonetheless, by the 1920s, Brazil was producing twice what it was able to export. Despite the Brazilian government's efforts to limit coffee production, surplus stocks and declining demand caused prices to fall even further in the 1930s.

With the onset of World War II, Latin American producers were cut off from their primary coffee buyers in Europe, leaving North America as their only market. In 1940, the United States and four-

Figure 1. World Coffee Prices, 1948–1991

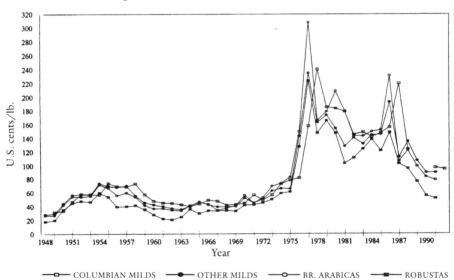

Source: Compiled from United Nations Monthly Commodity Price Bulletins, 1948–1991.

teen Latin American countries signed the first of five Inter-American Coffee Agreements, hoping to stabilize production and prices. Until that time, Europe's discriminating consumers bought coffees according to the quality produced by individual estates and processors. North American consumers were less particular, which allowed an oligopoly of U.S. firms to set a single price for all coffee produced in any given country, regardless of quality.

During the 1940s, coffee production fell in Brazil but increased elsewhere, particularly in Africa, where production trebled. Fortunately, demand also increased and so did prices. When Brazil's excess coffee stocks were depleted, the market price jumped from thirty-three cents per pound in 1949 to about fifty-four cents in 1950 (Rowe 1963:14). The biggest jump came in 1954, when a reported frost in Brazil sent New York dock prices for Brazilian Santos 4 to a high of nearly a dollar per pound.

The boom was brief. Reports of frost damage had been exaggerated, and by 1955 prices had already fallen by half. With production at an all-time high, no quick recovery in prices was on the horizon. By this time, many countries were heavily dependent on earnings from coffee exports and worried about the consequences of a continued decline in coffee revenues. There were several informal attempts at regulating production and enforcing export quotas, but none endured.

In 1958 representatives from thirty-six exporting nations, twenty-two importing countries, and thirteen other nations established the International Coffee Organization (ICO); a year later, they signed the first International Coffee Agreement (ICA). In 1962, the United States joined, motivated, some argue, by the escalating Cold War and a perceived need to stabilize Latin American economies against the threat of communism. This was the first in a series of five-year ICAs. As might be expected, this complex organization of producers and consumers is a highly political body. Voting power is based on "volume of interest," giving the largest producers (Brazil and Colombia) and the largest consumer (the United States) the most leverage (Mwandha, Nicholls, and Sargent 1985:90).[8]

Basically, the organization tried to manage cyclical imbalances between supply and demand by (1) controlling exports and imports so that prices did not fall below the 1962 level, (2) promoting coffee consumption, (3) adjusting production to demand, and (4) establishing policies concerning coffee stockpiling (Rowe 1963:187).

Until recently, exports were controlled by a quota system, in which each producer country received a specified exportable quota, and consumer countries agreed to import only coffee bearing ICO quota seals. The calculation of quotas was negotiable and varied with each five-year agreement; in general, though, quotas were based upon some percentage of previous production and took little account of variation in quality, apart from designating four basic groups. In descending order of quality, they are Colombian mild, other mild arabicas, unwashed arabicas, and robustas.

Colombian and other mild arabicas were rated highest because they are grown at higher altitudes, cultivated with better techniques, and processed via the wet method. Milds are generally preferred for brewed coffee, particularly in Europe. Robustas and Brazils, both of which are generally dry-processed, are used primarily for blending in off-the-shelf ground and instant coffees. Because of their neutral flavors, Brazils are preferred over robustas for blending with the better-quality milds, but most large companies use robustas because they are cheaper (Kummer 1990:118). The robusta bean also has a slightly higher caffeine content (2% as opposed to 1% in arabicas) and so is preferred for making instant coffees. At the 1962 conference, producers of other milds and robustas fought for quotas allocated according to the demand for coffee of those particular qualities, but Brazil, with its huge output of unwashed arabicas, wanted a pro rata allocation based solely on volume of production. Brazil prevailed (118; Mwandha, Nicholls, and Sargent 1985:121–22).

At the other end of the commodity chain is the tricky promotion of consumption. Though world demand has increased steadily for more than a thousand years, in the short term, coffee demand is fairly inelastic: that is, demand does not change much with changes in price. This is an advantage for producers when coffee prices rise, since on the one hand, coffee addicts (such as myself) do not readily lower consumption because of higher prices. On the other hand, during periods of oversupply, demand does not rapidly increase despite lower prices.

Adjusting production to fit world demand is equally difficult. The problems of supply and demand that plague the world coffee market present something of a "prisoner's dilemma" for producers. If each individual (or nation) produces as much as possible, a surplus accrues and prices drop for all. If some producers cooperate to limit production, then prices will rise, but the biggest profits will accrue to those who "defect," those who do not limit production and sales. The trick is knowing, and trusting, that other producers will cooperate. If a single farmer (or nation) limits production and others do not, then that producer risks losing doubly: through low prices caused by overproduction elsewhere and through lower output and income at home.

Despite market fluctuations, coffee brings a relatively high price, making it attractive for the individual farmer, who consequently tries to maximize production. Yet the dramatic increase in worldwide production (because of increases in production per hectare and in the number of producers) causes supply to outrun demand and prices to drop. For many, there are few options but to continue growing coffee. Leaving coffee can be expensive and risky: many coffee farmers, particularly those who have planted expensive hybrid trees, are constrained by heavy capital investments in this long-term tree crop. The ICO has attempted to limit production by promoting alternative crops, but farmers have been wary. Profitable (and legal) alternatives to coffee are not easy to find. For farmers who have made substantial investments in coffee, the costs of switching are high, as are national costs in terms of uncertain revenues and increased unemployment (Mwandha, Nicholls, and Sargent 1985:103).

In 1989, ICO members failed to reach a new agreement, dramatizing the difficulties in solving these problems in a manner acceptable to both producers and consumers. Commodity agreements can provide one "solution to a very basic global problem: how to reward the human effort which goes into the production of food and raw materials" (Gordon 1990:29). During the 1960s and early 1970s, commodity agreements were part of a general trend in world trade (others dealt with cotton, sugar, and petroleum). Commodity agreements have been credited to some extent with preventing the collapse of national economies heavily dependent on export production and thus averting the political and social upheaval likely to follow. But critics argue that they have done so by artificially maintaining these economies at the expense of consumers (Rowe 1963). The 1989 failure of the ICO should also be seen in light of broader political-economic trends, such as the end of the cold war (Talbot 2004) and growing neoliberal ideologies which oppose overt forms of market interference. This trend is propelled by the interests of the richer countries and their transnational corporations, but they have allies in developing countries. For example, opposition to renewing the ICA came as much from Brazil as from the United States.

With no international agreement, coffee prices dropped from roughly seventy cents per pound to forty-five cents per pound in 1989–1990; the resulting loss of export revenue for Third World coffee producers was estimated at $4 billion (Gordon 1990:28). Producers were at first optimistic that prices would recover within a year or two. In one report, economists predicted that, by the 1992–1993 harvest, coffee export earnings in Costa Rica would surpass their 1988–1989 levels (World Bank 1990:42).[9] Thus, despite unfavorable export prices, production continued to increase everywhere, allowing multinational corporations such as Nestlé and General Foods to stockpile coffee at extremely low prices ("Preocupa acaparamiento de tierras," *La Nación*, San José, 19 July 1990, 5A).

Informal efforts by producer nations to regulate world supply did manage to raise coffee prices temporarily. Coffee prices peaked at more than two dollars per pound in July 1994, though this was due in large part to frost in Brazil. Thereafter, prices declined again, to less than one dollar in December 1995 (IATP 1996a).

That same year, Brazil, Colombia, Costa Rica, El Salvador, Honduras, and Nicaragua signed a formal agreement to strictly limit coffee exports in order to bolster international prices (IATP 1995a); others, including Ecuador, Angola, Ivory Coast, Uganda, and Indonesia, joined later (IATP 1995b). The new Association of Coffee Producing Countries (ACPC), which represents most major coffee producers and 80 percent of the world's coffee production, plans to continue to manage supplies in order to support prices (IATP 1996b), but competition is keen, and they face an uphill battle against the giant buyers. Demand from the giant transnational coffee importers (including General Foods and Nestlé) has been low, as they continue to use up old stocks instead of buying fresh beans (IATP 1996a). Hence, connoisseurs detect stale coffee beans on the market, and the collapse of world prices does not get passed on to consumers in the form of significantly lower retail prices.[10]

How Do Households Cope?

Despite their relatively weak position in the modern world, family farmers persist worldwide. Careful and detailed studies of smallholders have shown how specialized skills, flexibility, and an intimate knowledge of local environments have contributed to the survival of farming households (see Attwood 1992; Bentley 1992; Netting 1981, 1993; Wilk 1991). Using both individual and collective strategies of adaptation, accommodation, and resistance, household producers continue to play active economic, social, and political roles in many contemporary societies. Though their activities may appear irrational to some economists and national policy planners, smallholder decisions about the allocation of resources and labor are often just efforts to make the best of difficult situations (see Ortiz 1973). As one writer, speaking for household weavers in Bolivia, put it, "If the legs on our stool are of different lengths, that is because the stage is tilted" (Eversole n.d.).

Though a "householdlike group or thing" can be found in every society (Wilk 1991:34), household composition, functions, dynamics, and activities vary from one society to another according to cultural codes, specific economic circumstances, personality differences, and demographic events (Freed and Freed 1983:313).[11] Thus, far from being like "so many potatoes in a sack," farming households differ not only in form and function, but also in their goals and in the ability to achieve them.

A number of activities are commonly associated with households worldwide, including "some combination of production, distribution (including pooling, sharing, exchange, and consumption), transmission (trusteeship and intergenerational transfer of property), biological and social reproduction, and co-residence (shared activity in constructing, maintaining, and occupying a dwelling)" (Netting 1993:59).

Much of this book is devoted to analyzing household economic strategies, but because individuals within households often have conflicting and competing goals, we cannot assume that any action or decision is agreeable to every member. Furthermore, "households, like decks of cards, have suits and hierarchies" (Folbre 1988:248). A general household strategy may emerge through negotiation or simply through the imposition of dominant interests, and some members of the household may not accept the outcome as appropriate or equitable. Nor are strategies set in stone. They constantly change as circumstances change both inside and outside the household. Household decisions are largely influenced by available resources, in particular land and labor. There is no single typical domestic cycle, but as household members are born, marry, migrate, age, become ill, and die, farming families must continually adjust their strategies to account for the numbers and skills of family members and the agrarian resources to which they have access (Netting 1993:87).[12]

Finding sufficient labor for production or sufficient employment for excess household labor is a basic component of any strategy. When labor is scarce, farming households might adjust production strategies by planting fewer labor-intensive crops (Barlett 1976, 1982); or they might find ways to supplement their labor via exchanges with extended family and neighbors, by forming cooperative work groups, or by hiring help. Households with insufficient land often supplement their incomes through local wage labor, small-scale craft production, or migration. Where household resources and institutional structures allow, education for some members can provide the key to secure, high-paying jobs in the formal sector, with wages potentially invested back in the family farm. For many farming households, a diversified strategy involving a combination of farming, wage labor, craft production, migration, and formal-sector employment (when possible) has become the norm (see Buechler and Buechler 1992; Netting 1993; Tice 1995). As Ortiz points out in her work with coffee farmers in Colombia, "in an uncertain situation (i.e., a situation where the statistical distribution of options is unknown) there is no clear single optimal strategy. There are only a number of satisfying (or adaptive) solutions with various costs and returns" (1990:305).

Factors outside the household play an equally important role in household economic decisions. The risky and uncertain nature of production and marketing is one of the prime concerns. Some farming households hedge against low market prices in one crop by planting several others. By diversifying, they can spread risks and stabilize incomes, but the success of that strategy depends on the suitability of the new crop to local conditions and the availability of markets (Godoy and Bennett 1989). Poorer farmers often live on the margin of disaster, with few resources to cushion them in times of crisis. They generally avoid new technologies or crops until the risks have been established and they feel they can afford to innovate (Cancian 1980; Guillet 1981; Johnson 1971; Wharton 1971).

Household producers also cope with risk and uncertainty by maintaining close social relations with other households. A history of friendship and reciprocity allows households to call on extended family and neighbors for cash loans or emergency food and shelter during hard times. Patron-client relations with large landowners, local merchants, or political bosses (offering credit, contacts, or protection in exchange for loyal support) provide some small-scale producers with indirect access to their patrons' resources and social networks (see Johnson 1971). In many places, access to land, irrigation water, machinery, credit, markets, and political favors procured through patrons can make or break such a producer. Strong personal relationships with buyers and suppliers can also help commodity producers to overcome some of the risks inherent in market transactions.[13]

These relationships might reduce risks and provide domestic producers with some measure of security, but confronting local elites, state officials, and transnational firms, who control access to markets and productive resources, often requires strategies of a different type. "Everyday resistance" to elite control and government interference often takes the form of foot dragging, feigned ignorance, tax evasion, pilfering, slander, and the like (Scott 1985; see also Olwig 1985). When all else fails, rebellion may seem the only option (Paige 1975; Smith 1989). Alternatively, under certain conditions, smallholders can create stable, effective coalitions (such as producers' organizations, political pressure groups, and unions) that provide them with a measure of political and economic control (see Attwood 1985; Esman and Uphoff 1984).

2

Coffee and the Farming Household

The rising demand for coffee that began in western Europe in the eighteenth century, along with the potential for wealth and power that the growing market implied, spurred production throughout colonial and postcolonial territories. Both consumption and production have steadily increased ever since. But how has this trend affected those who toil in the fields to provide the precious brew? Countries dependent on export commodities suffer from the instabilities of international commodity markets, but critics of export agriculture also contend that export crops (for example, coffee) are directly responsible for increases in poverty, extreme inequalities in wealth, and politically repressive regimes, such as are common in most of Central America. They argue that policies promoting export-oriented agriculture benefit primarily land-accumulating elites, at the expense of the rural majority who have "suffered from diminishing land access, food supply, and employment opportunities" (Brockett 1990:92).[1]

There is no doubt that since the mid-1800s the production of coffee as a major cash crop has dramatically altered the lives of smallholders throughout much of Latin America. But its effects have been varied, and it is misleading to suggest that export agriculture is solely responsible for the region's many social problems. "The nature of the coffee state and its posture toward small farmers and laborers differed substantially from one nation to the next, reflecting the practical experiences of coffee elites in the early coffee-growing districts and the problems encountered in projecting national policy into new areas of development"

(Williams 1994:224). Thus, although the coffee tree requires certain agricultural and technical practices to produce an exportable commodity, local context and historically conditioned demographics, social structures, and political cultures underlie the stark contrasts found among coffee-producing societies (Cardoso 1977; Paige 1987; Roseberry, Gudmundson, and Kutschbach 1995; Sheahan 1987).

In countries like Guatemala and El Salvador, large coffee plantations have created tremendous wealth for a few, while economic exploitation and political repression have led to misery for countless plantation workers and smallholders (Brockett 1990). In these countries, and others like them, coffee has become the "bitter grounds" for social unrest (North 1981). In dramatic contrast, coffee in Costa Rica is known as *el grano de oro* (the golden bean), so-called, some say, for the golden color of the washed and dried bean. Others attribute the term to the wealth that coffee has brought to the country—not only to large processing and exporting companies but also to a great many small-scale farmers and the populace at large, by providing the state with revenues for national social programs. Unlike the latifundistas who control production (and power) in neighboring countries, small household producers are the primary coffee producers in Costa Rica.

Though Costa Rica is not immune to social problems and injustices, the historical experience of Costa Rican smallholders with coffee has been relatively favorable, compared with the situation in neighboring countries. In Costa Rica, small and medium farming house-

T A B L E 1

Basic Indicators for Central America

Country	Population (in millions) (2003)	Life Expectancy (2000-2005)	Infant Mortality (per 1,000) (2003)	Maternal Mortality (per 100,000 live births) (2000)	Percent Adult Literacy (2003)	Rank by UN HDI[a] (2005)
Costa Rica	4.2	78.1	8	43	95.8	47
El Salvador	6.6	70.7	32	150	79.7	104
Honduras	8.8	67.6	32	110	80.0	116
Guatemala	12.0	67.1	35	240	69.1	117
Nicaragua	5.3	69.5	30	230	76.7	112

Source: United Nations Human Development Report (2005).

[a] The United Nations Human Development Index (HDI) combines national income with adult literacy, education, and life expectancy. Canada = 1; USA = 2; Niger = 174.

holds form a large and relatively prosperous rural middle class, sharing the rewards of coffee production—a high standard of living and high levels of human development—with large-scale farmers, processors, and exporters. (See tables 1 and 2 for a comparison of economic and social indicators among Central American nations.)

TABLE 2

Income and Social Investment in Central America

Country	Real GDP per Capita (PPP$)[a] (2003)	GNP per Capita (US$) (2003)	Public Expen. on Education (as % GNP) (2000-02)	Public Expen. on Health (as % GNP) (2002)
Costa Rica	9,606	4,352	5.1	6.1
El Salvador	4,781	2,277	2.9	3.6
Honduras	4,148	2,009	1.7[b]	2.3
Guatemala	2,665	1,001	4.0[b]	3.2
Nicaragua	3,262	745	3.1	3.9

Source: United Nations Human Development Reports (2005 and 2003).
[a] PPP$ (Purchasing Power Parities) United Nations international dollars that factor in buying power to allow for comparison.
[b] for 2000.

Local Context and History

Two factors have made Costa Rica's experience with agro-export production different from that of the rest of Central America. First, as a rugged territory with little gold or other readily exploitable resources, colonial Costa Rica was largely bypassed by Spanish colonists. Most settlers did not want to live in one of the smallest, poorest, and geographically and culturally most isolated provinces of the Audiencia de Guatemala (consisting of what is now southern Mexico, Guatemala, Honduras, Nicaragua, El Salvador, and Costa Rica);[2] those who did settle there found that they were frequently neglected by the Spanish Crown (Biesanz, Biesanz, and Biesanz 1982). Communication with administrative authorities in Santiago de Guatemala often took months, even years (Hall 1985:54).[3] On the positive side, Costa Ricans were able to operate independently, unhampered by distant authorities, and developed institutions and policies suited to local conditions.

Second, because the indigenous and Spanish colonial populations were extremely small, labor was scarce. *All* colonists needed to live and work on their farms rather than administer them from the cities, as was common elsewhere. The lack of a significant agricultural surplus (the consequence of little labor and few resources) precluded the establishment of large trading centers.[4] Elsewhere in the Audiencia, abundant natural resources and large indigenous populations lured many Spanish colonists, who forced indigenous peoples to produce cochineal, indigo, and cacao. Until the Spanish Crown banned the *encomienda* system around 1620, colonists were provided with lands and given the right to exact service and tribute from local inhabitants. Under that system, labor was often cruelly exploited. Able to produce only subsistence crops in the highlands, many Indians were forced to migrate to the coastal cacao plantations in order to pay tributes; there large numbers of them died from foreign diseases and unhealthful living conditions (MacLeod 1973:142; see also Brockett 1990).[5]

While colonists in Costa Rica were surviving on small-scale sales of beef, suet, flour, tallow, and hides to the merchants of Panama City (MacLeod 1973:274–75), colonists throughout the rest of the region were thriving from a cacao boom and producing little else. But crop diseases, external competition, poor transportation, and dramatic declines in indigenous populations led to the collapse of Central American cacao in the mid-1600s, and the region was flung into severe economic depression (95). Absentee Spanish landlords, who had previously resided in the cities, now fled to the countryside to ride out the hard times (301–2).

Not long after, cacao began to flourish in Costa Rica; tobacco followed shortly thereafter. In both cases, production was small-scale, and neither crop succeeded for long. The unhealthful climate of the lowland plantations and fierce invasions by pirates and Indians contributed to the demise of cacao. Already troubled by a scarcity of labor, the production of tobacco faltered when Spain imposed new controls and heavy taxes in 1766. Costa Ricans began to find smuggling more profitable than export production (Seligson 1980:12).

During these difficult times, the separate provinces within the Audiencia drew apart economically, amid rising resentment against Spanish authorities in Santiago de Guatemala. Throughout the region, export production died and was not revived on a large scale until shortly after independence from Spain in 1821. In this new era, Central American elites quickly responded to favorable international markets and pushed their nascent states toward policies promoting the production of agricultural exports: "Exports were the way of the future, and the role of the state in the economy was perceived, by and large, as a facilitator of export activities" (Lindo-Fuentes 1995:73). Coffee soon became a major export throughout the region; as its value rose, elites strove to gain control of land, labor, processing, and exporting (Paige 1987).

When coffee began to flourish in Costa Rica in the mid-1800s, it did so in an environment of relatively equitable land distribution and labor scarcity. This is not to say that Costa Rica was a classless paradise of yeoman farmers, soon to be spoiled by capitalist coffee production. Tangible differences existed in Costa Rica before the first coffee boom—not only between elites and peasants but also "within that same heterogeneous peasantry and among a surprisingly well-developed urban artisanry" (Gudmundson 1983:431). But when coffee began to flourish, low population densities and a shortage of labor led to high wages and technological innovations (such as mechanical processing), both of which contributed to Costa Rica's early affluence.[6] No doubt, some smallholders lost their lands through debt, but the majority of coffee producers remained small- and medium-scale farmers, forming the core of a strong "rural middle class" (Pérez Brignoli 1989:38).[7]

Elsewhere in Central America, the success of coffee as an export crop had different consequences for family farmers. In Guatemala, for example, the steep, mountainous highlands that previously had been deemed undesirable for cochineal and cacao and thus left to Indian communities were now recognized as prime coffee land. In the late 1850s, *ladinos* and European immigrants began invading communal lands and illegally planting coffee, which often led to violent retaliation by Indian communities (Cambranes 1985:72).

As the success of coffee exports brought the lure of profits, those in power in the new republics now had the political freedom to devise their own ways of increasing control over land and labor (Harris 1964:22). Laws previously enacted by the Spanish Crown to limit the exploitation of Indian land and labor were quickly overturned under postindependence liberal reforms designed to promote private property rights and create systems of debt peonage, ensuring a supply of cheap labor (Brockett 1990:23). For example, an 1878 decree in El Salvador stated that "access to common lands was no longer a right and that private title to such lands could be received upon cultivation of specified (export) crops" (25); yet indigenous and peasant communities lacked the capital required for coffee production and so were unable to retain their lands. In 1881–1882, communal lands were abolished altogether in El Salvador. In theory, indigenous communities retained the right to petition for title to their lands, but in practice they were disadvantaged by their lack of Spanish literacy and their long-standing second-class status. Though some small and medium farms survived, most land was consolidated into the hands of an oligarchy that came to be known as the "fourteen families" (25).

Rapid population growth and land scarcity forced wages down, and many land-poor and landless farm workers found agricultural wages insufficient to support their families (Barry 1987:107). Increasing landlessness and social inequality led to growing peasant unrest, land invasions, and even rebellions throughout most of Central America. The violent conflicts that have rocked Nicaragua, El Salvador, and Guatemala in recent decades are testimony to the continuing severity of these problems.

Costa Rica has not been immune to struggles between small farmers and wealthy elites, but the country's old pattern of land ownership and labor supply defined a more democratic and less polarized society, characterized by a larger middle-class coffee-farmer population than that found in other countries. In nineteenth-century Costa Rica, large estates did exist and exerted considerable influence over smaller farmers (Samper 1990:175), but the way that influence was manifested differed significantly. Costa Rican mercantile elites also possessed large agricultural properties, but unlike the latifundistas of Guatemala and El Salvador, their role in production was relatively insignificant (Pérez Brignoli 1989:39). The newly rising coffee elite did not seek to monopolize land and labor. Instead they found it more profitable to leave most of the land in the hands of small and medium producers and to put their efforts into the control of processing, export, and credit (Cazanga 1987:73; Paige 1987; Samper 1990; Winson 1984, 1989).

Why the Costa Rican elite failed to use coercive measures to increase their control of land and labor is not entirely clear, though it has been suggested that the "ethnic homogeneity of the population" may have been partly responsible (Seligson 1980:156). In Guatemala, El Salvador, and Mexico, elites could easily "justify" the application of coercive measures to their large indigenous populations by stereotyping indigenous people as lazy and deceitful. (Racist stereotyping and repressive policies have often proven mutually reinforcing, as in the antebellum U.S. South or in South Africa.) In the predominantly "European" population of Costa Rica, coercive laws to control land and labor might have been harder to justify and enforce.[8] Others have suggested that, because wealthy landowners ran their coffee farms and processing plants themselves, they maintained more direct personal contact with their laborers and were thus more amenable to political and social change (see Stone 1975).

It is also likely that open frontiers and rugged terrain would have made it impossible to enforce such laws, in any case. Until the 1930s, land was available on the frontiers, and farming families could easily relocate to unoccupied lands where elite control was difficult and costly. For the landless and land-poor, the monetary incentives of small-scale coffee production made relocation an attractive alternative to agricultural wage work (Gudmundson 1983:431). According to one historian, "Peasant-farmer access to land and successful involvement in commercial agriculture was one of the factors which made wage labor continue to be a scarce commodity through the early stages of agro-export growth, and thus restricted the establishment of very large coffee plantations during that period in Costa Rica" (Samper 1990:3). Though some elites also staked claims on uncultivated frontiers, their interest was more in speculation than production, and landless farmers found squatting on those uncultivated lands relatively easy (236).

Moreover, Costa Rican elites needed domestic producers to "stay put," not so much to supply labor for big coffee plantations, but to produce coffee that the elite could process and export. Hoping to keep small-scale producers from moving to the frontier and claiming their own lands, large-scale landowner-processors even "sold or gave land to attract settlers and potential laborers, made loans to the colonists and bought their harvests, effectively stimulating commodity production on domestic units"; in this way, elites contributed to the rise of a strong sector of commercial peasant farming while pursuing their own economic objectives (Samper 1990:245).

The Politics of Processing in Costa Rica

From Field to Factory

Costa Rica was one of the first countries to import and use coffee-processing equipment. By the mid-1800s the mechanical processing of coffee was well under way, and the country was producing a high quality coffee, avidly sought on the London market (Brockett 1990:27; Seligson 1980:19). Mechanized processing affected the structure of Costa Rica's coffee economy in a number of ways, not the least of which was by freeing labor to expand coffee production (Seligson 1980:19). But when coffee processed by the old method (of trampling by oxen) was no longer valued in the international market, farmers were forced to depend on factories to process their coffee (Winson 1989:21). Processing plants required large capital investments, which were usually within the means only of the wealthy Costa Ricans or foreign investors.

Unlike their counterparts in Colombia, who wash and pulp the cherries at home, farmers in Costa Rica sell their unprocessed cherries directly to the processing plants, or *beneficios*. The beneficio washes and de-pulps the cherries, then dries, mills, and markets the green coffee through licensed export companies frequently owned by the same firm. In the late 1800s, because farmers brought their cherries directly to the factory by ox cart or whatever means they could muster, they would sell their coffee to the closest beneficio. In any given locality, therefore, the beneficio enjoyed a monopsony. The advent of motorized transportation brought a change: with trucks and automobiles and better road networks, the beneficios were able to set up a system of *recibidores* (receiving stations) to expand their operations throughout the countryside, a system that initiated a phase of competition between beneficios. Producers benefitted from a larger choice of factories to which they could sell (Seligson 1980:33–34). This system is still in operation today. In the villages of Pérez Zeledón, recibidores from several competing firms often stand side by side. Farmers haul their coffee cherries to the receiving stations, where a beneficio employee measures the raw cherries in *fanegas* and *cajuelas* (standard measures of volume) and issues receipts. At the end of each day, trucks are sent around to collect the coffee from the recibidores and to take it to the beneficio for washing and processing. Once a week, farmers take their receipts to the beneficio offices, where they are paid. The final price for coffee cherries is not determined until nearly a year later, when the beneficio has sold all its beans and can calculate its earnings for the past season. Meanwhile, beneficios set an initial base price, which they pay to farmers in installments throughout the year. (Loan repayments are deducted from these installments.)

The beneficio is a powerful institution in Costa Rica's coffee industry, but the relationship between smallholders and processors is not entirely asymmetrical. Although the farmers must depend on the beneficios to process and market their coffee, few beneficio owners invest much in growing coffee. Most prefer to leave the risks of crop production to the farmers. To make a profit on the capital invested in expensive, modern machinery, factory owners need to process more coffee than they produce themselves and so rely heavily on small farmers for the bulk of their raw coffee. Still, processors have been known to collude to keep prices low, a major problem for farmers who have no alternative but to sell to the few beneficios operating in any one region.

The control of credit is useful for processors who want to ensure farmer patronage. The costs of producing export-quality coffee are high. Investments must be made in seedlings of high-yielding varieties, and fertilizers, pesticides, and harvest labor must be purchased in advance of the final coffee payment. Because coffee trees bear fruit only after the first three or four years, farmers must be able to survive that period without any return on their investment. For most small and medium producers, credit is essential for start-up and maintenance costs until the first harvest; many find they must borrow on a year-to-year basis to meet production costs.

Prior to World War II, financing for Costa Rican coffee was supplied by the London market. European buyers were more than willing to advance payments to ensure a steady supply of high-quality coffee. That credit was then distributed to farmers through the beneficios. The war put an end to this system, and the Costa Rican government has since supplied most of the credit to coffee growers. The beneficios still distribute the money to farmers, but financing comes through the Costa Rican National Bank (Seligson 1980:39); private beneficios also receive foreign credit from their transnational owners.

The Costa Rican government distributes credit to beneficios in three stages: the first installment is advanced to farmers to cover the costs of production (fertilizers, insecticides, weeding, pruning, and so forth) and the second to cover the cost of harvest labor; the third covers the beneficios' initial payments to farmers for their coffee cherries (until they begin to sell the coffee abroad).

The State as Regulator

During the late nineteenth and early twentieth centuries, the Costa Rican government adopted a laissez-faire policy toward the coffee industry. There was little taxation of coffee and no regulation of transactions between farmers, processors, and exporters. With respect to taxation, the entire industry—from small farmer to exporter—stood fast to avoid any form of taxes. And for many years, because of the influence of large coffee interests, they succeeded. Though a small tax on coffee (used to help reduce the country's foreign debt) came into effect in 1841, the first major coffee tax was not implemented until 1893; it was followed by a series of coffee taxes levied through the 1920s, as new noncoffee power bases developed in urban areas and the old coffee elite began to lose control of the political system (Seligson 1980:45–47).

This same laissez-faire policy was more of a problem for small farmers when it came to regulating the processing industry. Farmers had long argued that the processing factories colluded against them, setting high interest rates for loans and low prices for coffee cherries; increasingly they complained about the "trust of the *beneficiadoras*"

(Acuña Ortega 1986:115). As tensions mounted between farmers and beneficio owners in the early twentieth century, farmers in various parts of the country tried to organize locally. But it was not until the early 1930s, facing a collapse of world commodity prices, that coffee farmers united and pressured the government to intervene. Alone, smallholders might have had little hope of success, but larger growers also felt they were being treated unfairly. In 1933, amid a national and international economic crisis, the government stepped in and created the Instituto de Defensa del Cafe de Costa Rica, predecessor of today's Instituto del Cafe (ICAFE). The institute was designed to regulate all aspects of coffee production and marketing and regulate relations among the players. Among its first acts, it set a minimum price (based on the quality of coffee cherries received) that beneficios were required to pay to farmers and legislated the maximum percent of export earning that the beneficios could retain as profits (Seligson 1980:36).

Following the brief and relatively "peaceful" civil war of 1948, the new, reformist government began in earnest to increase its financial base through taxation of the lucrative coffee industry, though it was not an easy fight. In 1950, the state proposed a 2.25 percent tax on the market value of every fanega (one fanega = 256 kg) of coffee cherries. Because coffee prices at that time were high and still rising, the state argued that farmers would still be able to earn a fair income with their crop (Winson 1989:82). Nevertheless, the Association of Small Producers united with large growers and fought vigorously against the tax. In the end, a compromise ad valorem tax was settled upon, which in essence taxed processors rather than farmers, by lowering the share of the export price of coffee a beneficio could retain for profit from 16 percent to 9 percent.[9] In effect, the 7 percent difference was transferred from the processors to the state. Farmers did not see a direct benefit in increased crop prices, but they benefitted indirectly when the state invested in rural infrastructure such as roads, electrification, and sewage facilities (Winson 1989:85–86). According to Rowe, in the 1960s Costa Rican farmers received about 75 percent of the export value of their crop, a high percentage compared with what coffee farmers elsewhere received (1963:95).

Today, ICAFE oversees nearly every aspect of the coffee industry and is a powerful and highly political organization. Its board of directors includes one representative appointed by the state, two selected from a slate of three candidates proposed by farmer organizations (both cooperatives and other producer groups), one chosen from a slate of three proposed by processors (both cooperative and private), one selected from the domestic roasters, and one chosen by coffee exporters (Cazanga 1987:138).

Among its many responsibilities, the institute represents the country in international negotiations over coffee prices, ensures that all coffee farmers have access to credit, monitors national production, and oversees domestic sales and exports. Without ICAFE's permission, the Banco Nacional de Costa Rica (BNCR) cannot give export licenses or customs permits for export (Cazanga 1987:41). Domestic prices are regulated through semimonthly auctions, to which the beneficios bring their nonexportable coffee. This lower quality coffee is bought by domestic merchants and roasters. As a precaution against illegal exports, all coffee retained for domestic consumption is dyed a reddish color.

Maintaining the high quality of its export coffee is a prime concern of the Costa Rican state. Costa Rican coffee has always enjoyed a reputation for excellent quality, particularly in Europe, and keeping that reputation is one way for a small nation to hold its place in a glutted world market. ICAFE attempts to regulate quality in a variety of ways. For example, a 1989 Executive Decree states that "as of the 1990–91 crop, *beneficiadoras* will not receive coffee of the species *canephora*, known as robusta . . . in the interest of maintaining the quality and prestige of our coffee" (Ministerio de agricultura y ganaderia 1989).

The institute also strives to maintain quality by regulating the amount of green coffee that beneficios may accept from farmers. Theoretically, none is acceptable for export coffee, but in reality it is impossible for farmers to ensure that harvesters pick only ripe cherries. (This problem is discussed in detail in chapter 6.) ICAFE periodically sends inspectors to the recibidores of each beneficio to measure the amount of unripe coffee they are accepting from their clients. According to those with whom I spoke, there is an "unofficial" acceptance margin of 5 percent.

Unripe, green cherries do not yield a coffee of export quality, but they can be used for domestically consumed coffee. At the end of the harvest season, some beneficios will buy for domestic sale the *repela,* the few green cherries left on the trees, at about 70 percent of the price for ripe coffee.

Another way the institute attempts to control quality is by monitoring the use of chemical inputs, promoting balanced fertilizers and pesticides, and banning chemical ripening products. The latter hamper government efforts to control quality because they turn the cherries a ripe, red color, while inside the beans remain immature and bitter. But for many farmers, chemical "ripeners" are irresistible: a field that ripens uniformly (in appearance, at least) is much easier and less costly to harvest than a field that naturally ripens in stages over the course of several months.

Farmer Cooperatives

Although the state's creation of ICAFE was a positive step toward helping coffee farmers receive better treatment from the processors, many growers continued to feel that processors and exporters were receiving an unjustified proportion of the profits. As tensions mounted during the 1930s and 1940s, the concerns of small- and medium-scale farmers were taken up by the Centro para el Estudio de los Problemas Nacionales (CEPN, Center for the Study of National Problems), a group of intellectuals and young reform-minded politicians, including the renowned economist Rodrigo Facio.

As an alternative to the existing system, which favored coffee processors and exporters over producers, Facio promoted the creation of processing cooperatives. His interest in co-ops was part of a growing interest worldwide. In theory, cooperatives are egalitarian structures in which "all are equally workers and managers, and so exploitation is absent" (Nash and Hopkins 1976:8). A cooperative, unlike a private corporation, allows all shareholder-members equal voting power. The economies of scale created through cooperative organization should enable small producers to compete with larger and more powerful producers. In essence, co-ops should allow small producers to collectively increase production and economic output, thus providing new opportunities for the poor and contributing to social equity (see Attwood 1992).[10]

Facio argued that cooperatives would help Costa Rica's small- and medium-scale farmers by eliminating intermediaries between them and consumers, thus allowing farmers to receive a greater proportion of the sale price.[11] In addition, he predicted that cooperatives would stimulate an increase in members' standard of living and education, an increase in their individual savings, the formation of social funds, and the promotion of solidarity (Facio 1943, cited in Cazanga 1987:38–39).

Though a few cooperatives were formed earlier in Costa Rica, the first coffee cooperative, and the first to achieve any notable success, was the Cooperativa Industrial Agricola Victoria. The Victoria Cooperative was formed in 1943 in Grecia (a region in north central Costa Rica) to operate cane and coffee-processing firms that had been confiscated (as a consequence of the war) from their German owners and then handed over by the Costa Rican government to local small producers. About this time, the first formal piece of legislation concerning the promotion of cooperatives appeared; it was passed as part of the Social Guarantees Act of the reform-minded government of Rafael Calderón Guardia, though no specific plan concerning the formation or operation of cooperatives was laid out (Cazanga 1987:22).

According to Cazanga (1987:36–37), the government was willing to back the small-scale cane and coffee producers of the Victoria Cooperative for several reasons. First, the case had important political implications. The cooperative organizers had the backing of the CEPN, who saw this as something of a test case for the defense of small rural property owners. In addition, the prospective cooperative members were small and medium landowners who formed a potentially potent economic and political group.

Finally, these farmers were not looking to "cooperativize" land (which they already owned individually) but rather the processing factories. With the closing of the German-owned factories, they had lost buyers for their coffee and sugar. They needed processing facilities nearby and saw this as an opportunity to take over operations themselves. Thus, the "cooperativization" of the factories was ideologically acceptable to the government, because there would be no question of land redistribution. Costa Rica was experiencing, to a lesser degree, the rural unrest that was erupting into widespread violence elsewhere in Latin America, and larger estate owners were becoming nervous about what actions the state might take toward solving land problems. The Victoria Cooperative would fit within an otherwise capitalist economy and established no threatening precedent to larger landowners.[12]

Why the elites who controlled other processing and export enterprises did not attempt to block the formation of the Victoria Cooperative is unclear. But Calderón Guardia's reform-minded administration was strong, backed by a large agrarian middle class of small- and medium-scale farmers. Governmental support of the Victoria and subsequent cooperatives may attest to the dwindling political influence of old coffee elites.

The Alliance for Progress, which was U.S. president Kennedy's response to the political unrest in Latin America following the Cuban revolution of 1959, also actively promoted cooperatives throughout the region in the 1960s. At the time, it was believed that some form of agrarian reform and redistribution of resources to the poor, via the formation of cooperatives, would help to disperse tensions in the region. Thus, throughout Central America, agrarian reform programs included the formation of cooperatives in some form or other.

Stimulated not only by internal economic and political pressures, but also by the Alliance for Progress, the number of coffee cooperatives in Costa Rica grew rapidly in the 1960s. The majority were formed in newly emerging coffee regions, such as Pérez Zeledón, and did not infringe significantly on the territories of established private beneficios, though by the late 1960s, cooperatives had expanded even into the older coffee zones of the Meseta Central (Cazanga 1987:110).

The Costa Rican state provided various financial incentives for the formation of cooperatives and created a favorable environment within which they could operate. For example, under the 1968 Law of Cooperative Associations, cooperatives enjoy, among other privileges not granted to private firms, a ten-year exemption from property taxes; exemption from import duties on tools, machinery, replacement parts, and agricultural inputs not produced nationally in sufficient quantities to meet their needs; priority in access to transportation; and exemption from import duties incurred during the formation of the cooperative organization (Cazanga 1987). These tax advantages and exemptions allowed cooperatives to invest heavily in modern, more efficient machinery—a move many of the private beneficios were unable to make. Faced with competition from better-equipped cooperative factories, owners began to sell off some of their private beneficios to groups of producers wishing to form cooperatives (Cazanga 1987:109; Winson 1989:132–34). Some factory owners apparently sold their beneficios to cooperatives that they themselves had formed and consequently continued to control (Cazanga 1987:52).

Despite these advantages, in the 1950s and early 1960s, coffee cooperatives faced several problems. First, production was rapidly increasing, and by 1961 the Department of Cooperatives at the BNCR could no longer manage the sales of cooperative coffee. Second, coffee exporting was monopolized by large national and international firms. The cooperatives had no personnel technically qualified to manage the complex manipulations of coffee sales and were often cheated by private exporters. To survive, cooperatives desperately needed an integrating organization. In 1962 the BNCR helped create Fedecoop (the national Federation of Cooperatives). Cazanga argues that behind this impulse to create a cooperative federation was the political will of the modern bourgeois sectors to weaken the power of elites who controlled exports (1987:132).

In 1989 there were 350,000 cooperative members, representing 30 percent of the economically active population and producing 13 to 14 percent of the gross domestic product ("Cooperativismo sin respaldo," La Nación, San José, 5 April 1989, 5). Cooperative beneficios had increased their share of coffee processing from 11.5 percent in 1965–1966 to 34.1 percent in 1975–1976 (Torres Rivas 1978, cited in Winson 1989:133). Of the 110 beneficios registered with ICAFE for the 1989–1990 harvest year, 35 were cooperatives.

Coffee cooperatives are not required to become members of Fedecoop, though in 1979, twenty-eight of the thirty-one coffee cooperatives in Costa Rica were affiliated (Cazanga 1987:117, 136). The benefits of association with Fedecoop are many. In addition to the better prices gained through Fedecoop's international marketing of coffee, affiliated cooperatives also receive credit for production costs and technical assistance for farmers. Furthermore, Fedecoop imports agricultural supplies and equipment in bulk at low cost, distributing them to affiliated cooperatives, who in turn pass them along to their members. Perhaps one of the more notable achievements of Fedecoop was the establishment of a central factory in San José to undertake some of the final tasks of coffee processing and preparation for marketing (final cleaning, sorting, weighing, bagging, storage, and so forth). This factory uses extremely sophisticated technology and has reduced the expense of processing, particularly for smaller cooperatives.

With the creation of Fedecoop, cooperatives were able to enter the realm of coffee marketing and export and thus able to control yet another link in the chain that moves coffee from producer to consumer. The private beneficios continue to dominate the processing industry, but small-farmer cooperatives have become an integral part of the Costa Rican economy.

3

Los Cafeteros of Pérez Zeledón

New Horizons

The 130-kilometer journey from Costa Rica's capital, San José, to San Isidro, the municipal center of Pérez Zeledón, is a dramatic one (see fig. 2). The only direct route, the Pan-American Highway, winds its way through the cloud forests of the Talamanca Mountains and over cold dry tundra before descending steep, hairpin turns through more forest to the Valle del General. Today Pérez Zeledón is one of the fastest growing coffee-producing regions in Costa Rica,[1] and hundreds of people daily make the two-and-a-half-hour bus trip between San Isidro and San José. But coffee arrived relatively late in the valley. Before roads and motorized travel significantly decreased the length and dangers of the trip, few braved the rugged pass across the twenty-four-hundred-meter Cerro de la Muerte (the "Hill" of Death). It was not until the 1920s, when land became scare on the Meseta Central (the central plateau surrounding San José) and on the northern frontiers of Herédia and Alajuela, that poor settlers began to travel south over the Talamancas in search of affordable land.

Immigration increased in the 1930s with the first commercial airplane flights to San Isidro (Alfaro 1982:106). According to one early settler of that period, three weekly flights provided the only transport (other than mules and walking) to San Isidro, which at that time had only a handful of inhabitants and only two businesses. The earliest settlers in Pérez Zeledón produced maize and rice for subsistence. But like their nineteenth-century counterparts on the northern fron-

Figure 2. Location of Study Area

tiers, farmers in Pérez Zeledón produced some items for commercial exchange outside their home communities. Pigs were the most important commodity, though some families also raised cattle.

The construction of the Pan-American Highway in the 1940s brought the first significant wave of immigration. With increasing population and land shortages in the Meseta Central, the frontier of Pérez Zeledón provided a welcome opportunity for thousands. When the road reached San Isidro in 1944, it was unpaved but provided much easier passage over the Cerro de la Muerte than existing mule paths, according to Martin Fonseca, a founding member and first president of the local coffee cooperative. At that time uncultivated land and *tierra libre* ("free" land) were plentiful in the valley. These untitled lands could be claimed by anyone willing to work them, though a few claimed large tracts of land for speculative purposes. After 1960, it became increasingly difficult for family farmers to find land to homestead. Finally, the newly created Instituto de Tierras y

Colonización (Land and Colonization Institute) stepped in and bought much of this unworked land, redistributing it as small parcels to settlers until the mid-1970s.

Most new arrivals came from the overcrowded coffee zones of the north. Land in Pérez Zeledón was plentiful and suitable for coffee, but with no processing facilities and poor transportation, commercial coffee production was impossible. During this era, farmers produced rice, beans, cattle, sugarcane, and some coffee for home consumption. Many earned a modest cash income by feeding their corn to pigs, which they then herded over the mountains to the cities of Cartago and San José to sell or trade for goods that they brought back to San Isidro. Driving pigs over the mountains in this manner was so common that the Rio Quebradas, which ran along the old footpath, came to be known as the Rio de los Chanchos (River of the Pigs).

Recognizing the potential for coffee production in this region, the Banco Nacional built the first coffee-processing plant in 1949. This plant and the improved road drew a flood of immigrants from the crowded north. Some twenty thousand people arrived between 1950 and 1958 (Altenburg, Hein, and Weller 1990:238). Though farmers continued to grow corn, beans, and rice for subsistence, el grano de oro soon became the upper valley's primary crop. By 1960, production had increased tremendously, prompting Jorge Zeledón, a Costa Rican entrepreneur, to build a second beneficio, the San Jorge. In 1962, an Italian firm bought the first factory from the Banco Nacional, and a German businessman built a third factory in the Palmares district just outside San Isidro. During that same year, a group of small coffee farmers formed the canton's first coffee-processing cooperative and bought their own beneficio (see chapter 5).

Pérez Zeledón Today

Today, the canton of Pérez Zeledón comprises eleven districts and encompasses an area of approximately 1,905 square kilometers. Most of the 81,500 residents (as of 1990) live in the district of San Isidro surrounding the market town of the same name (population 28,000). The rest live in small hamlets and villages scattered throughout the northern end of the valley and the foothills of the surrounding Talamanca and Coastal Ridge Mountains. Because of its position as a gateway north through the mountains to San José, San Isidro is an important market center for the entire southern Región Brunca of Costa Rica.

In 1990–1991, the town included a branch of the Universidad Autonoma, a technical school, a hospital, and a municipal sports facility. Branch offices of government agencies such as the Institute for Agrarian Development, the Ministry of Agriculture and Animal Husbandry, and the Ministry of Public Works and Transportation were also located there, as well as several banks and hotels and numerous service enterprises, such as snack bars, dry-goods and grocery stores, and a variety of repair shops. The only other industries in the canton were a small cooperative lumber mill, which processed timber primarily from the virgin forests near the Panamanian border, and one small, foreign-owned garment factory. Coffee production and processing were unquestionably the mainstay of the canton's economy. Altenburg, Hein, and Weller suggest that, although the yields and the quality of coffee from this region are below those of the coffee grown in the Central Valley, coffee production in Pérez Zeledón continues to increase because the poor soils and steep slopes are not well suited for the cultivation of other commercial crops (1990:240).[2]

Four coffee-processing companies were buying and processing coffee in the canton: Coopeagri (as the cooperative is now known), Beneficiadora La Meseta, Beneficio El General, and Beneficio El Aguila. A recent arrival on the scene, Peters, S.A., bought coffee cherries but did not have a processing plant in the canton. It trucked the cherries it bought from farmers in Pérez Zeledón to its factories near San José. As table 3 shows, for the 1988–1989 harvest, the four local factories processed a total of 600,692.6 double hectoliters of green coffee,

TABLE 3

Coffee Processing by Beneficios in Pérez Zeledón
(1988–1989 Harvest Season)

Beneficio	No. Clients (1990)	Processing Capacity (double hl)	Coffee Bought (double hl)	Own Coffee Processed (double hl)	Total Coffee Processed (double hl)	Percent of Total Canton Processing (double hl)
El General	4,500	300,000	165,969.5	1,116.0	167,085.5	27.8
La Meseta	4,000	200,000	180,539.7	0.0	180,539.7	30.1
El Aguila	2,600	150,000	91,540.3	0.0	91,540.3	15.2
Peters	1,500	0	n/a	0.0	0.0	—
Coopeagri	3,970	200,000	159,869.8	1,657.3	161,527.1	26.9
Total	16,570	850,000	597,919.3	2,773.3	600,692.6	100.0

Source: ICAFE 1989, Coffee Totals Declared by Beneficios, 1988–89 Crop.
Note: 1 double hectoliter (double hl) = 128 kg = approx. 0.5 fanegas.

approximately 8 percent of the country's total. Of this, El General processed 28 percent, La Meseta 30 percent, El Aguila 15 percent, and Coopeagri 27 percent.

Sugarcane is the canton's second largest commercial crop. Cane is either processed into *dulce* (a crude brown sugar) in domestic *trapiches* (cane crushers) or into commercial white sugar in Coopeagri's *ingenio* (sugar refinery). To a lesser extent, farmers also raise cattle for beef and dairy products. Because of the lack of slaughtering and packing facilities in the valley, farmers must ship their beef cattle to the Central Valley for processing. Coopeagri's small milk-processing plant provides a market for a limited supply of milk.

Two plantations, owned by multinational corporations, should also be mentioned. The Finca Santa Fe, partly owned by a former national minister of agriculture, is a 1,380-hectare farm that began planting coffee (and some sugarcane) in 1988. The Pindeco pineapple plantation, located in Buenos Aires in the neighboring province of Puntarenas, is close enough for residents in the southern districts of Pérez Zeledón to commute to work there.

Farming Households in Palomas and Santa Cruz

The Communities

On the surface, Santa Cruz and Palomas appear quite different from each other.[3] The long, scattered community of Santa Cruz lies nestled along a narrow valley cut by a small river and flanked by the steep foothills of the Talamancas; Palomas is a more compact community perched on broader foothills at a slightly lower elevation. Santa Cruz has a reputation as a stronghold of cooperative supporters, whereas Palomas is noted for the opposite. This contrast was one factor that led me to choose these two villages for research, though the contrast later proved less significant than I had anticipated.

Although these differences are important, the communities are alike in many ways. First, both are farming communities. In each, coffee is by far the primary crop, with sugarcane a distant second. In Palomas, where the land is generally more level, a few farmers have large fields where they grow sugarcane to sell to Coopeagri for processing into refined white sugar.

Farmers in Santa Cruz do not grow sugarcane for industrial refining. Since sugarcane is heavy and bulky and since the fields are several kilometers from the nearest paved road and more than twenty-five kilometers from the ingenio, farmers find the costs of transportation prohibitive. Instead, a few grow sugarcane that they process into dulce in domestic trapiches. Dulce is produced both for home consumption (it is a staple in most Costa Rican households) and for sale, either to local merchants or at the weekly market in San Isidro. There are five trapiches in Santa Cruz; the sole trapiche in Palomas has not been used for many years.

Second, as those in the rest of Pérez Zeledón, most residents of Santa Cruz and Palomas migrated from the densely populated cantons of the Meseta Central during the 1950s, 1960s, and 1970s. More than two-thirds of all adults (71% in Palomas, 69% in Santa Cruz) were born outside their current residential communities; half of these (about 35% of the total of each community) were born outside Pérez Zeledón. The average length of residence for immigrants was 15.5 years in Palomas and 20.1 years in Santa Cruz.[4]

Finally, both Santa Cruz and Palomas are the largest communities (population 400–500) within their respective districts and serve as centers for social and economic activities. Both communities resemble similar-sized villages found almost anywhere in highland Costa Rica. Each has a new cement-block church and elementary school, a children's playground, a small health center with weekly outpatient service, a community center, a soccer field, and a public telephone. Although electricity is provided and maintained by the national Costa Rican Electrical Institute, the domestic supply of water is managed by local water committees. The committees receive funding and technical advice from the Departamiento de Agua y Aquaductos (AyA—Department of Water and Aqueducts), but community members are responsible for building, maintaining, and collecting payments for their water systems.

In 1990–91, Palomas and Santa Cruz each had recibidores from three coffee-processing companies. In Palomas they were Coopeagri, El General, and El Aguila; in Santa Cruz, Coopeagri, El General, and La Meseta. La Meseta and Peters also had collecting stations within practical hauling distance of Palomas, but neither Peters nor El Aguila had recibidores within practical distance for the farmers of Santa Cruz.[5]

Residents in both communities purchase daily supplies in small, family-run *pulperías* (small general stores) that supply a variety of food and sundry goods and offer credit (which residents appreciate, particularly in the cash-strapped periods prior to coffee payments). But prices tend to be high, so most families send someone weekly to San Isidro to cash their coffee receipts and purchase the bulk of their supplies. Buses run three times daily between San Isidro and both

Santa Cruz and Palomas. Though the condition of the roads and the distance from San Isidro vary, in each case the trip takes about forty-five minutes. People buy their groceries and sundry items either in San Isidro's municipal marketplace (a large warehouse with about twenty or thirty market stalls), in one of the town's three small *supermercados*, or in one of several family-run grocery stores. In 1990, the government lifted restrictions on selling produce in street markets, so today farmers can also buy and sell a variety of garden vegetables and other household staples in the street market held every Friday and Saturday.

Families spend leisure time watching television, listening to music, kicking a ball around the soccer field, chatting and eating at the *soda* (snack bar), or (for men) having a *copa* (drink) in one of the two cantinas in each community. By far the biggest pastime is to sit with family and friends and catch up on the latest gossip.

As throughout Costa Rica, the Catholic Church plays a substantial role in the lives of most villagers. Protestant sects are beginning to make a breakthrough in some parts of rural Costa Rica, but their presence is minimal.[6] Sunday Mass is the main religious activity and a prime social event. Even those who do not actually enter the church will congregate outside on the church grounds. The entire community lingers after Mass: children play, parents visit with friends and relatives, teenagers congregate to gossip and get acquainted, young sweethearts hold hands and stroll around the church.

Annual religious celebrations bring families from throughout each district together. During Holy Week, the entire country shuts down: shops and offices close, local buses stop running, and half the population flocks to the beaches. In Palomas and Santa Cruz, throughout the week families gather to attend special religious services or to say the rosary at home. Special meals and picnics are common on Good Friday.

Religious fiestas for each town's patron saints are the second most important holidays in the annual cycle. These two- or three-day affairs of games, riding competitions, disco dancing, and feasting are planned months in advance and eagerly awaited by young and old alike. In Palomas, the celebration ends with parishioners parading around the town plaza to receive the priest's blessing and sprinkling of holy water. Those who own horses, cars, and trucks parade them behind the pedestrians and receive a special blessing to protect these valuable assets for the coming year.

Neither Santa Cruz nor Palomas has a formal local administrative body to govern affairs within the community, but each has an *asociación de desarrollo comunal* (community development association or ADC). These associations, run by elected boards, organize and implement grassroots community improvement projects, but they have no legislative or taxing powers. As part of the province of San José, Pérez Zeledón is represented in the National Legislative Assembly by elected delegates. For the most part, delegates have been elected from the urban areas around San José, though in 1990 the province elected three delegates from Pérez Zeledón. Regionally, the municipality of San Isidro administers the entire canton through an elected municipal council. Each of the eleven districts elects a nonvoting delegate to represent it at weekly municipality meetings in San Isidro.⁷

The most obvious manifestation of the state in these communities is the Guardia Rural (rural police), though its responsibilities are limited. The two officers assigned to keep the peace in each community carry no weapons and deal primarily with drunkenness, rowdiness, and thefts. Theoretically, the policemen are not politically connected, but rural guards are almost always supporters of the party in power at the national level. They are appointed from among local applicants or brought in from the outside when it suits the party in power. Legally, rural guards cannot be fired because of political affiliation, but when a new party comes to office, they frequently are moved to distant posts. After a few such moves away from their families, most resign voluntarily.

Economic Stratification

Life in Santa Cruz and Palomas ebbs and flows with the cycle of agricultural tasks. Social and economic differences among the people in these communities are not great but are nonetheless evident. Of the 97 households in my initial census of Palomas, 16 supported themselves through nonagricultural activities: teaching, construction work, small businesses, and so forth. The remaining 81 households (84%) supported themselves primarily through agricultural activities; of these, 29 were landless laborers and 52 were landowning coffee farmers. Similarly, in Santa Cruz I found that of a total of 86 households, 12 supported themselves through nonagricultural activities; of the remaining 74 agriculture-based households (86%), 7 were landless and 67 were landowning coffee farmers. Landholdings ranged in size from 0.17 hectares to over 69 hectares, but only four farms in each community were larger than 35 hectares. In Palomas, two of these were owned by absentee landlords. As figure 3 indicates, most farms were smaller than 3.45 hectares.

The great majority of landless agricultural households in both communities were not permanent residents (who might have lost land to large farmers and been forced to turn to wage labor). Rather, they were migrants who came from other parts of the country for seasonal harvest work. What their situation was there is unclear, but one young couple told me they were doing migrant field work only until their own two hectares of recently planted coffee in a neighboring district came to fruit. For the most part, these transient workers were young families who rented houses for less than one year, then left to work in other parts of the country (though many returned on a yearly basis). Not counting the transients, only ten households (12%) in Palomas and five (7%) in Santa Cruz were resident agricultural workers with no land.[8]

Since my objective was to study coffee-farming households, I did not select landless households for intensive study, though I did conduct an additional short interview with each one and collected information informally as a participant observer. In choosing farming households for in-depth study, I reasoned that the ratio of land to available adult labor was likely to be an important factor in household

Figure 3. Comparison of Landholdings by Community

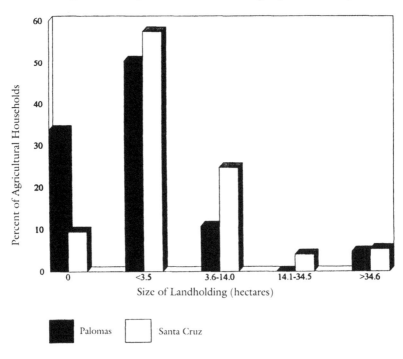

Source: Author's village survey, 1990–1991.

economic strategies. Using data gathered from my initial census, I categorized the 119 resident landowning, coffee-farming households according to the occupations of all members ages twelve through sixty-five, distinguishing among (a) "marginal" households, in which members farmed but also worked regularly for wages, (b) "self-sufficient" farm families, in which members worked the family farm themselves, with neither regular wages nor full-time employees to assist, and (c) those few "employer" households that had the need and resources to hire full-time workers (as opposed to the occasional day laborer) to help them farm.

I then drew a stratified random sample of seventy-eight coffee-producing households (65.5%) for in-depth study (thirty-six households in Palomas and forty-two in Santa Cruz). Because they were so few, I included all resident "employer" households (except two absentee large landowners in Palomas) in the sample but randomly selected households from the other categories in roughly the same proportions as found in the community as a whole. As I collected further data, several households had to be reclassified. Table 4 shows the number of households in the sample after final classification.[9] Though employer households tended to have larger farms, the median farm size for sample households in both communities was just over two hectares.[10] As might be expected, marginal households had more people on average but tended to have smaller landholdings (see tables 5 and 6).

Despite these differences in farm size, most families own modest

TABLE 4

Sample Households by Category of Labor Use
(Number and Percentage)

Community	"Marginal" Labor-Selling Households	"Self-Sufficient" Family Farmers	"Employer" Households
Palomas (N = 36)	22 (61.1%)	11 (30.6%)	3 (8.3%)
Santa Cruz (N = 40)	21 (52.5%)	17 (42.5%)	2 (5.0%)
Total (N = 76)	43 (56.6%)	28 (36.8%)	5 (6.6%)

Source: Author's sample survey, 1990–1991.

three- to four-room wooden houses with corrugated tin roofs and wood floors. In the last decade, roughly half a dozen families in each community have built concrete block houses with tile floors. Whatever the construction of the house, it is surrounded by a flower garden, and potted plants adorn its porches. Vegetable gardens are few, but tropical fruit and nut trees are found in every yard: banana, mango, citrus, cashew, guava, litchi, carambola, and others. A few women grow small patches of medicinal and culinary herbs.

TABLE 5

Median Landholding of Sample Households by Category of Labor Use
(Hectares)

Community	"Marginal" Labor-Selling Households	"Self-Sufficient" Family Farmers	"Employer" Households[a]	Median for Sample Households in Community
Palomas (N = 36)	1.04	4.00	41.26	2.07
Santa Cruz (N = 40)	1.21	4.00	49.82	2.07

Source: Author's sample survey, 1990–1991.
[a] Due to the small number of cases, average, not median, is used.

TABLE 6

Median Household Size by Category of Labor Use
(Number of Persons)

Community	"Marginal" Labor-Selling Households	"Self-Sufficient" Family Farmers	"Employer" Households[a]
Palomas (N = 36)	5.0	4.5	3.0
Santa Cruz (N = 40)	5.0	4.5	4.5
Total	5.0	4.5	3.8

Source: Author's sample survey, 1990–1991.
[a] Because of the small number of cases, average, not median, is used.

With one or two exceptions, all houses have electricity, indoor plumbing, and potable running water. About one-third of the households still cook with wood, which family members gather from forests and coffee fields; the rest have converted to electric hot plates and stoves. (Many families keep a wood-burning stove as a backup and for preparation of foods that "just don't taste the same" when cooked with electricity.) Black beans, rice, plantains, and yucca are dietary staples; I estimate that about half of all households eat some kind of meat or poultry at least once a week.

Inside nearly every house, radios and television sets provide constant accompaniment to daily activities. About three-quarters of the households have refrigerators and small appliances such as blenders and electric irons, which help make domestic work easier. A few have also purchased small washing machines. Motor vehicles are still rare. (In 1991, there were nine in Palomas and six in Santa Cruz.)

Household Composition and Structure

Households in Santa Cruz and Palomas were comprised predominantly of nuclear families (70%). Extended-family households—those consisting of a conjugal pair, their children, and other lineal relatives (parents, grandchildren, or both)—made up 15 percent of each community, and reduced-family households (those that lack a conjugal pair) accounted for an additional 15 percent.

Marriage within the Catholic Church is the only union recognized by the church, but common-law unions *(uniones libres)* are widespread, accounting for more than half of conjugal partnerships. Although these unions are recognized by the community, formal marriage provides status, and middle-class families actively discourage their daughters from living with partners rather than marrying. In many cases, arrival of the first child encourages a couple to marry. Each year, the Catholic Church gives premarital classes for all who wish to wed. During my stay, the week before classes began in Palomas, the priest lectured at Mass on the importance of marrying within the church and urged all those living together—regardless of how long they might have done so or how many children they might already have—to take the classes and marry. Not all did, but no one was discouraged from attending church services for neglecting to marry.

The preferred arrangement is for a couple (married either legally or by common law) to establish an independent household, and most couples manage to do so. Children and their new families often reside next to their parents, forming "kindred clusters." But each household is run separately, with members mostly cooking and eating in their own homes and managing finances independently.

Regardless of the amount of formal economic cooperation between parents, children, and siblings, members of related households interact frequently on a day-to-day basis. Children often are sent to borrow the odd cup of sugar or rice from their grandmother or aunt, and when daily chores are finished, several generations will congregate in one house or another to drink coffee, watch television, and gossip.

Familial ties, especially between mothers and children, are generally very strong; conjugal bonds are less so. Though divorce is not recognized by the Catholic Church, and couples married within the church appear to be more stable than others, both church-sanctioned marriages and common-law unions frequently end in separation. A legally married woman is by law entitled to support from her estranged husband. Her rights are likely to be enforced if she has a strong local kin group to support her claim. In the breakup of a common-law union, the woman has few rights. Without strong support from her natal family, a common-law wife finds it difficult to uphold claims on property, and it is left to the discretion of the husband whether to continue to support his offspring.

For example, for fifteen years Roberto Zamora and his common-law wife, Marisol Vasquez, supported their family of five children with the small but adequate income from his .69 hectares of coffee. When Roberto abandoned his family to start a new life working on the banana plantations in Limón, Marisol attempted to work the farm herself. But the land was in his name, and she was unable to obtain loans to pay for fertilizers and pesticides. As a common-law spouse and with no family nearby to support her claims, there was little she could do to get title to the land (though we shall see in chapter 4 how she eventually managed to do so), and she had no way to coerce Roberto to help support their children. Consequently, she was forced to work at various wage-labor jobs, including the strenuous task of harvesting sugarcane.

When men and women begin new long-term relationships after separation, conflicting responsibilities to new and old partners and children sometimes require deft juggling, as the case of Ramon Bermudez demonstrates. Ramon and Marixa had been married for eight years and had four children when he met Teresa, who had recently returned to Palomas with her four-year-old daughter after she and her husband of six years had decided to separate. Ramon and Teresa moved in together and started a family of their own. Still, after two children and nearly ten years of living with Teresa, Ramon remains legally, and in many ways practically, Marixa's husband. Marixa does not let him shirk his responsibilities to her and her children, and she has a large extended family in the community to ensure that he does not.

Though Ramon eats and sleeps in the house he shares with Teresa and their two children, three or four times a week he visits Marixa to tend the coffee fields, to make repairs to the house, and to see his other children. Marixa keeps all income from these coffee fields. Ramon, Teresa, and their children live on his paycheck from his part-time job as a security guard at the Finca Santa Fe plus the income from Teresa's .69 hectares of coffee that Ramon also works. Both Marixa and Teresa spoke of Ramon as their husband and (at least publicly) each insisted that he lived exclusively in her household. Ramon is a busy man.

Although most households in Santa Cruz and Palomas had a resident conjugal pair, many did not. Most of the reduced households consisted of a woman and children or grandchildren. Female-headed households made up 12 percent of all households in Santa Cruz and 14 percent in Palomas. In a few cases single men lived with their children or grandchildren. In two cases, elderly couples brought their orphaned grandchildren to live with them. The children were cared for and loved, and the elderly couples acquired family help for farm and domestic chores.

Few people live entirely alone. An adult child usually takes the responsibility of living with an aging single parent (or having that parent live with him or her). If a child is not available, an unmarried grandchild, nephew, or niece might move in. Twenty-two-year-old Jesus Mora's common-law wife left him with their three-year-old daughter. Unable to manage on his own, he moved in with his (deceased) father's maiden sister. She helped with child care; he helped her with her coffee field.

Family is the main support system in times of crisis, but when kin are unavailable or unable to care for a family in need, friends and neighbors rally to help. When Victor Cazanga's wife, Flore, fell ill, he was hard-pressed to care for their five young children and continue working as a day laborer on a nearby farm. Because they had only recently moved to Palomas and had no relatives nearby to help them through their crisis, several women in town took turns preparing food and cleaning for the family until Flore was back on her feet.

Families, friends, and neighbors frequently exchange goods on an informal basis. Thus, surplus goods—especially food that may otherwise spoil—are put to good use, and support networks are formed and strengthened. In Palomas, my "adoptive mother" doña Lila frequently took bunches of bananas to her friend and neighbor doña

Teresa; a week or so later doña Teresa would reciprocate with a sack of oranges or a bottle of homemade black-banana vinegar.

This system of informal exchange applied to services as well. For example, if someone had a purchase too large to carry on the bus or if an illness required immediate doctor's care, don Fernando would chauffeur him or her between Palomas and San Isidro in his 1972 Datsun hatchback. (He drove many women to the hospital who were about to give birth.) Though passengers usually gave him a few colónes to cover the cost of gasoline, he charged nothing and his help was considered a favor, which would some day, in some way, be repaid. Likewise, mothers, daughters, and sisters from different households often shared child-care duties and exchanged labor for the more strenuous household tasks.

Within the realm of coffee production, such informal exchanges were rare. Households with insufficient labor, such as female-headed households or those with only very young children, might make sharecropping or other arrangements with brothers, fathers, or other male relatives. But in general, the goods, services, and labor related to coffee production were exchanged on a cash basis or on strict principles of balanced reciprocity. Terms and time of repayment were clearly agreed upon in advance. Even among kin, those who received help in their coffee fields found some immediate way to compensate for services rendered. For example, Sidei, a single mother of two small children, could not care for the two hectares of coffee her widowed father gave her. Her father and an unmarried brother (living with the father) tended and harvested her coffee for her. In exchange, she cooked, cleaned, and otherwise cared on a daily basis for them, even though she lived apart in her own home.

In the farming communities of Santa Cruz and Palomas, some married children continued to work closely with their parents, sharing labor and resources, whereas others ran their farms quite independently. The nature of economic relations between households of parents and married children and among individuals within households varied a great deal. How they affected men and women, young and old, is the subject of chapter 4.

Typical rural
Costa Rican home.

Coffee harvester
with cajuela
basket.

Coffee harvesters
waiting for day's
harvest to be
measured.

Farmer's daughter (center) supervises daily measuring of harvest.

Coopeagri supermarket and supply store, San Isidro.

4

The Political Economy of Coffee-Farming Households

Decisions about the use of household resources and income often form part of a cooperative strategy pertaining to common goals of maintaining the household and improving the standard of living. Yet individuals within households frequently have dramatically different and sometimes competing goals (see Agarwal 1989b, 1994; Sen 1990). Members of the household conduct "complex negotiations of mutual gain and shared interest" (White 1992:135); but when goals conflict, access to household resources and "shares of family income are determined in part by individuals' bargaining power within the household" (Netting 1993:81, citing Folbre 1984).[1] In market-oriented agrarian societies, an individual's position at the bargaining table, so to speak, is enhanced by direct contributions to production and household income via land and labor (see Boserup 1970; Jaquette 1990; Miller 1982).

Divided We Stand: Coffee and the Gender Division of Labor

Household Labor and the Coffee Cycle

As elsewhere in Costa Rica, most households in Santa Cruz and Palomas maintain a strict gender division of labor, based on cultural constructions of appropriate work, which vary according to age, sex, and stage in life cycle. Apart from the coffee harvest, when all hands are urgently needed, agricultural production and marketing are considered the domain of adult males. Though not all farmers perform every task, and the timing of tasks varies from area to area, in Pérez Zeledón, the cycle of agricultural tasks related to coffee production is basically as follows. From late January through mid-August, farmers are occupied "cleaning" their coffee fields, which involves pruning good trees, removing very old or dead trees, and weeding. Pruning is done with a small handsaw, and cut branches are stacked to dry for use as firewood. Coffee wood is an important fuel source for many families who still cook with wood. Even if the coffee field is not nearby, the wood eventually must be brought home, by cart, wheelbarrow (if one is available), or carrying it on the back.

From March through early May, some farmers spray their coffee trees with an insecticide and a liquid fertilizer for strengthening leaves. (Because this is expensive, most farmers in Santa Cruz and Palomas do not apply foliar fertilizer.) In early May farmers also begin to prune and plant shade trees. Though some new coffee varieties are said to grow best without shade, older varieties require partial shade. Banana and plantain are among the preferred shade trees, but deciduous trees, such as the *poro,* are also used. The fruit from the shade trees is consumed by the family or given to friends and neighbors; it is rarely sold.

With the onset of the rainy season in mid-May, farmers begin to apply ground fertilizer. In 1990–1991, farmers used chemical fertilizers exclusively, despite their rising costs. With no animals other than the occasional horse, pig, milk cow, or a few free-ranging chickens, these farms produce little organic waste. Most beneficios now deliver chemical fertilizers directly to the farm, usually without charging for transportation, but unless farmers own or can borrow a wheelbarrow, they must haul the fifty-kilogram sacks on their backs through the narrow rows of coffee trees.[2] Some farmers also apply a recommended second dose of fertilizer in mid-August, though about half said they could not afford to do so.

During the early weeks of the rainy season, farmers also begin to plant new coffee, a task that can last until July, depending on the number of trees to be planted. Every year, some coffee trees die, and others need to be replaced because they have become too old to produce well. If a new field is to be planted, the task is even greater. Though a few farmers grow seedlings in special nursery plots for their own use or to sell to other farmers, most purchase seedlings from other farmers or from the beneficios. In 1990, seedlings sold for about fifteen colónes (about 17¢) each.

During these eight months of the year when coffee is not being harvested, the workload is relatively light. According to one study, farms of one to five hectares (the size of most farms in Pérez Zeledón) require about 642 hours of maintenance work (weeding, pruning, fertilizing, and so forth) per hectare per year (ICAFE 1988). That is, one hectare of coffee requires about twenty hours per week for routine maintenance, making it feasible for one person to care adequately for about two hectares of coffee.

During slack periods, men can be seen fixing roofs or porches or making other house repairs. Men are responsible for weeding the heavy growth around the house, and if the household uses a wood-burning stove, men and older boys are usually charged with cutting wood, though women and younger children often collect smaller branches and twigs. Among those who own motor vehicles, the men of the household operate and maintain them.[3]

Women generally work in their homes, where their responsibilities are many. They take their *oficios domesticos* (domestic duties) very seriously, believing that the maintenance of home and family is an important contribution to the household's production of coffee. As among the middle-class Guatemalan households described by Bossen, "a woman resembles a 'shareholder' in the household 'corporation'" (1984:256). It is to her advantage to support the efforts of male field workers because she shares some of the rewards of their work. Likewise, men benefit from prepared meals, an organized and meticulously clean home, and well-kept children, which are the realization of a desired standard of living for all.[4] Domestic work is seen as a necessary complement to agricultural work. Though domestic duties are not easy (and do not provide the same rewards as farming or wage work, such as monetary income, freedom of movement, and public authority), women said they preferred household work to agricultural work, which they described as difficult and dirty. Work in the ornamental (and sometimes vegetable) gardens that surround most homes was seen as an exception.

A woman's responsibilities of feeding, clothing, and maintaining the home for those who labor directly in coffee production involve many hours of work. Setting aside the constant care required by infants and toddlers, I estimate that the upkeep of the average household requires approximately seventy hours of weekly labor: thirty-five hours of food preparation, twenty hours of cleaning, and fifteen hours of washing, mending, and ironing clothes. Older children, particularly daughters, are recruited early to assist with household chores. Teenage sons might help in the fields if needed.

On a typical day, work starts early. If the family's coffee fields are far from the house, a woman will rise around three-thirty or four o'clock, wash, dress, and begin preparing the light meal that her husband and/or sons will take with them to the fields. She must also prepare breakfast, which usually consists of *agua dulce* (hot water with milk and raw brown sugar) or coffee, accompanied by bread or *gallo pinto* (rice and black beans). Men rise around four-thirty or five, dress, eat, and prepare to leave for the fields by about six o'clock. If the fields are close to home, the woman also can sleep until about five o'clock because the mid-morning meal can be prepared later in the morning and taken to the fields either by herself or a child so that those working in the fields can eat around nine.

Once the field workers have left the house, the woman will prepare breakfast for the rest of her family, who have by that time also gotten out of bed. Following breakfast, even in the humblest dwelling, floors are swept and washed on a daily basis and waxed by hand two or three times a week. Shopping is generally done on a weekly basis, usually on Friday, the market day in San Isidro. Both men and women make the forty-five-minute bus trip, frequently together.

Except for the affluent few who have washing machines, women wash their laundry by hand in large outdoor sinks and hang it outside on lines to dry; during the rainy season it must be whisked into the house when storms threaten. Depending on the size of the household and the method of washing (machine or hand), a woman may spend anywhere from ten to twenty hours per week doing laundry. As with their homes, Costa Ricans are particular about personal cleanliness and appearance. Clothes must be clean, mended, and ironed in order to meet social standards.

Around eleven o'clock in the morning, women begin cooking the main midday meal, which is eaten when the men return home for the day. (Rarely do they prepare food or drink for hired laborers.) During most of the year, this meal is eaten around noon or one o'clock, though during harvest season field workers often do not return until two o'clock or later.

After eating, the men who have been working in the fields will wash and often catch a quick nap, and the women will continue with their unfinished household chores. Though small children always require attention, by mid-afternoon the women can usually take a short break from their domestic chores. The afternoon break is a popular ritual that frequently involves visiting family or friends, sitting on the front porch chatting with neighbors and passers-by, or just watching television. Men occasionally participate, but these coffee breaks are generally female-oriented. Men might take the afternoon to do small chores around the house, visit with their friends, or socialize in the cantina. Around six o'clock, women prepare a final (somewhat smaller) meal, which is followed by visiting or watching television. Most people are in bed and asleep by eight or nine in the evening.

Just as men rarely undertake domestic duties, women rarely participate in routine agricultural work. In less than 9 percent of my sample did women do any routine field work. In households where male labor is in short supply (where there are few or no sons of working age), wives and daughters are sometimes called upon to help with agricultural tasks such as weeding and pruning, but I heard of no cases of women helping with the application of fertilizer—either granular fertilizer, which is broadcast, or foliar fertilizer, which requires carrying a heavy spray tank. For example, Maria Vargas and her husband, Martin Coto, owned two hectares of coffee that was still too young to produce enough to support the family. So Martin and their teenage son worked full-time as agricultural laborers on a nearby farm. Because the time they had available to work their own land was limited, Maria did most of the weeding, planting, and harvesting while her eldest daughter (age fourteen) looked after the two younger children at home. Maria left the fertilizing to her husband and son.

It is clear that child-care responsibilities greatly influence the division of labor. Younger women, both those who remain within their natal households and those who are married but have no small children, contribute more to agricultural tasks than older women or those with small children. Though other arrangements can be and sometimes are made for child care, there is a strong belief that children are best cared for at home. Women with breastfeeding infants were astonished when I suggested that they take their babies to the fields. Women with toddlers explained that they must find someone to care for their children or take them to the fields. Coffee fields are often steep and shelter poisonous snakes and other dangers; small children (under five or six) must be closely supervised. All the women I met who had at one time helped in the fields had quit when their first child was born.

For years, Doris Valentes helped her father with the family's seven-hectare farm (she had no brothers). Neither she nor her only sister did any routine maintenance work in the fields, but by the time she was seventeen (in 1990), Doris was managing the entire harvest: supervising harvesters, measuring the coffee at the end of the day, keeping accounts, and driving the coffee in the family truck to the recibidor, where she supervised the measuring of the crop and collected the receipts. She also routinely helped with such tasks as vaccinating the family's few head of cattle and running errands in the family truck. She was her father's "right-hand-man." Then in 1992 she married and had a child. "How can I help my father now?" she said. "With my baby I am much too busy." Fortunately for her father, Doris's new husband had no land of his own and gladly took her place.

In households with no adult males, one might expect to find women doing routine tasks in the fields by necessity, but this scenario was rarely the case. Because the number of female-headed households in my sample was small (only eight) and their circumstances were quite varied, the reasons for their lack of participation in field work were not entirely clear or consistent. Three women with relatively large landholdings could afford to hire *peones* to do routine maintenance and harvesting in their fields; two others, whose husbands were away working in the United States, arranged for their brothers to tend their fields in return for a share of the crop. The women in the remaining three of those eight households had little or no access to male family labor, and they could not afford to hire help. None had very young children, yet they did little of the work themselves. Consequently, their coffee fields were in poor shape and their yields extremely low.

Marisol Vasquez is a case in point. When her common-law husband, Roberto, abandoned her years ago, he left her to support their five children and her elderly mother. Her household quickly became one of the poorest in Palomas. Yet Marisol said that, despite their circumstances, neither she nor her daughters did any maintenance work in the cafetal (just over one-half hectare) that Roberto had left. "That is men's work," she explained. "It is just too heavy for us." In 1990–1991, their field produced about one-quarter of the average yield.

Most women and men echoed Marisol's biological explanation for the lack of female participation in field work. Yet women elsewhere in the world undertake heavy agricultural tasks, and women in Pérez Zeledón *do* undertake heavy work of other kinds. (For years Marisol collected and sold firewood and harvested sugarcane.)

Even when women are interested in deviating from culturally appropriate work, their opportunities are limited by other factors. Agarwal (1989, 1992) found that a number of social and cultural barriers prevent women from farming in India. Clearly, similar mechanisms are at work in Pérez Zeledón. For example, I observed that women farmers were often less confident than men about their farming abilities and tended to be less knowledgeable about the technical aspects of farming. Most farming information is passed from father to son and through informal male networks, from which women are generally excluded. Men and women generally socialize in different spheres—men frequently in the cantina or on the football field, both of which exclude "respectable" women. Even if she were to be accepted among men in the cantina or on the football field, a woman would lose status and perhaps also lose access to informal networks of mutual aid and information sharing among women. Furthermore, agricultural agencies and farmers' organizations do not encourage women to attend agricultural extension courses, and women have a much harder time getting credit from banks and agricultural businesses than men do.[5]

Since the majority of farming households have a surplus of adult male labor for routine field work, and because a woman's status depends on her skills as an *ama de casa* (housekeeper) and child-care provider, it is not surprising to find most people adhering to this strict division of labor, even when it might seem economically rational to do otherwise. Yet, in an economy dominated by commercial farming, this means that opportunities for single women farmers like Marisol (or women from land-poor and landless households who may need or want agricultural wage work) to raise their incomes are severely limited.

The Coffee Harvest

Costa Rican farm women spend most of the year contributing to the household with their domestic support. But as in other Latin American coffee-producing nations, their labor (and that of older children) is indispensable at harvest time (Bossen 1984; Cardoso 1977; Machado 1977; Reinhardt 1988; Wolf 1956). During the three-to-four-month harvest period (roughly September–December), labor needs are enormous. Coffee does not lend itself to mechanical harvesting, so men, women, and older children are all mobilized to ensure that none of the crop goes to waste. (Children younger than six or seven rarely harvest, because they are difficult to supervise in the fields.) Once picked, coffee cherries must be transported to the receiving stations within twenty-four hours. There farmers collect receipts for their coffee, which they later exchange for payment at the beneficio offices in San Isidro.

Though the government actively promotes coffee picking as a national pastime and "patriotic duty," it is nonetheless difficult and tiring work. To be able to avoid coffee picking is a sign of affluence. Wealthier farming households (usually farms with more than fourteen hectares of coffee) prefer to hire all their harvest labor, though men, and occasionally women, supervise the harvest in order to keep coffee-pickers from adding unwanted green cherries and "trash" (leaves and twigs) to the ripe coffee. In Santa Cruz and Palomas, 50 percent of the sample households were able to harvest their crop using only household labor; 47 percent and 44 percent, respectively, harvested with both family and hired labor. Only 3 percent in Santa Cruz and 6 percent in Palomas used hired labor alone to harvest their crop.

In both villages, competition for harvest labor is intense. Farmers make verbal agreements with harvesters as early in the season as possible, though a few are often still frantically searching for labor as the harvest begins. Smaller-scale farmers, whose harvest-labor needs are modest, may find coffee-pickers locally among friends, neighbors, and relatives or in nearby communities, particularly since harvest times vary between villages at different altitudes. Men and women from households with very small crops will harvest for others locally, though farmers in Santa Cruz commented on the difficulty of finding harvest workers from within the community: "Everyone has his own bit of coffee land, and no one has the time to harvest for others."

The Costa Rican government has legislated in various ways to ensure that farmers have enough labor for the coffee harvest. Unharvested coffee is lost revenue for the state, as well as farmers ("Persiste falta de recolectores," *La Nación*, San José, 14 Dec. 1990, 5A; "₡1.000 millones de pérdidas en café," *La Nación*, San José, 23 Jan. 1991, 5A; "Falta de mano de obra," *Estrella del Sur,* San Isidro, Costa Rica, 15–31 Jan. 1991, 20). In 1990, the government built child-care centers in some parts of the country to allow "housewives to participate in the harvest of coffee, while their children are cared for by child-care experts" ("Guarderías en fincas," *La Nación*, San José, 14 Dec. 1990, 5A). There are no such centers in Santa Cruz or Palomas, so women with young children must either take them along or find others to mind their children. Because relatives and friends are usually out harvesting coffee themselves, most mothers with young children just stay home.

To free older children for the harvest, the Costa Rican government schedules the school vacation to coincide with the peak harvest season on the Meseta Central (December–March). But again, this schedule has done little to help farmers in Pérez Zeledón, where the peak harvest arrives in October and November, when children are still in school. Although poorer families remove their children from school so that they can earn money during the coffee harvest, many families are reluctant to do so.[6]

People from other parts of the country come to Pérez Zeledón each year to harvest coffee. Most of them come from the Coto Brus region near the Panama border. For years, farmers in both Santa Cruz and Palomas hired Nicaraguan families from the refugee camp in

Buenos Aires (Puntarenas). When those refugees returned home in 1991, farmers had to scout about for new workers.

Some farmers make contracts with workers from other parts of the country well in advance of the harvest season; such arrangements entail providing living space for the workers. Thus, during the preharvest season, men must repair workers' houses (usually simple wooden frame houses) or, if need be, build new ones. Because competition for harvest labor can be fierce, providing a comfortable living space (a house with at least access to good water and firewood) often makes the difference between finding labor and being caught short. The lack of sufficient help can mean losing much of the crop. In Palomas, one large absentee landowner has given at least three families free housing for the entire year on the sole condition that they agree to work for him during the harvest season at normal rates of pay. During the remainder of the year, they are free to work where they wish.

Some farmers in Palomas complained that the Finca Santa Fe was "stealing" all their workers by paying higher piece rates. (In 1990–1991, the Finca Santa Fe paid one hundred colónes per cajuela [a standard-sized basket used for the collection of coffee], whereas smaller-scale farmers could pay only the "normal" rate of sixty colónes.) Workers told me, though, that conditions at the Finca Santa Fe and on large estates elsewhere were very impersonal, housing arrangements (in barrack-type sleeping quarters) uncomfortable, and thefts among workers high (of both personal property and coffee picked). For these reasons, many migrant workers preferred to work for smaller, family operations, and many returned to the same family farms in Palomas and Santa Cruz year after year.

The fact that coffee does not ripen uniformly poses other problems for farmers. During the first four to six weeks, maturation is particularly slow, with just a few cherries ripening each day. Coffee pickers dislike harvesting this *granilla*, as it is called. It is difficult to pick the few ripe cherries from among the many green ones, so harvesters, who are paid according to the volume of coffee picked, cannot earn much in a day. For this reason, households that do not have enough labor to pick the granilla themselves must pay a higher piece rate during this part of the season or else risk losing the early crop.

Land Ownership and Acquisition

As might be expected in a society where farming is perceived and practiced as primarily a male activity, in both Santa Cruz and Palomas land is distributed unevenly between males and females. In 1991, 71 percent of landowners were men, and men held title to 82 percent of the land; 29 percent of landowners were women; women held title to 18 percent of the land (table 7). In 39 percent of sample households, women held title to at least some land. Of these women, thirteen were the sole landowners in their households: seven were living with a co-resident spouse; six were single heads of household.

There are several ways in which a person can acquire land. Until recently, Pérez Zeledón was one of Costa Rica's most active agricultural frontiers, and some of the earliest immigrants to Santa Cruz and Palomas acquired lands through homesteading or through agrarian reform programs, in which the government redistributed the nonproductive lands of large landowners. But most residents of Santa Cruz and Palomas arrived during the 1960s and 1970s, by which time little tierra libre was available and reform lands had already been redistributed. Thus, homesteaded lands accounted for only 2.5 percent of the land owned by sample households.

As is often the case when a capital-intensive export crop such as coffee predominates in a region crowded with small farmers, land today is rarely available to rent or sharecrop. This is neither surprising nor unusual. Both Barlett (1982), in her study of farmers in Puriscal,

TABLE 7

Mode of Land Acquisition by Gender:
Number of Landowners and Area of Landholdings
in Sample Households in Palomas and Santa Cruz

Mode of Acquisition	Number of Landowners			Area (Hectares)			Hectares/ Person		
	Males	Females	Total	Males	Females	Total	Males	Females	Total
Inherited from parent	34	20	54	59.77	24.67	84.44	1.76	1.23	1.56
Inherited from spouse	0	5	5	0.00	42.61	42.61	0.00	8.52	8.52
Inherited from other	1	0	1	1.00	0.00	1.00	1.00	0.00	1.00
Bought	36	6	42	357.56	3.62	361.18	9.93	0.61	8.60
Bought jointly[a]	8	2	10	42.08	2.86	44.95	5.26	1.43	4.50
Transfered from spouse	2	2	24	1.73	29.84	31.57	0.87	14.92	7.84
Traded	2	0	2	1.04	0.00	1.04	0.52	0.00	0.52
Homesteaded	1	0	1	14.49	0.00	14.49	14.49	0.00	14.49
Total	84	35	119	477.67	103.60	581.27	5.69	2.96	4.88
(percent)	(70.6)	(29.4)	(100.0)	(82.2)	(17.8)	(100.0)			

Source: Author's sample survey, 1990–1991.

[a] For analytical purposes, in this table the area of lands bought jointly was divided equally among co-owners.

Costa Rica, in the 1970s, and Ortiz (1973), in her work in the 1960s with Paéz coffee farmers in Colombia, found that the scarcity of land was such that land had to be either bought or inherited. At the time of my study in Pérez Zeledón, sons (and occasionally daughters) who had not yet legally inherited were often "given" parcels of land to work either independently or cooperatively with their parents, but loaning, renting, or sharecropping with those who had no future claim on the land was rare. Farmers told me that there just was not enough land to rent or loan out. Though the Brazilian *colono* system (where large plantation owners provide landless farmers with small plots of land in exchange for coffee care) was practiced for a time in the east-central canton of Turrialba (Loomis 1953; Norris 1953; Holloway 1977), in Pérez Zeledón farms have never been sufficiently large nor labor in such short supply that such a system has been necessary or practical.

Sixty-two percent of all land owned in the sample households was bought by the current owners. Nearly all of that purchased land (98%) was bought by men (either alone or jointly with another person). Male control of income from coffee production probably accounts for the fact that men purchase far more land than women. Four of the six women who bought land (only 2% of all purchased lands) had first inherited elsewhere; they then sold their inherited land and used the money to buy new property (either alone or with their spouses) in Pérez Zeledón. It is likely that purchases by men often were financed in a similar manner. Many men who immigrated to Pérez Zeledón may have sold their rights to family land in the north (to older brothers, for example), using the capital to purchase relatively inexpensive land in Pérez Zeledón. (Further investigation would establish how frequently this actually occurred.)

The other principal means by which land is acquired is through inheritance. Costa Rican law dictates that sons and daughters inherit equally from their parents, but as table 7 shows, in practice land is not evenly inherited by men and women: only 37 percent of those who inherited land from a parent were women. They inherited an average of 1.23 hectares, whereas men inherited an average of 1.76 hectares. Though women in this region continue to inherit land, they do so less often than their brothers. It appears that many daughters of Palomas and Santa Cruz, like their mothers who left the Central Valley with no inheritance, are beginning to "give up" (by choice or "persuasion") their rights to family lands in favor of a brother or brothers.

Daughters may not be inheriting equally in Pérez Zeledón, but neither are sons, though they are favored over daughters. Despite official inheritance laws, such findings are not surprising. During the latter half of the nineteenth and the first half of the twentieth centuries, similar changes in patterns of land inheritance occurred in Herédia, the province just north of San José. Historical studies show that as the coffee economy expanded throughout the Central Valley, and as population grew and land became more scarce, families increasingly urged some heirs either to hold shared rights on undivided farms or to sell inheritance rights to other heirs or third parties (Samper 1990:220). More well-to-do families increasingly provided "advances" on inheritance to help children migrate to new frontiers. Although formal accounts of the distribution of inheritance varied little over time, in reality, inheritance rights were "sometimes a legal fiction, disguising the actual exclusion of certain heirs, especially women" (221; see also Gudmundson 1995a).[7]

With diminishing farm size and land scarcity, farming families in Pérez Zeledón regularly face similar choices regarding the distribution of property among their children. Like their historical counterparts in Herédia, farming households in Pérez Zeledón have three options: to favor one or a few heirs over others, to finance out-migration of some heirs in the hope of avoiding conflict, or to divide the farm equally into small lots (Gudmundson 1995a:124). The relatively large proportion of self-supporting family farms in Santa Cruz and Palomas (over 41%) is likely due to the availability (until recently) of tierra libre in this frontier region, but it may also be the result of decisions to restrict partibility in order to preserve family lands intact, as happened in Herédia during the early part of the century.[8]

Title to land is also acquired through the death of a spouse or the dissolution of a marriage, though the latter is not common. Among sample households, only three women (and no men) acquired lands by either manner. These three women held 41.5 percent of all female-owned lands in the sample, but most of it was acquired by one woman in Palomas when she legally separated from her husband, a wealthy landowner who now lives in San José but who still oversees the farming of her (and their children's) lands. It is more common for agricultural lands to be inherited directly by sons, bypassing the widow.

Sometimes land titles are transferred inter vivos from one family member to another. There are several reasons for doing so. First, and most common, title is transferred from parents to children in anticipation of inheritance. This practice is becoming more usual, primarily to avoid future inheritance taxes and lengthy and costly probate. In other cases, women transfer their land titles to their husbands and vice versa. For example, when Mayella Cárdenas's father died, she inherited 1.5 hectares of land in the canton of Terrazú (in central Costa Rica). Because she was already married and living in Pérez Zeledón, she sold the land and bought 1.7 hectares near her home in Palomas. Two years later she transferred the title of that land to her husband so that he could use it as collateral for loans to buy more land. (Banks are more likely to loan to men, and legal title is a prerequisite for most bank loans).

Conversely, in some cases, men put the legal title of their lands into their wives' names. For example, in Santa Cruz, Oldimar Quezada and Franklin Montoya transferred title of their farms (14.5 hectares and 18.0 hectares, respectively) to their wives. But like the *benami* practices found in Bangladesh and India, transfer of title is nominal, to avoid taxation (see White 1992). In eight households (10.5%), title to land was held jointly by spouses, fathers and sons, brothers and sisters, mothers and daughters, or in larger combinations. One farm in Santa Cruz was owned jointly by a local farmer and a Chilean financier. (Unless affordable credit becomes more accessible in Costa Rica, this type of arrangement is likely to become more common.)

In two cases, families have registered their lands as small, jointly owned firms. This move to incorporate household farms into small companies is new and, I was told, not explicitly allowed for under the Costa Rican tax code. Nevertheless, others told me that they were also considering incorporation. When a farm becomes a legal company, adult workers can receive salaries for their labor (including women's domestic support work), which can be deducted as expenses from the firm's earnings. It will be interesting to see whether this practice becomes more common, among what kinds of households, and how it affects gender relations within the household.

Finally, it is worth noting that land is sometimes obtained through guile. For example, when Marisol Vasquez, whom we met earlier, was abandoned by Roberto Zamora after fifteen years of living *conjunto*, she did not have title to their coffee field and so could neither use it as collateral for production loans nor sell it. As a common-law wife, her claim to the property was weak, and she had no family nearby to support her claim. Finally, she convinced Roberto's sister, with whom she remained on good terms, to help her gain legal title to his land. Though it is unclear exactly how they managed to do so, Marisol is now legal owner of the cafetal. According to Marisol, Roberto was, of course, angry when he discovered what had happened, but because he had abandoned his family, he dared not make a fuss. It is impossible to know exactly what tactics were employed in any such transaction; nonetheless, this case not only demonstrates that land is sometimes obtained through surreptitious methods but also underscores the importance of legal ownership for economic security.[9]

Property and the Politics of Decision Making

Labor contributions to production certainly bolster one's position within the household. As those in cash-crop systems elsewhere, women in Pérez Zeledón invest substantial labor in domestic upkeep and harvesting, but their work is considered "support work"; men's year-round direct contributions to coffee production are used to legitimize their overall greater authority in farming households and their greater control of both productive resources and income from coffee sales, which they manage. But the importance of field labor can be exaggerated. As we have seen, women from wealthier households are precisely those who can (and do) escape work in the fields. Yet many of these women, as well as those from less well-to-do households, hold substantial sway in their households. In fact, if we hold labor relatively constant—by comparing decision-making power of women with women and that of men with men—the importance of land in household negotiations and decision making becomes more clear.

Gender

Though women overall own much less land than men, my data show that even when they perform no field labor, women who bring land into their conjugal households have considerably more decision-making power regarding both production and consumption than do their landless counterparts. For example, forty-year-old Hannia Gamboa has not worked in her household's coffee fields since the birth of her first child, twenty years ago. When she married Flavio Valentes, a landless farmer, the seven hectares of coffee that she inherited from her father was all they had to live on. Flavio took over the day-to-day running of the farm, while Hannia manages the domestic duties. But he constantly seeks her opinion on long-term strategies, and they discuss all major decisions together.

In a similar situation, Lidia Ovares inherited 1.7 hectares of coffee from her father upon his death in 1952. (Her only brother inherited the same amount of land.) Her husband, Juan Castillo, owned none. Like Flavio Valentes, Juan does all the work in the coffee fields, but no financial decision is made without consulting Lidia. She was formerly a school teacher and manages their operations by keeping detailed accounts of production expenses and income. Juan is more knowledgeable about the technical aspects of coffee production, and Lidia listens with care when he makes a suggestion concerning their crop. She most often agrees with his suggestions, but he nevertheless brings all problems to Lidia, and together they decide what course of action to take. Lidia is not particularly wealthy, but the combination of education and land ownership have made her one of the most respected women in Palomas.

Husband and wife hold joint title to land in just two sample households (both in Santa Cruz). In both cases, decision-making power also seems to be jointly shared, though one might defer to the expertise of the other. For example, shortly after they married and moved to Santa Cruz, Julio Balboa and Petronila Chavez together bought 2.75 hectares of coffee. (It is unclear where the money to purchase this land initially came from.) Like most other women, Petronila does no work in the coffee fields, except for a day or two of harvesting. Yet she and Julio discuss all major decisions concerning household production and consumption. She is free to purchase small items (such as clothes, cosmetics, knickknacks, and so forth) for herself and the household at her discretion, though she is expected to use her skills and good judgment not to exceed the family's means.

In contrast, women with no claim to land generally have less influence in household economic decisions. Twenty-six-year-old Rocio Castillo explained her situation:

> My father was a coffee farmer in Santa Maria de Dota [a populous canton near San José]. When he died, the farm was divided among my four brothers—with just five manzanas [3.5 hectares], there was not enough land for me and my two sisters. They had no money for us either, so I came to Santa Cruz and married Jesús, who had four manzanas [2.75 hectares] of coffee. I don't work in the cafetales, except each year I harvest coffee on one manzana [0.69 hectares] with our two oldest children. Jesús lets us use the profits from this manzana of coffee as we wish.

She goes on to say, however, that Jesús has the final word on where to sell the crop.

> For years I have sold my coffee to Coopeagri because they pay higher prices and I believe in their goals; Jesús always sells the rest of the crop to El General. But last year [1991], Jesús said that I could no longer sell my coffee to the cooperative. He does not like it, and their recibidor is too far from our fields. I will receive less money for my coffee at El General, but I cannot go against the wishes of my husband. The land is really his, and it is for him to decide.

It is important to distinguish between de jure ownership and de facto control. Although de jure property ownership bestows a measure of legitimacy and decision-making authority on the owner, it does not guarantee total control of the property: "De facto landholding rights that are recognized and respected by one's neighbors may be more functionally important than de jure legal rights established by national governments" (Netting 1993:157).[10] Community recognition of rights may legitimize control of property by individuals who do not have legal title; a strong network of family and friends can ensure that those rights are protected. This is particularly evident in cases where titles are transferred to husbands or wives for bureaucratic purposes.

After Mayella Cárdenas transferred the title of her 1.5 hectares to her husband, they had better access to credit, but the process of decision making within the household changed little. Mayella still does no regular maintenance work in the coffee fields nor even helps harvest the coffee; nevertheless, she is consulted in all major decisions regarding use of the family's land and of loans obtained when the land is used as collateral. She is free to spend money on the daily running of the household and small personal items as she pleases, though all major household expenditures are discussed together by the family.

Like women who have never held title to land, women who have land registered in their names only for tax purposes seem to have little influence in household economic decisions. Even though these women may have legal title to large parcels of land, their husbands conceptually remain the landowners and continue to control the land and make all production decisions.

For example, as noted earlier, Celia Marin holds title to the eighteen hectares of land that her husband, Franklin Montoya, transferred to her in 1970. But it is clear that the land is hers in title only. Franklin continues to control the family income and makes all decisions regarding both production and household consumption. Celia must ask Franklin for money for even the smallest purchase for herself or the household. She might have held a stronger position if her labor had been crucial to the production of the household's coffee or sugar, but during the year I conducted fieldwork, her sons and daughters-in-law provided more than enough labor to keep the farm running smoothly. With her children grown and married (all but one son), her work within the home was less valued. She fed her husband and son and cleaned the house, but overall, Celia's contributions to the domestic economy were minimal.

When a husband puts title to land in his wife's name for tax purposes, she is unlikely to sell or mortgage it for her own investment, not only for fear of reprisal from her husband, but because she knows she will get no support for her actions from the community, where he is recognized as the true owner. Likewise, when a woman transfers or sells her inheritance, and land is bought in her husband's name, community recognition of her claim to the property serves as a deterrent to potential abuses on the part of the husband—even in cases of immigrant women like Mayella Cárdenas, who live in communities with no immediate kin outside their marital households. Thus, de jure land ownership provides some women with a greater measure of power within the household, but community recognition of a person's rights to land is equally essential.

Generation

Young men who work daily in the coffee fields certainly make enormous contributions to coffee production, but their ability to formulate their own economic strategies also depends a great deal on rights to land. Though men overall own more land than women, I found that fewer younger men owned land, and they owned less. Of the eighty-four male landowners in my sample, the average size of landholding for men younger than twenty-five was 1.4 hectares; men of age twenty-five to forty-four owned an average of 6.7 hectares; and men forty-five and over averaged 7.7 hectares. (Of thirty-five female landowners, the figures were 1.4, 1.1, and 9.7 hectares for the same age groups.)

Until children (even married children living in separate households) obtain full and unobstructed rights to land, their ability to formulate their own economic strategies is limited by their relationship with their parents (or others who provide access to land). Children who are given de facto rights to portions of their parents' property are freer to formulate their own strategies than those who have only partial use rights or no rights at all.

The economic relationships between parents and the households of married children vary greatly and depend in large part on how family resources are divided. There is no clear norm dictating when parents transfer control or title to family property to their children. In a few cases, while parents are still living, children receive clear title to family lands, but usually parents simply provide use rights.

The nature of those rights also varies from family to family and seems to be closely related to the way in which production is organized. In what I shall term *independently oriented* families, parents and children typically share capital goods such as trucks and tools, but children have full use rights to portions of their parents' land and make all decisions regarding the specific uses of land, labor, and incomes as they see fit. In *cooperatively oriented* families, the parental and married children's households combine labor and productive resources to farm parents' lands together. In these cases, children are "given" specific plots of land to farm and may use the earnings as they please, but parents (specifically the father) make most decisions concerning the use of capital goods, land, and labor.

The Muñoz family in Palomas is an example of an independently oriented family. Roberto Muñoz is fifty-four years old and considered a successful farmer. He and five of his seven sons farm seventeen hectares of land. All but one son, who is single and continues to live at home, are married (or cohabiting) and maintain their own households. (The other two sons have gone to the United States to work; their only daughter lives with her husband in a nearby community.) When his sons began to show an interest in and ability for farming, Roberto "gave" each one 2.75 hectares to farm as his own, though Roberto retained title. In 1990, he began the lengthy and expensive process of legally transferring the title of each parcel to his sons.

According to Roberto and his sons (and confirmed by my own observations), though they have always shared information and the family truck, each has been responsible for his own farm; they make their own decisions about what and when to plant and do not share labor. During harvesttime, when labor is most crucial and most in demand, each household is responsible for finding its own workers, though one son told me that if he gets in a bind his father will "loan" him his peones for a day or two. The son, of course, must pay the laborers himself.

Although very much like the Muñozes, Franklin Montoya's family is cooperatively oriented. Franklin is a man in his mid-forties and considered a successful farmer. He and his wife, Celia, have five sons and three daughters. Like the Muñoz family, all children but one son are married and maintain separate households. Like Roberto Muñoz, Franklin Montoya allows his unmarried son, three married sons, and one married daughter to farm small parcels of the family's land. Unlike the Muñozes, the Montoyas share not only capital equipment but also labor. On a daily basis they exchange labor for all chores, as well as share the costs for upkeep of the family's truck and oxen. Harvesting is done by members of all five households working cooperatively on each plot. Franklin describes his working arrangement with his children as "cooperative," but he maintains firm control over the land (the title belongs to his wife, Celia) and the family's labor. Children are free to use the proceeds from "their" fields as they wish, but Franklin coordinates all production and marketing activities.

These cooperative and independent strategies provide advantages and disadvantages for parents and children alike. In the cooperative arrangement, on the one hand, each household in the working kin group has access to productive land, labor, and capital equipment, and the risks of production are shared by all. In this way, parents and children work to ensure a secure living for one another. However, managing large areas of farmland and supervising individuals from several households, whose needs, aspirations, and temperaments may vary considerably, can be a tiresome and time-consuming task for parents. For children, depending upon the goodwill of their parents for access to land can be frustrating. Without control of land, dependent children are unable to make basic production and consumption decisions for themselves and their families.

In the independent arrangement, on the other hand, parents are not burdened with the problems of managing all the land and coordinating all the labor from several households; children have greater control over production and can invest their labor and resources as they choose. But while each household reaps the rewards of its own efforts, each also bears the risks and costs of production on its own.

Though some parents allow their grown children considerably more freedom in making decisions regarding the use of the family's productive resources than others, most parents at least provide their future heirs with usufruct rights to land whenever possible. But in a few extreme cases, children are cut off from all use of property until after the parents' death.

For example, upon the death of her husband in 1980, Aña Quiros inherited fourteen hectares of good agricultural land, but for reasons that remain unclear, rather than permit her children to farm the land, she allowed it to return to forest. Meanwhile, her six sons and one daughter remained landless. Her sons were forced to work as local day laborers; her daughter, a single mother with seven young children, was particularly hard-pressed to support her family, relying primarily on income from a boarder she took into her home. When Aña died in 1991, the land went through a lengthy and costly probate, eventually being divided among the eagerly awaiting heirs. When I expressed my amazement that anyone would let so much land go idle while children struggled to survive, I was told by one granddaughter that Aña would not allow her children to work the land while she was alive because she was afraid that once she did so, they would stop looking after her. Perhaps Aña feared that as an elderly widow her legal claim to the land would be insufficient to maintain control over the property once her children (the recognized heirs to the land) began farming the land themselves.

Fortunately for most children, this was an unusual case. Most parents try to ensure that their children (at least their sons) have access to productive land, and parents with larger properties rely on their children's labor to help work that land. Why some parents prefer to retain control over land and their married children's labor, while others relinquish control early, is unclear. There are no cultural norms that prescribe how and when parents should relinquish control of their property. As Netting found among Swiss farmers (1981:170), in Santa Cruz and Palomas tensions and conflict arise as expectant heirs await their inheritances and the ability to control their own property. As in the case of Aña Quiros, it is likely that individual circumstances and temperaments had as much to do with the control and transmission of property as did state and customary law.

Pinpointing the causal factors underlying decision-making power within and among economically related farming households is not an easy task. The cases presented here illustrate the complexity and variability of households and the difficulty of separating material factors from sociocultural factors. Notions of appropriate work (and the value placed on that work); the ownership, transmission, and control of land; and opportunities to gain other valuable (e.g., technical and/or managerial) skills are regulated by socially and culturally constructed norms. Bargaining power, opportunities, expectations, and ambitions of men and women, young and old, vary accordingly.

The data from farming households in Palomas and Santa Cruz suggest that, in agrarian economies (where land is the key productive resource), an individual's ability to influence decisions pertaining to the use of household resources and income is significantly enhanced if he or she has rights to land. Community recognition of pre-existing rights legitimizes control of property by individuals who do not have legal title; a strong network of family and friends can ensure that those rights are protected.

Still, there are a number of barriers that discourage women, and sometimes men, from exercising their legal claims to land or from controlling and independently farming land to which they have access. Social, cultural, and economic factors that funnel women's labor primarily into domestic work and restrict their access to agricultural information, technology, and credit also limit their ability to own and use land (see Agarwal 1989; Boserup 1970; Bossen 1995; Lockwood 1989).

In Pérez Zeledón, a region with few employment opportunities outside of agriculture, economic security within both the household and community remains strongly tied to ownership and control of land. Women's already tenuous connection to coffee production is likely to make it increasingly difficult for them to pursue claims to land in the future. As population increases, coffee production expands, and land becomes increasingly scarce, we shall likely see increased stratification both within households (as women inherit less land) and among households (as some sons inherit at the expense of other sons and daughters). Nevertheless, as we shall see in chapter 7, many families are beginning to compensate daughters and some sons in other ways, particularly with greater education. Should the regional economy diversify, new opportunities for nonagricultural skills may present themselves, and incomes from skilled wage work could offset in significant ways disparities in land ownership and control.

Part
Two

Strategies for Survival
and Mobility

5

Against the Wind

Local Organizations and Change

It is necessary for farmers to unite. . . .

In our age, isolated voices are like voices given to the wind.

—Coopeagri

Over the past two decades, a great deal of attention has been given to grassroots, participatory, community-level development. Scholars and planners have increasingly turned to various types of local organizations, such as producer cooperatives and community associations, for solutions to local problems (Berger and Neuhaus 1984; Cernea 1988; Esman and Uphoff 1984; Korten and Klauss 1984).

I had not been long in Palomas and Santa Cruz when I discovered a striking enthusiasm for defining and solving community problems through collective, grassroots efforts. My interest in how the canton's coffee-processing cooperative might contribute to the well-being of small farmers was largely responsible for bringing me to Pérez Zeledón in the first place. But I was surprised to find that within these communities there were also a number of active community associations dedicated to improving economic and social conditions at the local level. Most prominent were the formally organized ADCs. It was clear that farmers' collective efforts to strengthen their position in the coffee market and to improve village conditions were part of overall household strategies for survival and mobility.

Coopeagri: *Beneficiando[1]* Pérez Zeledón

La Niña Is Born

For years, farmers in Pérez Zeledón, like those throughout the country, endured consistently late payments for their crops and other poor treatment from the beneficios. Then in 1962, prompted by the growing awareness and promotion of cooperatives that was emerging throughout Latin America at the time, a group of 391 smallholders joined together to form the canton's first (and to date only) coffee-processing cooperative, the Cooperativa Caficultura de Pérez Zeledón. They first rented and later bought the San Jorge beneficio, which had recently gone bankrupt. By pooling their resources and collectively owning and operating their own beneficio, coffee farmers hoped to better their situation vis-à-vis the transnational corporations and the international coffee market, improve farming and marketing conditions, and earn higher incomes.

The early founders of Cooperativa Caficultura were deeply committed to their cooperative. Years later, one writer described the organization with parental pride and affection, referring to the cooperative as *"la niña,"* a child that was nurtured and protected: "'La niña' was robust . . . because the associates defended her from the attacks of her enemies. . . . Now in the present there is no lack of an enemy here or there, but they can't do her damage because they are very weak and 'la niña' is very gallant, favored, and protected" (Mora Zuñiga 1987:13–14).

But opposition to the cooperative was strong, and even the smallholders who stood to benefit the most from a cooperative processing factory were reluctant to support the fledgling organization, for both ideological and economic reasons. The 1960s Cold War ideological battles that were being fought at the global level were finding their way into the Costa Rican countryside. Many farmers believed *cooperativismo* to be a form of communism and were afraid of losing control over their land and their labor.[2] Some simply ignored the cooperative; others openly opposed it. One member of the cooperative's first Education Committee recalled how he was once roughly grabbed by another patron in a village cantina. His attacker raised his fist, shouting "Communist!" When the co-op member asked for an explanation, the angry man replied: "Because you say all of us with coffee *must* become members of the cooperative" (Mora Zuñiga 1987:11).

Organizers did manage to recruit many farmers into the cooperative, but participation rates were low at first; frequently meetings were arranged in communities and no one showed up. Many would join and then quit soon after. There were even incidents of sabotage, as when an entire stock of processed coffee was completely destroyed by being drenched with oil (Mora Zuñiga 1987:5–6, 10). The culprit was never caught. One can only speculate, but among others, the private beneficios had surely wanted the co-op to fail.

Farmers also feared economic disaster. Despite the favorable operating environment that the state provided for co-ops, Costa Rican newspapers were full of accounts of failures. One problem was that many cooperatives formed in the 1960s naively bought beneficios that had previously declared bankruptcy because of overwhelming debts. Attempting to recoup some of their losses, banks sold these factories to cooperatives at inflated prices (Cazanga 1987:108). Thus, although low interest rates and liberal terms of repayment helped the new enterprises to get started, many cooperatives were burdened with crushing debts from the outset. Afflicted also with frequent mismanagement, corruption, and lack of member participation, coffee cooperatives did not have a good reputation.

Ideology, Structure, and Policy

Coopeagri, as the co-op is now known, is a large, agro-industrial business that operates a modern coffee-processing facility in a highly competitive capitalist environment. In this respect it is much like the four private beneficios in the canton; but as a cooperative, Coopeagri operates according to specific legal and ideological principles that set it apart from its private competitors.

Like cooperatives elsewhere, Coopeagri defines itself in terms of an ideology that promotes mutual self-help efforts aimed at improving economic opportunities for the less powerful segments of society. This ideology of cooperativismo pervades presentations to the public at large (such as its weekly radio program), as well as annual reports to its membership, but it goes beyond rhetoric to form the operational basis of the cooperative as a business organization.

As regulated by Costa Rican law, Coopeagri is owned and operated by farmer members. The relationship between coffee farmers and Coopeagri is more formal than that between farmers and the private beneficios and entails a stronger commitment from both parties. Selling coffee to the latter is quite simple: the farmer merely delivers coffee cherries to the recibidor and collects a receipt that is cashed at the company's offices in San Isidro. But to sell coffee to Coopeagri, a producer must first join the cooperative by making a formal application for membership, then attending a two-hour orientation lecture that outlines the general ideology of cooperativismo and acquaints the potential member with the specific operations of Coopeagri and the benefits and responsibilities of membership. In theory, each cooperative member is a shareholder, an owner of the organization, and is committed to share the responsibilities as well as the benefits of membership.

There are two kinds of members in Coopeagri: producers and employees. The former include all those who produce a product—coffee, sugar, milk—that they wish to market through the cooperative; the latter include those who are paid to work in various capacities within the cooperative, such as the beneficio manager, people who work in the processing factory and on the co-op's several small farms, and office clerks. In 1990, Coopeagri had 3,967 coffee producers, 615 sugarcane producers, 107 milk producers, and 160 employee members (Coopeagri 1991:23). Each member, regardless of type of membership or size of landholding, has one vote.

One condition of membership for agricultural producers is proof of legal access to land, such as a copy of a deed of sale, a rental contract, or a loan agreement. In addition, all applicants must present two recommendations, one from the local coordinator and one from the delegate for his or her area of residence. These recommendations are usually a mere formality and involve no more than a signature on the application. The final requirement for membership is a one-time fee of one thousand colónes (in 1990, about ten dollars).

The terms of membership are simple. First, each producer agrees to sell his or her product exclusively to the cooperative. In the case of sugar and milk, Coopeagri owns the only processing factories in the region, and farmers have little choice but to sell to the co-op. Coffee farmers have more choice and, as we shall see, for various reasons do not always honor this agreement.

Second, the cooperative may deduct 5 percent of the annual value of each member's product (or wages, in the case of worker members) and place it in the member's savings account.[3] This money can be withdrawn only upon termination of one's membership. In the meantime, members' savings are used by the cooperative as working capital to provide loans to producer members to help finance agricultural production and other operating costs. The policy for providing interest on members' savings has varied over the years, depending on the financial status of the cooperative and members' desires. If the cooperative has surplus funds, members can vote that some of that money be used to pay interest on their savings, as they did at the 1991 General Assembly. (Members can also vote to distribute surpluses in the form of cash dividends or to reinvest them in expanding Coopeagri operations.)

Membership in Coopeagri can be terminated by the member at any time, by submitting a letter to the administration renouncing membership. At the end of the fiscal year, the cooperative determines what, if any, outstanding debts the member may still have. Once the debts have been paid, the member is free to leave the cooperative, and his or her savings are repaid (though not always in one lump sum). Associates who renounce their membership with Coopeagri must wait five years from the date of termination before petitioning again for membership. In practice, many members quit when the family requires the savings to meet expenses; then a different member of the household joins so that the household can continue to receive the benefits of cooperative membership.

To run their business, farmers elect from among themselves an administrative board of directors. By law, the General Assembly meets once a year to review operations, discuss problems, and elect representatives for a number of administrative committees. In cooperatives with a small membership (in the hundreds of members), all members are entitled to attend the annual General Assembly, but in large cooperatives such as Coopeagri, which had a membership of more than four thousand in 1990, the presence of every member would make the proceedings cumbersome and less effective. Hence, the law allows for a system of elected representatives: for each twenty-five members, local constituencies elect one delegate (and one supplemental delegate) to represent them at the annual General Assembly.

In addition to the local delegates, members elect local coordinators (one for every fifty members). Every three months, coordinators meet at Coopeagri's offices in San Isidro to discuss members' concerns. They then report to their members the results of the meetings. A few coordinators hold regular meetings in their areas, but I was told that those usually are not well attended. Because of the small and intimate nature of rural communities, most coordinators and their constituents pass information back and forth to one another informally, on a day-to-day basis.

Each February, prior to the annual General Assembly, the board of directors and management personnel meet with members in each district of Pérez Zeledón. Official reports are tendered concerning the status of the cooperative, and then members' comments, concerns, and suggestions are heard. It is a lengthy process, which continues until all who wish to speak have been heard. Although participation at the annual General Assembly is restricted to coordinators and delegates, at these local meetings members are encouraged to openly voice their opinions—and none seemed shy in doing so.

Development practitioners and cooperative idealists frequently have envisioned cooperatives as institutions for distributing social services and providing a means for social and political empowerment (Apthorpe 1971:79). The cooperative ideology fits well with an increasing emphasis on grassroots, participatory, community-level development (see Chambers 1983; Stull and Schensul 1987). These ideological principles have also guided Coopeagri, but it has always placed a strong emphasis on improving the economic situation of its members by trying to operate a profitable economic organization. Farmers in Pérez Zeledón are quick to say that "cooperativismo must be in the pocket as well as in the heart," an idea that Coopeagri has astutely put into action. Since its inception, the cooperative has been concerned with operating a beneficio that would "generate net revenues and thus improve incomes and marketing conditions for the small and medium coffee producers in Pérez Zeledón" (Coopeagri 1989:7).

Though coffee processing has been its main purpose, through the years Coopeagri has expanded its activities and services to become one of the country's largest multipurpose cooperatives and a model cooperative in Latin America. In 1969, it established a supermarket, and in 1974, it bought the canton's only sugar refinery, with the hope of expanding the economic opportunities of farmers in the region.[4] Cane producers who were close enough to take advantage of the factory now had a new and more profitable outlet for their cane, and many substantially increased their production.

Unfortunately, as has happened to many coffee cooperatives in Costa Rica, in the late 1970s Coopeagri ran into a number of organizational and management problems and nearly collapsed. Cooperatives worldwide have a varied track record. Internal factionalism, corruption, mismanagement, low participation rates, poor economic planning, and bureaucratic interference have contributed to the failure of many cooperatives (Baviskar and Attwood 1995; Eckstein 1970; Van den Berghe and Peters 1988). Though Coopeagri's diversification policy is aimed at providing economic stability by spreading risks, with the purchase of the sugar refinery came a number of unanticipated costs, both financial and managerial.

The first few years of operation of the sugar refinery were extremely difficult. By 1979, it was losing money, and coffee producers complained as the cooperative began to funnel funds from other departments into the failing sugar factory. Despite, or perhaps because of, heavy investment in upgrading the sugar factory's machinery, Coopeagri's debts were so great that Infocoop (the National Institute for the Promotion of Cooperatives) threatened to declare Coopeagri insolvent. Though closing the sugar refinery would have cut losses, the leaders and many members (cane farmers in particular) were concerned about the loss of this alternative industry in the valley.[5]

Fortunately, the disaster provoked drastic changes in the management of the cooperative that have been crucial in keeping the organization alive. According to Guillermo Quesada, the beneficio manager from 1986 to 1992, Coopeagri suffered from management problems common to many Costa Rican cooperatives. Managers were selected from among the farmer members, who for the most part have little or no business training. Moreover, pay is low, because cooperatives try to keep costs down. The result is that inexperienced, unqualified, underpaid people are put into positions of managing technically complicated and expensive business operations.

To solve that problem, the board of directors proposed, and members agreed, to hire a university-educated, professional manager to run the beneficio and a qualified chemical engineer to take over the sugar factory. In addition, the new managers ran their departments independently, with a coordinating manager overseeing general operations. The new arrangement was instrumental in Coopeagri's recovery. It allowed managers to specialize, it no longer burdened a single person with running the entire cooperative's diverse enterprises, and it tightened accountability.

Despite the costs of diversification, Coopeagri has continued to expand its operations. In 1980, members voted to open an agricultural supply store and in 1984 to buy a local milk-processing plant, which produces not only a variety of milk products but also fruit juices (both from purchased syrups and from local fruits). Through a deal with the Swedish consortium of consumer cooperatives, Cecoop (Centro Cooperativa), Coopeagri also acquired a *supermobil,* a large van equipped as a mobile supermarket, which visits several rural communities each week, bringing goods that are often not available in the local pulperias. Eventually, Coopeagri also plans to build small grocery stores in several communities (land has already been bought in five districts).

In 1983, the co-op established its Women's Group, the brainstorm of one dynamic and energetic woman, Marcelly Orozco. The Women's Group evolved after Coopeagri set up a refugee center for the people of Buena Vista, who had suffered severe losses from a large earthquake. According to Orozco, the Buena Vista women, assisted by men and women of Coopeagri, worked hard to put their lives back together and rebuild the community. Inspired by their success, women from other communities expressed interest in helping others and formed similar local groups. Coopeagri's support for the Women's Group was, no doubt, also facilitated by the fact that Marcelly Orozco was the wife of the president.

Orozco says her goals include "awakening" women to the fact that they are human beings who form a vital part of society, but the primary focus of the group thus far has been to teach marketable artisan and craft skills to rural women who have few other opportunities to earn income. The group's nearly two hundred members in eighteen communities meet weekly in their communities to learn and practice new techniques, compare products, and discuss problems and future projects. The co-op also offers workshops on community development, at which women identify problems within their own communities and design solutions that draw predominantly on local resources and skills.

Finally, in the early 1990s, the cooperative established a number of small experimental farms for the production of macadamia nuts and has been working with the national government to channel funds into reforestation projects. These projects employ about one hundred landless agricultural laborers, who enjoy benefits as Coopeagri members.

Coopeagri's basic aims are to deliver the highest possible price for crops and to offer agricultural inputs to its members at low cost, but it also offers its members a variety of other benefits not provided by private competitors. They include agricultural and veterinary consulting services and a medical clinic—all free of charge for members and at low cost for their families. Though loans have always been made to producers to cover production costs, the cooperative is currently in the process of creating a separate credit and loan branch, which will allow members to apply for credit to invest in other projects, such as home improvements.

The Odd Couple: *"Solidadismo"* and *Sindicalismo*

Coopeagri stands out as one of the economically most successful agricultural cooperatives in Costa Rica, but it is also exceptional in another important way. Unlike most cooperatives in Latin America, Coopeagri has developed. what it calls an integrated rural development plan, which goes beyond agricultural industries to improve life in Pérez Zeledón in other ways. The most unusual thing about this farmers' cooperative is that, in addition to helping agricultural producers, it has placed the problem of landless agricultural laborers on the agenda.

In 1991, with the help of the Institute for Agrarian Development (IDA), Coopeagri was negotiating with the Costa Rican government to acquire nearly two thousand hectares of land. The co-op plans to give landless laborers ninety-nine-year leases on small plots of that land, along with guarantees of credit and technical assistance. These long-term tenants would be encouraged to grow sugarcane, coffee, and macadamia nuts, which Coopeagri would purchase, process, and export, and basic grains, which the cooperative would purchase, process, and sell locally in its supermarkets.

Coopeagri has been able to extend its agenda in large part because of a close relationship, dating from 1977, with the Union de Productores Independientes de Agroproductos Varios (UPIAV, Union of Independent Producers of Various Agricultural Products), a local syndicate of farmers and agricultural workers. Many of the co-op's elected leaders are also union leaders, a state of affairs that has caused a stir not only in Pérez Zeledón but also throughout Costa Rica.

Historically in Costa Rica, the syndicate movement, *sindicalismo,* has been at odds with the "*solidadismo*" movement, with which cooperatives are normally associated. Ideologically, *sindicatos* (labor unions) organize workers in opposition to capitalists and managers; most of Costa Rica's syndicates arose in the coastal banana plantations during the 1930s and were strongly backed by the Costa Rican Communist Party. Solidadismo, in contrast, aims to avoid worker-management conflict through cooperation rather than confrontation. Most syndicate leaders see the solidadismo movement as capitalist co-optation of workers; solidadismo leaders feel that syndicates are unreasonably confrontational.

UPIAV's Marxist orientation in the 1970s worried some of Coopeagri's members, particularly the president at that time, Martin Fonseca. He told me that when Coopeagri and UPIAV members first proposed joining forces, he was concerned that official agencies might be reluctant to lend the co-op money because of its association with a syndicate. He also was worried about what he perceived to be an innate conflict of interest between the two groups. "Syndicates are more for salaried workers and not producers, and the cooperative is an organization of producers. The two should be kept separate because they have different interests," he explained. Though UPIAV today is much less ideologically Marxist than it was twenty years ago, many people in Pérez Zeledón still fear it because of a perceived communist connection.

Despite these concerns, UPIAV and Coopeagri have been able to coordinate their respective political and economic agendas. Over the past twenty years, this partnership has successfully pressured various governmental agencies—such as the Costa Rican Coffee Institute, the Ministry of Agriculture and Animal Husbandry, and the Ministry of Public Works and Transport—to speed infrastructural improvements within the canton that have benefitted farmers and workers alike. Such is their influence that in July 1990, Costa Rican president Rafael Calderón Guardia himself came to San Isidro to meet with Coopeagri and UPIAV leaders to discuss their development agenda for the canton.

Community Development Associations

In years of good coffee prices, most households in Pérez Zeledón prosper, and the state uses coffee taxes to provide rural communities with primary schools and teachers, health clinics, clean drinking water, and graded roads. These are not inconsequential accomplishments. Nevertheless, in the dry season, the dust from unpaved roads covers houses, trees, and clothes; in the rainy season, roads become mud pits, a definite liability to farmers trying to transport crops. Community health clinics provide access to doctors, but only once a week; schools frequently lack enough books and supplies, and parents feel facilities could be radically improved; teenagers have little in the way of recreational facilities; and the list goes on.

Although cooperative efforts in coffee processing and marketing benefit farming households in many ways, these types of community improvement require collective action at the local level. The most active local associations in Santa Cruz and Palomas are the ADCs. Formed under the direction of, and modestly financed by, DINADECO (the National Institute for Community Development), the main mission of these grassroots associations is to identify community needs and then design and implement self-help projects. It is through the ADCs that rural residents have the most voice in shaping their own communities. DINADECO workers monitor ADC accounting practices and elections to ensure that proper democratic procedures are followed, but they do not participate in either identifying community needs or designing solutions.

Associations in both Palomas and Santa Cruz were active during the time of my research; I was told, though, that the Palomas association had recently been disbanded and reformed. A new board was elected following serious factional problems and rumors of poor accounting practices (no accusations of outright fraud had been made). Despite its short time in operation (since April 1990), the new association had numerous projects under way: acquiring land for a new cemetery; paving the road from the highway to the village center (and eventually beyond); creating a new town plaza; and transforming the weekly health center into a permanent clinic, where medical staff would be available daily.

The Santa Cruz association also had plans to improve its road and upgrade its health center, but most of the time and energy of its board of directors was devoted to the creation of a large sports and commercial center, which is considered one of the ADC's major accomplishments. Many parents worry about increasing alcohol and drug abuse in the community. At the moment, apart from Sunday soccer games, teenagers have few places where they can meet to socialize and have fun. Such a center, they hope, will help to occupy young men and women in healthy ways. Surrounding the covered gymnasium are a number of small shops that can be rented as workshops or stalls for marketing produce, crafts, prepared foods, and so forth.

The construction of this multimillion-colón building involved a great deal of planning and creative fund-raising. The association held numerous raffles plus a large annual fiesta with food, games, and dancing, which brought merrymakers and their money from neighboring communities for kilometers around. The former ADC president used his political connections in San José to get funds from various government agencies, and community residents donated time and labor to building their new center.

The community development associations operate on a democratic basis. During the period when I was conducting my research, support and participation, particularly in Palomas, was quite high. Membership is open to all, though by law associations must have a minimum of one hundred members and a maximum of fifteen hundred. Every four years a board of directors is elected. Projects are often designed by the elected board members, but they are revised, voted on, and implemented by association members.

Much of the success of the ADCs depends on their leaders, their commitment to improving their communities, their political savvy and connections, and their ability to mobilize community support. It is the charisma and energy of its board members that usually determines the success of an ADC. The directors have no legislative powers, but they have a great deal of influence on how projects are organized, coordinated, and implemented. Directors are among the most respected members of the community but are not necessarily the most wealthy. One of the board members of the Palomas association is a landless laborer who works as a peone for a local farmer. In 1991, the same association elected as president a woman with just less than one hectare of land.

Although the community development associations in both Palomas and Santa Cruz accomplished much, they operated quite differently. In Palomas, in addition to the three men and two women on the board of directors, fifteen to twenty-five people regularly attended the semimonthly meetings. In Santa Cruz, only the board of directors (made up of five men) attended the meetings regularly; other members would occasionally drop by if they had particular issues to discuss.

Nonetheless, there was a much better turnout at the 1991 elections in Santa Cruz (more than 200) than in Palomas (about 80). Elections in Palomas were a sedate affair. There was no enthusiasm for nominating people as directors, and many of those nominated declined, claiming they would support projects but could not spare time from other activities to work as board members. The Palomas ADC had such trouble getting someone to accept the nomination for president—the previous president was resigning for health reasons—that the DINADECO observer declared the association would be disbanded if it could not find anyone to serve. Finally, the board's former treasurer was nominated and elected president. (Though I know of no other association with a female president, several women at that meeting were nominated for president, and having a female president seemed to be no great concern for anyone.)

The 1991 election meeting in Santa Cruz was a different affair altogether.[6] There, organized groups arrived agitated and ready to oust the previous board. Despite the incumbent board's tremendous accomplishments (particularly with the sports complex), people were worried about the huge debts the community was incurring as a result of that project and the lack of attention to other issues. Debate was lively and very political. In the end, the previous board, primarily supporters of the PLN (the National Liberation Party), was replaced by a board comprised more of USC (Christian Social Party) supporters. Though the previous board had accomplished much, the USC was currently holding power in the national government, and so people felt that the association stood a better chance of obtaining additional government funding with more USC supporters on the board. (There was no such discussion during the Palomas meeting.)

One reason ADCs have been successful is that they are not entirely without resources. DINADECO receives a yearly budget equivalent to 2 percent of the national income tax. From this fund, each ADC receives approximately 50,000 colónes (about U.S.$580) per year for project expenses. For most projects, DINADECO requires the associations to obtain matching funds from outside agencies or from community resources. Armed only with small annual budgets, members of the community work and scheme to obtain additional matching funds and other types of support and resources from various Costa Rican and international aid agencies (and visiting anthropologists). They are quite good at doing this.[7]

For example, when I arrived in Palomas, one of the most pressing problems was the overflowing cemetery. People joked that no one was allowed to die, because there was not room to bury any more bodies. The association approached a large, absentee landowner and persuaded him to donate a field for a new cemetery. (The same man had previously donated the grounds for the new church.) Once he agreed to donate the land, a cemetery committee was formed to take charge of clearing the land of sugarcane and arranging the transfer of title. Within two months the new cemetery was clear, and the villagers had raised nearly enough money to pay for the cost of transferring the title.

The most common way for ADCs (and other organizations) to raise funds for projects is through raffles. These are usually small in scale and quite simply organized. The group sets a goal of the amount of money it needs to raise, purchases numbered tickets in San Isidro (raffles are extremely common throughout Costa Rica and ticket books are easy to come by), and sets a date for the drawing. They then sell tickets door-to-door throughout the community and in any surrounding communities that may have an interest in the project. (School or health center improvements, for example, may benefit many nearby hamlets). The price of a ticket ranges from twenty to five hundred colónes, depending on the size of the project being financed.

Money prizes are the most common, but occasionally, if a group has access to something like a nice handcrafted item or an inexpensive radio, such goods are raffled off. The organization does not conduct its own drawing (that is not only more work but can leave the group open to accusations of cheating); according to convention, local raffle drawings are made to coincide with the Sunday national lottery drawings. Thus, if twenty-seven is the winning number drawn in the national lottery, it is also the winning number for local raffles whose drawings were arranged for that date.

Raffles are such a popular means of raising funds for projects that in any given week (particularly during harvest season, when people have more cash) there will likely be at least one raffle. As one villager told me, the three things most characteristic of Ticos are that they are fierce football fans, earnest *politiqueros* (petty politicians; that is, they love to immerse themselves in politics), and enthusiastic lottery players. Tico enthusiasm for the lottery is evident on every street corner, where dozens of vendors hawk the two national lotteries' weekly tickets. Everyone has his or her favorite numbers, and almost anyone can tell you the winning numbers from last week's drawing.

Although most farmers are generally cautious about risk taking, the desire to win a substantial prize for a small risk has made the raffle a popular method of raising funds. Raffles have another advantage for fund-raising: people know they are also supporting projects that will benefit their community. Even those who may not want to play the national lotteries will buy raffle tickets because they are "for a good cause." Most tickets are relatively cheap, and sooner or later everyone gets around to supporting one project or another.

Raffles have raised funds for a number of projects in Santa Cruz and Palomas. The Santa Cruz ADC held numerous raffles over several years to raise funds for its sports complex. In 1990–1991, the Palomas ADC held frequent raffles to pay for transferring the land title for the new cemetery, the proposed health clinic, uniforms for the village soccer team and improvements to the soccer field, and road improvements (during weekly Mass, the priest also called for special donations to improve and pave the road to the village). The elementary school committee also organized several raffles to raise money for books and classroom materials. In a particularly inspiring example of grassroots effort, a neighboring hamlet (too small for an official ADC of its own) organized a series of raffles over several years to raise money to build its own elementary school. The local people could get no government funding for the school (though the state did agree to provide a teacher), so it was primarily through raffles and other fund-raising efforts of their own that they eventually were able to construct the school.

The high degree of community participation seems to reflect the nation's long-standing democratic tradition, one that Costa Ricans take for granted. During one ADC meeting I attended, a villager suggested that they invite Costa Rican president Rafael Calderón to come and discuss the possibility of paving the road. To my knowledge, President Calderón never came, but the fact that this idea met with great approval and no skepticism demonstrates the confidence that Costa Ricans have in their community development program and in the democratic process.

6

To Market, To Market

Though ox-trampled coffee satisfied the London coffee market of the nineteenth century, today's consumers demand coffee processed with more technically sophisticated equipment. Because of the technical requirements of wet-processing and the way processing is organized in Costa Rica, for all practical purposes coffee farmers have but one market for their raw coffee cherries: local beneficios that process and then, through subsidiary companies, market their coffee. To get the most from their coffee crops, farmers in Pérez Zeledón must devise multifaceted marketing strategies to contend with the large, mostly multinational processing factories, the vagaries of the international market, and the composition, resource base, and individual needs of their particular households.

Cooperative Strategies in a Competitive Industry

By organizing and collectively buying their own coffee-processing factory, small farmers in Pérez Zeledón hoped to retain a larger percentage of the coffee profit for themselves. But in order to turn the theoretical benefits of cooperation into tangible rewards, it was necessary to create a business that could survive tough competition, in both local and international arenas. After their near bankruptcy in the late 1970s, the first step Coopeagri members took toward recovery was to reorganize management and improve accountability. But that was not enough.

Competition among the five processing factories in Pérez Zeledón is keen. To get the best return on large capital investments in modern processing equipment, these factories must try to run as close to maximum capacity as possible. Like most processing companies in Costa Rica, the beneficios of Pérez Zeledón have few, if any, estates where they grow coffee; they must therefore rely on small-scale, independent coffee farmers to provide them with enough coffee to make their facilities profitable.

Table 3 shows that in 1990–1991 none of the beneficios in Pérez Zeledón were processing at full capacity—and that was not an unusual year. Though the actual processing of coffee is much the same in all beneficios, the high demand for raw coffee has created tremendous competition among the five processors in Pérez Zeledón. As in private business, a cooperative's competitive edge may come from undercutting monopolies; eliminating costly middlemen through better coordination of activities; improving packing, grading, storing, and shipping practices; reducing transportation costs; reducing production costs (for example, lowering the costs of farm inputs); or increasing productivity by providing technical assistance and better access to credit (Scott and Fletcher 1969:216; see also Helm 1968:33). Competition within the canton for farmers' coffee cherries spurred the processing factories to enhance their support services; through such improvements as collecting coffee cherries at village recibidores and delivering fertilizer free of transportation charges, each beneficio has tried to make itself more attractive to farmers than its competitors. Certainly, one of the greatest attractions for farmers is the price they receive for their coffee crop.

Processing and exporting companies in Costa Rica have no substantial influence on the international price of coffee, but it is their business to try to receive the best price possible. In the late 1980s, shortly after its near collapse, Coopeagri worked to decrease marketing costs and devised an aggressive marketing strategy that allowed it to compete more successfully in the tough international coffee market and thus to pay farmers in Pérez Zeledón higher prices for their coffee. Here is what it did.

First, the co-op focused on improving the quality of its processed coffee. When the ICO failed to renew its agreement in 1988, the old quota system disappeared. As a result, coffee quality took on even more importance in negotiations. Today's buyers are looking for reliable, high-quality coffee suppliers. Though coffee quality is partly determined by altitude and soils, the ripeness of the cherry also affects the quality of the end product—immature cherries produce bitter coffee. Government regulations stipulate that no green cherries are to be accepted, but farmers told me this was an unrealistic goal and that a crop with 5 percent green coffee was unofficially acceptable. Coopeagri was the first (and for several years the only) beneficio in Pérez Zeledón to respond to the new market demand for better-quality coffee: it strictly limited (to 3%) the amount of green coffee it would accept from its farmers. In this way, it was able to produce a higher-quality coffee, which it hoped would sell better in the more quality-conscious world market.

Next, Coopeagri developed brand-name labels for three grades of export-quality coffee and produced a colorful brochure as an advertising aid. It also began again to separately process and sell coffee from the higher altitudes, a practice that was common in the 1960s and early 1970s but was discontinued because the costs involved are higher and the marketplace at the time did not sufficiently reward the distinction.

The final price that a seller can obtain for coffee is also affected by the general nature of commodity transactions. The coffee seller and buyer each bring to the transaction different information about the value of the product: the buyer has an intimate knowledge of world demand and market prices, while the seller has an intimate knowledge of the coffee offered for sale (e.g., exactly how ripe the cherries are and what percentage is leaves and other "trash"). In such situations, the possibility exists for both buyer and seller to deceive one another, and transactions are often engulfed in cheating and manipulation as each party attempts to take advantage of the other (Williamson 1975, cited in Acheson 1985:126).

There are two ways to deal with this problem. The first is to build mutual trust through personalized, long-term business relationships. As Plattner points out, such trust helps to "reduce risk in transactions that would otherwise be too uncertain or expensive to undertake," allowing both parties to "stabilize and regularize their incomes" (1989:209, 213; see also Acheson 1985). But under Costa Rican law, only licensed companies may sell coffee abroad. About half of all private beneficios also own exporting companies that market their coffee internationally (World Bank 1990:23); Fedecoop usually handles exporting for the cooperative beneficios. To eliminate some of the intermediaries and reduce transaction costs, Coopeagri petitioned for the right to negotiate directly with overseas buyers. Today, Coopeagri managers have direct, personal contacts with buyers in Holland, Sweden, and Japan in the hope of building long-lasting business relationships. Managers now fly overseas to meet personally with buyers rather than conducting their business by telephone, as they did in the past. Fedecoop still brokers the transaction (as it must by law), but for its efforts, Coopeagri retains a greater percentage of the market price than it did previously.

The other way to deal with the problem of cheating and manipulation (and thus ultimately obtaining a better price) is through access to better market information. Since they began to focus their efforts on direct marketing overseas, Coopeagri managers have discovered the need for accurate and up-to-date market information and so have invested in a sophisticated computer system. Initially, computers were purchased to establish an interdepartmental network to facilitate accounting and coordinate day-to-day operations. In 1990, the co-op was hooked into an international commodities satellite network that allowed managers to follow changes in the market around the world on a moment-to-moment basis. Such market information is enormously beneficial in helping sellers decide when and where to sell. According to the beneficio manager, undertaking this responsibility may be risky, but rewards are great.

Finally, though it is the international market price that ultimately dictates coffee prices, factory policies and local competition also affect in a small way the price farmers receive for their crop. In addition to reducing transaction costs and improving coffee quality, Coopeagri also distributes "profits" back to its farmer-members in the form of higher cherry prices (unlike the private factories, which strive to keep costs to a minimum by paying the lowest possible price to farmers). In eight out of ten years from 1980 to 1990, Coopeagri paid the highest cherry prices in Pérez Zeledón.

Weighing the Benefits of Cooperative and Private Factories

Ideology versus Pragmatic Concerns

Today Coopeagri is held up as a model cooperative throughout Latin America—and for good reason. Not only does it provide farmers with a number of auxiliary services that the private factories do not, but in addition, for the 1990–1991 harvest, the co-op paid farmers an average of 14 percent more per fanega of coffee than any other beneficio in the canton and 292 colónes per ton above the national average for their sugar (Coopeagri 1991:9).[1] These prices indicate Coopeagri's ability to compete both locally and internationally and demonstrate that smallholders can collectively strengthen their position in wider economic arenas and improve their household incomes.

Yet, for the 1990–1991 harvest season (and this was a typical year), more than half of all households in each category of farming household ("marginal," "self-sufficient," and "employer") sold their coffee exclusively to private factories; of those who sold to Coopeagri, 42 percent also sold to a private factory (see table 8). Those figures suggest that, though collective efforts may provide significant benefits for farmers and their families, ultimately each farming household constructs its production and marketing strategies alone, based upon resources, circumstances, and conditions peculiar to each domestic situation. The question arises, then, What factors lead some farmers to take advantage of Coopeagri's "success" (i.e., high prices) while others do not?[2]

TABLE 8

Beneficio Use by Category of Labor Use
(Percentage of Sample Households)

Category of Household	Co-op Only	Co-op + Private	Single Private	Multiple Private	Total Co-op Users	Total Private Only Users	Total
"Marginal" households (N = 43)	25.6	18.6	48.8	7.0	44.2	55.8	100.0
"Self-Sufficient" households (N = 28)	25.0	17.9	50.0	7.1	42.9	57.1	100.0
"Employer" households (N = 5)	20.0	20.0	40.0	20.0	40.0	60.0	100.0

Source: Author's sample survey, 1990–1991.

One might assume that farmers join cooperatives because of ideological goals of mutual self-help, cooperation, and equity. When I began my research, I thought that Santa Cruz's reputation as muy coopertivista and Palomas's as anticooperative would be reflected in household economic strategies and the ability of community members to work toward common goals. (The average number of years of cooperative membership for farmers in Santa Cruz [7.29 years] is nearly twice that of farmers in Palomas [3.27 years]). But overall this reputation turned out not to reflect significant differences in farmers' strategies. Of the thirty-three cooperative members in my sample, only five (15%) gave ideological reasons for joining the cooperative. The remaining twenty-eight (85%) gave neither ideology nor the services offered as a result of the ideology as reasons for using the co-operative.[3] They cited economic reasons: "It pays better."

Three farmers told me that cooperative ideology was the very reason they did *not* join. "Oh, no, I just don't go for any of *that* business," I was told. Though fears of collectivization and communism are not as rampant as they were in the early 1960s, many remain fearful of cooperativismo, often confusing cooperatives with syndicates. Because the Communist Party has been active in organizing labor into unions in other parts of the country (particularly on the banana plantations), many coffee farmers fear that somehow cooperatives, by extension, are communist and that they will lead to land collectivization and cooperative farming.

Overall, few farmers cited ideological reasons (either pro or con) as serious marketing criteria. Instead, farmers in both communities consistently discussed more practical concerns. Despite the significant role that cooperatives play in the Costa Rican economy, many people still believe that joining a cooperative is risky. "Cooperatives in Costa Rica have a bad reputation," one man told me. And to some extent, that reputation is earned. Not all Costa Rican cooperatives have been as successful as Coopeagri (which itself nearly failed). One board member of a small coffee cooperative in the canton of Turrialba told me of the tremendous problems their organization was having in keeping its members and of severe financial difficulties they were facing as a result. Such difficulties can lead to bankruptcy and dissolution, as happened in 1992 to Coopeleco in the town of San Pablo (southeast of San José). For two years Coopeleco was unable to pay farmers for their crops. Not surprising, riots ensued when farmers discovered that their cooperative was bankrupt and they had forever lost that income, collectively totaling millions of colónes ("Angry Farmers Loot Cooperative," *Tico Times,* San José, 8 May 1992, 26). These examples are not rare.

Factory Policies and Harvest Labor

Processing factories vary in their compliance with government regulations regarding green coffee. Because of the policies Coopeagri has adopted to improve its overall coffee quality, co-op members have had to limit more strictly the amount of green coffee they can accept from coffee pickers. For farmers who use hired labor, costs are high in terms of the time and effort required to find, supervise, and pay nonfamily labor who will conscientiously harvest the coffee crop. These farmers often find it difficult to get anyone to work for them because coffee pickers can easily find work for the same wages harvesting for farmers whose standards are not so high. Until 1990, the price Coopeagri paid for quality coffee was only slightly higher than what the other factories paid—not enough to make it worthwhile for farmers to pay higher wages to their coffee pickers for more selective picking. Nearly one-third of the farmers who sold to private factories cited Coopeagri's policy of accepting only fully ripened cherries as the main reason for either not joining or quitting the cooperative.

Three farmers in my sample used only hired labor to harvest their crops; two of them sold their coffee only to private factories (see table 9). The third, Carlos Cifuentes, is a co-op member—one of the few farmers I met with a strong ideological commitment to the cooperative movement. Yet he also sells more than half his coffee to a private factory! He took great care to explain to me how the cooperative belongs to its members, generates money that stays within the country, and helps the region by providing competition for the multinational firms that dominate the industry. "But with all the labor I have to manage, I can't control for the quality as well as they [Coopeagri] want, and so I must sell the lower quality coffee to a private factory," he added. This dilemma suggests that those households with small or medium landholdings and enough family labor to harvest their own crop would take advantage of the cooperative's higher coffee prices, whereas those who hire most of their harvest labor would tend to use the less discriminating private factories. But 63 percent of the sample households using only family labor to harvest their crop sold entirely to private factories, as did 49 percent of households using a mixture of family and hired labor (see table 9).

TABLE 9

Beneficio Use by Type of Harvest Labor, 1990–1991
(Percentage of Sample Households)

Type of Labor	Co-op Only	Co-op + Private	Single Private	Multiple Private	Total Co-op	Total Private
Family only (N = 38)	21.0	15.8	60.5	2.6	36.8	63.1
Family and hired (N = 35)	31.4	20.0	37.1	11.4	51.4	48.5
Hired only (N = 3)	0.0	33.3	33.3	33.3	33.3	66.6

Source: Author's sample survey, 1990–1991.

Marketing and the Marginal Household

If we examine factory use by household coffee yields, we see that nearly two-thirds of those producing twenty fanegas (the median yield for sample households in 1990) or less sell to the private factories and not the cooperative (table 10). This suggests that there are other factors at work. Although larger farmers must consider problems of hired labor, those with smaller farms, who are likely to have enough family labor for careful coffee harvesting, are often those with the fewest available resources. For these households, the line between survival and disaster is a fine one. Even for family members, picking only fully ripened coffee cherries is a difficult and time-consuming task. Because Coopeagri's cherry price is not always significantly greater than that paid by private factories, many marginal farmers might find it more profitable to spend the extra time and effort picking coffee for someone else, for wages.

Furthermore, Coopeagri might pay higher prices than most private factories, but there are costs involved that may make it prohibitive for marginal households to join. For example, to join the co-op, each member must pay a small fee. In addition, the co-op withholds 5 percent of each farmer's payment and deposits it in the farmer's savings account (used by the co-op as "social capital" until the farmer terminates his or her membership). Once the 5 percent is deducted,

T A B L E   1 0

Beneficio Use by Coffee Yield, 1990–1991

(Percentage of Sample Households)

Yield (fanegas)	Co-op Only	Co-op + Private	Single Private	Multiple Private	Total Co-op Users	Total Private Users	Total
0–20 (N = 38)	28.9	7.9	63.2	0.0	36.8	63.2	100.0
21–60 (N = 21)	23.8	23.8	47.6	4.8	47.6	52.4	100.0
>60 (N = 17)	17.6	35.3	23.5	23.5	52.9	47.1	100.0
Total (N = 76)	25.0	18.4	50.0	6.6	43.4	56.6	100.0

Source: Author's sample survey, 1990–1991.

Coopeagri's prices appear to be roughly the same as (and sometimes less than) what the private factories offer. Applied to even as little as twenty fanegas of coffee, this deduction could make a substantial difference to households already struggling to make ends meet (see table 11). As several farmers told me, the mandatory 5 percent deduction "evens things out." Though members' savings ultimately would be returned to them upon termination of one's membership, poorer farmers said they could not afford the luxury of long-term savings; they needed the money right away. (Moreover, for years, those savings did not collect interest.)

Credit and Cash Flows. To maintain high yields and quality, Costa Rican farmers invest in expensive hybrid trees, fertilizers, and pesticides. Younger farmers in particular frequently face serious cash flow shortages and must rely on credit to survive. As mentioned in chapter 2, in Costa Rica credit for coffee production is funneled through the

TABLE 11

Comparison of Coopeagri Coffee Prices and
Nearest Competitor's in Pérez Zeledón, 1979–1990
(Colónes/Fanega)

Year	Coopeagri Price	Coopeagri Minus 5%	Nearest Competitor	Difference/ Fanega	Difference per 20 Fanegas[a]
1990[b]	4,936.62	4,689.79	4,409.10	280.69	5,613.80
1989[b]	5,145.96	4,888.66	n/a	n/a	n/a
1988	4,910.06	4,664.56	4,571.88	92.68	1,853.60
1987[b]	4,150.00	3,942.50	4,085.76	-143.26	-2,865.20
1986[b]	5,840.00	5,548.00	5,715.50	-167.50	-3,350.00
1985	3,328.90	3,162.46	3,169.00	-6.54	-130.80
1984	2,649.28	2,516.82	2,702.92	-186.10	-3,722.00
1983	2,213.68	2,103.00	2,070.14	32.86	657.20
1982	2,523.68	2,397.50	2,189.16	208.34	4,166.80
1981	1,260.60	1,197.57	1,206.48	-8.91	-178.20
1980	868.34	824.92	922.74	-97.82	-1,956.40
1979	740.64	703.61	737.40	-33.79	-675.80

Source: ICAFE 1979–1989, *Liquidaciones Final.*
Note: Italics indicate highest price for that year.
[a] Median yield of sample households.
[b] Source: Factory managers and clients.

beneficios to the farmers, usually in three stages throughout the year. All beneficios loan money to producers to help with production costs, but the amounts and terms vary from factory to factory.

For example, in 1991, Coopeagri was offering loans at 28 percent annual interest while the private beneficios were charging around 31.5 percent. The private beneficios also required interest to be paid for the entire year, regardless of how long the farmer actually took to repay the loan. In contrast, Coopeagri charged interest only for the length of time the money was used.[4]

Though interest rates and terms may be better, the process of getting a loan from Coopeagri is more bureaucratic and cumbersome than obtaining one from any of the private beneficios. Once a farmer has made a formal application for a loan, the co-op sends an agent to survey the farmer's coffee fields, to ensure that he will have the means to repay the loan. Loans are given strictly to cover production costs at a fixed rate, based on the yield from the previous year or the anticipated yield for the coming year. (Coopeagri officials say they limit the amount loaned to farmers not only because they are concerned about the financial health of the cooperative but also because they do not want to encourage farmers to overextend themselves.) The farmer must then wait while his or her application is reviewed by a loan committee. The entire process is lengthy, and farmers can wait from fifteen to thirty days before receiving the money. Over one-quarter of sample households interviewed said the bureaucracy and difficulty of obtaining loans was a major reason for not using the cooperative.

Obtaining a loan from the private beneficios is much easier. Farmers usually receive the loan, or "advance," within a day or two of their request. Though the private beneficios are also concerned with being fully repaid, they are often willing to extend larger amounts than the cooperative. These loans are likewise supposed to cover agricultural costs, but with larger amounts available and less strict accountability, farmers often use the loans for other ventures such as financing home improvements or a child's wedding or education. This is less easily done (though not impossible) with loans from the cooperative.

Credit is also the most common reason why farming households sell to more than one factory. In 1990, 17 percent of the sample households in Santa Cruz and 35 percent of those in Palomas sold to more than one processing factory.[5] The issue of quality control and of hired harvest labor has led some cooperative members, such as Carlos Cifuentes, to patronize more than one beneficio, but obtaining more credit is the primary reason for selling coffee to more than one factory. Credit in Costa Rica, as in much of the developing world, is expensive—in 1991, bank rates were running from about 38 to 45 percent. Beneficios not only have more affordable rates than banks, but they are also one of the few sources of credit available to families with scant resources and little collateral. One man, who resides most of the year in Cartago, where he runs an electronics shop, said his primary reason for keeping his coffee fields in Pérez Zeledón is that it is easier for him to finance his electronics business with loans from the coffee factories than from the banks!

For most households, though, taking care of their families and farms is their main financial concern. In addition to agricultural inputs for coffee, farming families have a number of other expenses that they often cannot cover with small or nonexistent cash reserves: weddings, funerals, house repairs and furnishings, or opportunities to buy more land. If they cannot get all the credit they want or need from one beneficio, they will apply to an additional beneficio for a loan (usually in the name of a different family member). In order to meet at least some repayment obligations, the household is then obliged to sell some coffee to each of those factories. For example, Doris Valverde and Victor Soto consider themselves "muy coopertavista." They told me they "would never think of leaving" Coopeagri. Nevertheless, when they needed money to send their daughter to college, they took an additional loan from a private factory. They must now sell a part of their crop every year to that factory, while the rest goes to Coopeagri.

Rodolfo Coto and his wife, Amable Calero, have loans from three processing factories and so must sell coffee to those factories. They are also long-time Coopeagri patrons, but when 4.5 hectares of good land was offered for sale, they took out loans with both La Meseta and Peters, so that their sons could have land of their own to farm. They said that Peters's (temporary) high prices also convinced them to sell most of their coffee to that firm in 1990–1991. So, although they say they have a strong ideological commitment to Coopeagri, they have patronized other factories during the past several years to take advantage of changing markets for both land and coffee.

Credit is a double-edged sword. Once a beneficio grants a loan, the farmer is committed to selling coffee to that factory until the loan is repaid. Though farmers have a number of strategies for extending repayment, and factories are not eager to foreclose, in the end farmers must pay the debt or face forfeiture of their lands.

For example, Beneficio Ubando says that when he bought his farm in 1976, the previous owner was using El General. El General gave more generous loans than the other factories, and so that is the factory Ubando also chose when he took over the farm. In 1990–1991, he realized that he could increase his income significantly by selling to

Coopeagri but found that he could not leave El General because he had too many debts there. El General was pressuring him to repay his loan in full, and he was obliged to sell them his entire crop that year.

Hector Barbosa explained that, because prices in general were so low and expenses high, they were forced to sell their 1990–1991 crop to more than one factory—not to receive more credit but to avoid paying some of their existing debt. Loans are repaid as a percentage of every fanega sold to the factory, so in order to maximize their income, Hector sold fifty fanegas to the factory that had given them their loan (28% of which was withheld for debt repayment). But he kept back six fanegas of coffee, which he sold to another factory to which he owed nothing (thus taking home full payment for each of those six fanegas).

Debt patronage is not unique to users of the private beneficios. Though Coopeagri has stricter credit policies, they also have heavily indebted co-op members. A case in point is the Coto family, who had been growing coffee for just four years: "We only seem to be paying and paying. I hope soon we will get to see some profit." Nevertheless, without credit most farming households could not survive.

Security. One way of facilitating access to credit is to establish and maintain long-term relationships with a processing factory.[6] Transactions between farmers and processors are potentially fraught with mistrust and uncertainty. Processors must trust the farmers to deliver coffee free of twigs, leaves, and unripe cherries and to repay their debts in a timely manner (by continuing to supply them with coffee). Farmers must trust the factory to measure their coffee fairly. And because the final price of one year's crop is not known until well into the next coffee season (after farmers have sold all their coffee to the beneficios), farmers must be able to trust both the selling and management abilities of the factories to which they sell (not to mention the honesty of their accounting methods). At the time of sale, farmers know only what the beneficios have paid in previous years. A beneficio with a reputation for low prices or cheating will find it more difficult to attract badly needed clients. Thus, farmers and processing factories both can benefit from a stable relationship in which there is an implicit agreement to share the ups and downs of the market.

It is clear that the longer a farmer has been with a beneficio, the greater the trust on both sides. A good relationship not only makes it easier for farmers to obtain credit, but it also can reduce some of the risks of coffee production. Particularly for marginal farmers, the security of such a relationship may prove vital in times of crisis. For a reliable client of eight or ten years, a factory manager may provide extra credit, defer a loan payment, or continue to deliver fertilizer despite outstanding debts, but he is less likely to do so for a new client or one he knows nothing about.

Maria Mondragon learned the value of long-term factory patronage firsthand. She owns one hectare of land, which her only son, Juan, farms with the help of her new son-in-law, José. They sell their coffee to El General, as her husband did before his death a few years ago. She explains that when her husband was sick and could not work, El General was very understanding and helped the family make it through that difficult time. The company did not immediately call in her husband's outstanding debts, and they even helped her with funeral expenses.

Rafael Bermudez's remarks clearly demonstrate the weight that these relationships carry in farmers' strategies. He, his son, and his elderly father farm just over two hectares of coffee in Santa Cruz. For as long as he can remember, they have sold their coffee to El General and have never wanted to change. Very simply he says, "The co-op really may be better, but it is best just to stay with the same factory." His point is that stability creates an important margin of security.

Others I spoke with also emphasized the importance of establishing a trusting and secure relationship with a processing factory. For example, Hector Solano and his family have been selling their coffee to El Aguila and La Meseta for the past ten years, but in order to take advantage of the Peters company's extremely high prices in 1990–1991, they sold nearly half of their crop to that factory. Despite earning somewhere between six hundred and nine hundred colónes more per fanega with Peters, Solano said that he did not sell their *entire* crop to that firm because he had a "good relationship" with both El Aguila and La Meseta. The companies were easy to work with and "treated him well," and so he did not want to "just drop" them. He knew that, in order to build up a clientele, Peters was offering extremely high prices temporarily during its start-up years in Pérez Zeledón. All farmers told me that this was a passing phenomenon—they had seen the same thing happen when El Aguila set up operations. Hector did not want to jeopardize his well-established relationships until he was confident he could rely on the new company to provide him consistently with the same kind of service he received from his long-time buyers.

Reaping the benefits from a long-term relationship is more difficult for younger or new farmers, who lack the years of experience that older farmers have. One way they can facilitate the acquisition of loans and ensure "good treatment" is to ride on the reputation of a close relative (spouse, parent, or sibling) who has already established a good working relationship with a factory. Farmers frequently remarked that they sold their crop to a particular factory because "that is the one my father uses," or "that is the one my husband used." For example, José Valverdeu is a founding member of Coopeagri who lives in Santa Cruz. His son, his three brothers, and his three sisters, all living in separate households, also sell their coffee to the cooperative. In Palomas, Horacio Ubando, his two brothers, his two sons, his daughter, and his brother's son all maintain separate households and all sell their coffee to El General.

TABLE 12

Factory Use by Community, 1990–1991 Harvest
(Percentage of Sample Households)

Factory Use	Palomas (N = 36)	Santa Cruz (N = 40)	Both Communities (N = 76)
Coopeagri only	8.3	40.0	25.0
Coopeagri + private	19.4	17.5	18.4
Single private	55.6	42.5	48.7
Multiple private	16.7	0.0	7.9
Total co-op users	27.7	57.5	43.4
Total private only users	72.3	42.5	56.6
Total	100.0	100.0	100.0

Source: Author's sample survey, 1990–1991.

Since Santa Cruz farmers did not espouse a stronger cooperative ideology than farmers in Palomas, and marginal households in the two communities did not show marked differences in beneficio use, the practice of choosing a beneficio according to kin ties could account for the much greater percentage of sample households in Santa Cruz (57.5%) who patronize Coopeagri, as compared to the percentage in Palomas (27.7%) (see table 12). Santa Cruz is home to two of Coopeagri's founding members, whereas none live in Palomas. Their presence and their large kindreds could account for the larger number of cooperative members in that community.

Finally, having close family members with good factory relationships can bring other benefits as well. Martin Cascantes is twenty-six years old. He and his wife have only one-quarter of a hectare of coffee, which they sell to El General. He said he chose the factory because it was the one his father always used, but another advantage, besides the long-standing relationship, also developed: "My brother had a job working at the recibidor for five months of the year. He is gone and now I have that job." With such a small field, Cascantes does not need to devote much time to his coffee; and in an area with few job opportunities, a secure job for five months of the year is a real bonus.

Factory Patronage Is Not Forever

Coffee farmers in Pérez Zeledón use long-term, family-based relationships with the beneficios to deal with problems of credit, risk, and security. But they are not merely rigid, tradition-bound producers who do only as their families have always done. As conditions change, so do marketing strategies. Despite the benefits of a long-term relationship, when farmers perceive that transaction costs, credit opportunities, cherry prices, and security are better at a factory other than the one they currently use, they will sell their coffee there.

Nevertheless, change involves risks, and changing beneficios is not a decision made lightly. For the 1990–1991 harvest, only nineteen sample households (24%) sold some of their crop to a processing factory that they had not used in 1989–1990. Most of those households continued to sell coffee to at least one of the same beneficios they had used the previous year. The need for additional credit was the sole reason for adding a new factory, whereas dissatisfaction with a beneficio (in three cases, with the co-op) was the main reason for dropping a factory.

Only five households (all in Palomas) sold their 1990–1991 crop to completely different factories than they had used in the previous year. Reasons for switching varied. Maria Chavez said she changed because she was dissatisfied with the company she had been using previously: "They were too slow with their payments." Two others were obliged to change beneficios because their previous processor, La Meseta, had removed its recibidor from the community, and they found it too costly to transport their coffee to the nearest recibidor in a neighboring hamlet.

The remaining two households, those of the Muñoz-Ruiz family and one of their sons (note again the family relationship), dropped their old factories completely in order to sell all their coffee for the high prices the new Peters company was offering. Leaving their old factories completely, as the two Muñoz households did, is quite unusual. As noted earlier, other households also took advantage of

Peters's high prices, but they continued to sell to their "regular" factories as well. The Muñozes, though not large farmers, have just over seventeen hectares that they work among themselves and are comfortably well-off. Perhaps for this reason, they felt they could afford the risks of abandoning a factory with which they had a long-term relationship for an "unknown."

The vast majority of farmers are more cautious, but the case of the Muñoz households demonstrates that farmers are concerned with short-term prices and profits as well as long-term security. When Coopeagri announced its final prices for the 1990–1991 harvest, at least three co-op members in the sample who had not sold all their coffee to Coopeagri openly lamented that decision. "I lost a lot by not selling all my coffee there [to Coopeagri] this year," said one. "Next year we will sell all we can to Coopeagri."

Unlike the Peters company, which most farmers agreed would soon drop its prices, Coopeagri has a long record of paying farmers well. Though there is no guarantee it will continue doing so, farmers know that the co-op's record is good, and many are now seriously considering joining. Beneficio Ubando explained that because of his debts with El General, he has not been able to leave that factory entirely, but the high prices paid by Coopeagri this year have convinced him to join at last. He told me that he would continue to sell part of his crop to El General until his debts were paid off but that he was convinced the cooperative was the better buyer.

The great variety of coffee-marketing strategies found among coffee farmers in Pérez Zeledón underscores the heterogeneous nature of these farming communities and the complexity of formulating household survival strategies. In Palomas and Santa Cruz, coffee-producing households attempt to maximize both income and security through marketing strategies that incorporate the power of cooperation and the needs of the individual household. For some households, the costs related to cooperative membership—in terms of harvest labor, working capital deductions and membership fees, and stricter and more bureaucratic credit policies—outweigh the benefits of slightly higher coffee prices, services, social programs, and lower interest rates.

By taking advantage of opportunities that might appear in a constantly changing environment of prices, services, credit, and labor, farming households in Pérez Zeledón have managed, for the most part, to make coffee work for them. Yet, despite these efforts, as international market prices continue to fall and land becomes scarcer, many are discovering that livelihood strategies based on coffee production alone do not suffice.

7

When Coffee Is Not Enough

Coping with Diminishing Returns

With the failure in 1989 of the International Coffee Organization to renew its agreement, coffee prices fell dramatically as producer countries dumped their surpluses on the world market. In 1990, the world market price for coffee (U.S.$76.82, or 7,082 colónes, per 46 kg sack) was down 19 percent from the 1988–1989 price of U.S.$95.20 ("Preocupa acaparamiento de tierras," *La Nación*, San José, 19 July 1990, 5A). Costa Rican farmers were at first optimistic: analysts predicted that, as the market began to differentiate according to quality, Costa Rica's fine coffees would soon fetch even higher prices than before. But by 1991, prices had yet to recover. Not only were coffee prices low, but costs of production continued to increase. Imported chemical fertilizers, herbicides, and pesticides contribute to Costa Rica's high yields, but they have always been expensive and are becoming even more so. Under pressure from the International Monetary Fund, Costa Rica gradually lowered its import duties, but in 1990, it devalued the colón. Although devaluation brought farmers higher colón prices for their coffee, it also increased the price of imports such as fuel (for transportation), fertilizers, herbicides, and pesticides. In May 1990 alone, the price of agrochemicals rose 17 percent ("Precio de abonos aumentó 20%," *La Nación*, San José, 23 May 1990, 31A).

Farming expenses vary, depending on the size of the farm, but I estimate production costs for a typical farming household in Santa Cruz or Palomas at about 560 colónes per fanega (including interest payments but excluding costs of land, family labor, and equipment).[1] Property taxes in Costa Rica are extremely low (about 0.3%), few people pay personal income tax, and all enjoy the security of relatively good public health care; but sales taxes are heavy and import duties high (Biesanz, Biesanz, and Biesanz 1982:199–200). Under such a regressive tax system, those at the bottom of the ladder are hardest hit during these difficult times. Although small pensions, savings, or investments have cushioned the blow for a handful of farmers in Palomas and Santa Cruz, most coffee-producing households must make do in other ways.[2]

Beyond these influences, Mother Nature, the ally and enemy of all farmers, ultimately determines costs and profits. When periodic frosts (unknown in Costa Rica) ruin the coffee harvest in Brazil, Costa Rican farmers cheer. But farmers everywhere know that natural catastrophes are always lurking around the corner. For example, during the late 1980s and early 1990s, a nematode began spreading through Costa Rica, destroying thousands of coffee trees. Extension agents of the Ministry of Agriculture and Animal Husbandry say they have no way to control the pest. The plague has yet to reach Pérez Zeledón, but farmers know that it is just a matter of time. Meanwhile, they wait and watch as disease and disaster creep closer.

One of the first steps farmers take to deal with economic crises is to adjust their production strategies, often choosing to cut back on applications of expensive fertilizers, herbicides, and pesticides. In many cases, there is hardly a choice: less income simply means farmers must cut back on chemical inputs. The five processing companies in Pérez Zeledón (both private and cooperative) lend money for chemical fertilizers and other agricultural inputs, and many farmers continue to borrow in order to apply them to their crops. Others have found that they can afford no more credit: "When I go to receive payment for my crop, after the loan payments are deducted, there is no money to bring home," one farmer said. As a result of rising costs, during the 1990–1991 growing season, 80 percent of farmers in the sample cut back on applications of chemical inputs, though that meant reduced yields and still lower incomes.

This situation might seem to open an opportunity for organic coffee farming, but organic methods are relatively new in Costa Rica, and few farmers can afford the considerable risks involved: yields are lower and potential losses from disease and pests are greater. The market for organic coffee is still small, and processing factories and banks will not issue loans to buy organic fertilizers. In Pérez Zeledón, farmers do not keep enough livestock to provide homegrown organic fertilizer, nor are there other reliable sources of organic fertilizers that could be transported to their farms at reasonable cost. So, at the moment, farmers must either use expensive chemical fertilizers or suffer reduced yields and lower incomes.

With soaring costs and plummeting prices, profits are rapidly diminishing. In 1990, net yearly income from coffee for a typical household (producing twenty fanegas of coffee) was 78,800 colónes, about U.S.$856 or U.S.$71 per month.[3] (A day laborer could earn about U.S.$60 per month; per capita GNP in 1992 was U.S.$2,010 [United Nations Development Programme 1995]). To put such an income in perspective, in 1990 a family of four could purchase what is known locally as *la canasta basica* (the basic food basket: rice, flour, corn, beans, milk, and sugar) and minimal clothing and utility expenses. During the boom of the 1970s, the same farming household was also likely able to build a cement block house or buy a new truck, furniture, or more land.

Diminishing returns on coffee, coupled with increasing population and land scarcity, have meant that farming households throughout the country now struggle with inadequate incomes and chronic underemployment. Yet, despite this dismal scenario, few farmers in Palomas and Santa Cruz have abandoned farming altogether. Instead, they have chosen to weather the storm by supplementing their dwindling coffee incomes.

Changing Course

Agricultural Diversification

Although coffee continues to be the primary crop, those who can afford to do so sometimes diversify farm production in order to spread the risks of crop and market failures and to stabilize their incomes. As table 13 shows, sugarcane was the second most important crop for 16 percent of the farmers and occupied slightly more than 20 percent of the land. Growing cane was more popular in Palomas because of the flatter terrain and because the village is only a few miles from the canton's only sugar refinery. In Santa Cruz, some farmers plant small patches of sugarcane for dulce. A few farmers have also ventured into fruit and vegetable production. Most households in Santa Cruz and Palomas, though, have been slow to diversify (see fig. 4). There are several reasons why they have not done so. First, coffee is a long-term crop with a life span of twenty to thirty years. Encouraged by market booms and an enthusiastic government, most farmers have planted all their available land in coffee. Although the flexibility of the family farm has been found elsewhere to be one of its greatest strengths (Netting 1993), modern coffee farmers in Costa Rica are constrained by heavy capital investments, particularly in expensive hybrid coffee trees. As Reinhardt notes with regard to Colombian farmers, this introduction of fixed capital into the family farm reduces "its ability to reallocate resources quickly in response to changing market conditions" (1988:231).

TABLE 13

Land Use of Sample Households by Community

Land Use	Palomas		Santa Cruz	
	Area (ha)	Percent Total Area	Area (ha)	Percent Total Area
Coffee	123.50	57.7	79.67	21.2
Sugar (dulce)	.50	0.2	13.80	3.7
Sugar (refined)	35.90	16.8	—	—
Fruit	.52	0.2	5.49	1.5
Vegetables	1.04	0.5	3.76	1.0
Pasture[a]	9.32	4.4	173.02	46.2
Forest/scrub	4.31	2.0	95.08	25.4
Other	38.99	18.2	0.32	<0.1
Rented/Loaned Out	—	—	3.62	0.9
Total	214.08	100.0	374.76	100.0

Source: Author's sample survey, 1990–1991.
[a] Grasslands, not necessarily with livestock.

For the same reason, the "exit option" (reverting to subsistence farming when markets are unfavorable) is not a realistic alternative. A retreat into subsistence farming would require tearing up years of investment in coffee in order to produce subsistence crops in poor tropical soils requiring large amounts of expensive fertilizers, and land is too scarce for shifting cultivation. Furthermore, Costa Rican coffee farmers are unlikely to revert to subsistence production except in the direst circumstances. In what Wilk calls the "ratchet effect," years of good coffee prices have ratcheted standards of living upward: "Even if it is physically possible for the farmer to return to subsistence production, the products of his labor now have less value and he cannot sat-isfy his family's (and his own) needs any more" (1991:141). Thus, the majority of farming households, who have few resources other than years of investment in their small coffee fields, are unlikely to leave coffee until they perceive the benefit-risk ratio of the alternatives to outweigh that of coffee.

Marketing problems have also made it difficult for farmers in Pérez Zeledón to take advantage of new export opportunities. Costa Rica's production of nontraditional exports such as ornamental plants, flow-ers, pineapple, melons, and tropical fruits jumped from $88.6 million to $188.8 million between 1989 and 1994 (EIU 1995). But distance from processing and shipping centers has made it nearly impossible for farmers in Pérez Zeledón to compete, and previous disasters have made them wary of the risks. Enthusiastic government agencies and NGOs (non-governmental organizations) have often promoted alternative

Figure 4. Production Diversity of Sample Households

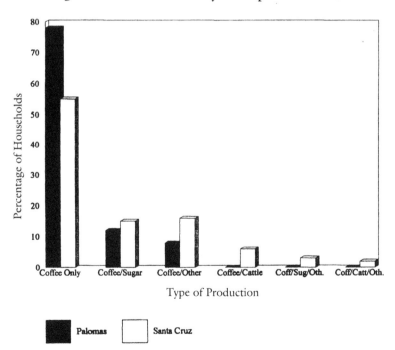

Source: Author's Sample Survey, 1990–1991.

crops, which desperate farmers have adopted, only to see them fail because they were unsuitable for the local environment, because processing facilities were not available locally, or because envisioned markets were inaccessible or had vanished by the time the crop matured.

For example, in the 1970s, agricultural extension agents convinced several farmers in Santa Cruz and Palomas to plant pineapples. But markets failed to materialize, and pineapple did not fare well at these higher elevations (700–1000 meters). In the 1980s, government agents encouraged farmers to plant an ornamental cane, known locally as *caña de india,* a popular houseplant in North America. Lured by prospects of selling an easy-to-grow plant to a large and profitable North American market, about 10 percent of the farmers in my sample planted small plots (usually less than one-third hectare) of caña de india. But when the plants reached maturity, the market was saturated. The price had fallen so low, and transport costs to the shipping port of Limón had risen so high, that there was no commercial value to the crop. Caña de india now serves primarily as (quite good) living fence posts for farmers' fields. Finally, the story of Flavio Valentes, which opened this book, is a classic example of an alluring, yet risky, coffee alternative: easy-care livestock. Good government loans were available, and high profits were predicted. Yet, the lack of processing facilities locally, a short-lived lucrative pig market in San José, and devastating pig disease nearly bankrupted a family that thought it could quickly and easily recoup its coffee losses.

Since 1989, when the state relaxed laws regulating the sale of produce on the streets, more farmers in Pérez Zeledón have begun to grow vegetables and fruits for the new street market in San Isidro. Eager to leave behind the worries of coffee, in late 1990 Pablo Mirales sold his one hectare of coffee trees a month before the harvest. He was willing to do so because coffee was "no longer a good crop." Plagues were decreasing yields, economic reforms were increasing the costs of inputs, and world coffee prices were falling as production worldwide increased, he explained. When an eager buyer offered a good price for his land and trees, he said, "It was my chance to get out and into something else. I won't ever go back to coffee." But to take advantage of new markets, he kept one hectare of citrus trees and planned to buy more land in the mountains (where it is cheaper) to grow garden vegetables such as lettuce, carrots, and radishes.

Despite Mirales's confidence, the risks of fruit and vegetable production are great, as Franklin Herrero and his son soon discovered. When I talked with Franklin in August 1990, he waxed enthusiastic about the 1.5 hectares of tomatoes and chiles he and his son had just planted. They had fitted a large water tank on their truck so that they could irrigate in the dry months, when their labor was not needed for coffee; by April, they would have a crop of garden vegetables to sell in the new street market in San Isidro. When I saw him again the following April, he had abandoned vegetable production altogether: the crops were too delicate and spoiled quickly, he said.

Pedro Mora had a similarly disappointing experience that year. He planted just over one-half hectare in beans, which he planned to sell to a local pulperia. But unusually heavy and untimely rains ruined his crop, and he did not harvest a single bean, even though he applied expensive chemical fertilizers.

Many farmers have concluded that food crops, including the Latin American staples of corn and beans, can no longer be grown on these poor tropical soils. Others have conceded that those crops could be grown, but they believe they require such large amounts of fertilizers and pesticides that growing them, especially with market prices so low, would be unprofitable. Today, a few farmers in the valley make sharecropping arrangements with friends or relatives who live at higher elevations, where forest land is still plentiful, to grow a little corn and beans for home consumption. As happens with many tropical soils, though, these lands lose their fertility within two to three years. After that, either crops must be rotated or the fields must be fallowed or fertilized. There is just not enough virgin land left to continue to support much shifting cultivation. Most agree that it is cheaper to buy corn and beans than to grow them.

Sample households in Palomas and Santa Cruz own a considerable amount of land that they describe as pasture or *potrero* (grazing land for horses). Yet, few of these farmers own much livestock. Because cattle require less supervision or labor than field crops, those who can afford to do so have begun to "bank" their extra cash in a head or two of cattle, which they graze on their remote pasture lands at higher altitudes.[4] The cattle can be sold later to pay a debt, help finance a child's education, pay for a child's wedding, or buy a new stove or refrigerator.

It is unlikely that farmers in Palomas and Santa Cruz will expand their cattle production significantly in the near future. Coopeagri runs a milk-processing factory in the valley, but the pastures are hours away on extremely poor roads, making dairy a nonviable option. Furthermore, marketing costs for beef are very high. (The small demand for meat in each community is met by resident butchers—two in Palomas and one in Santa Cruz—who raise small herds specifically for that purpose.) Farmers who wish to raise cattle as a commercial sideline must truck them to market in San José. Should a slaughterhouse be established in Pérez Zeledón, cattle production might increase.

But since the mid-1980s, sluggish export demand, soaring interest rates, and veterinary costs, combined with stagnant prices, have made cattle a losing proposition for farmers in other parts of the country (Edelman 1989:4). Beef and dairy markets are not yet well developed, nor are they any more stable than the coffee market. Thus, although they complained about how much money they were losing with coffee, during the time of my field research most farmers in Pérez Zeledón felt that coffee continued to be their best option.

Wage Labor

Farming households in Pérez Zeledón face a dilemma. Under current conditions, they find it increasingly difficult to support themselves as they would like with coffee production, but the costs and risks of leaving coffee prevent most of them from turning to other market crops. Instead, most farming households supplement their coffee incomes with wage work. Yet employment opportunities in this still rather isolated canton are few.

The primary way of earning extra cash is through coffee harvesting for others. In Palomas and Santa Cruz, 46 percent and 26 percent of the sample households, respectively, included at least one person who harvested coffee for others. During the harvest season (roughly September through January), when demand for labor is high, men, women, and older children can easily earn four to five dollars per day harvesting coffee for friends and neighbors (1990–1991 figures). (A day laborer earned about U.S.$3.50 per day in 1990.) Because even slight variations in altitude affect the ripening of the crop, small-scale farmers can easily find work harvesting for others before and after their own crop is harvested. Once the peak harvest season in Pérez Zeledón is over, many landless and land-poor workers (particularly from Palomas) migrate to the Meseta Central for the peak harvest there. In some households, only the younger, childless men and women (ages fourteen to twenty-five) make the trek north to harvest, but in others the entire family packs its belongings, closes its house, and travels north for two or three months (November–January) of harvesting in the Meseta. In 1991, 13 percent of all sample households in Palomas sent at least one member to harvest coffee outside the canton; none in Santa Cruz did so.

Outside the harvest season, some men find work in the cafetales of other farmers; most are employed as *jornaleros*, workers hired on a day-to-day basis to complete a certain task. Permanent agricultural wage work as a peon is becoming increasingly difficult to find. Larger farmers who in the past employed workers as peones say that the social insurance payments employers must pay by law make it too costly for them to continue hiring permanent workers. Those who once had permanent employment find that they are now being hired by the same farmers for the same work, but on short-term contracts. Sugarcane provides some opportunities for wage labor, especially in Palomas, where the crop is grown in large fields for factory refining. There, farmers must mobilize large amounts of labor for a short period of seasonal harvesting. In Santa Cruz, sugarcane is grown for dulce on a few patches of land scattered through the valley. Dulce-producing households harvest their cane bit by bit and do not need to hire labor. A half-dozen or so residents of Palomas have found routine agricultural wage work (both as peones and as jornaleros) at the Pindeco pineapple plantation in Buenos Aires, Puntarenas, and the nearby Finca Santa Fe. No such opportunities exist for the residents of Santa Cruz.

In both Palomas and Santa Cruz, wage labor outside agriculture, either for men or women, is nearly nonexistent. Apart from positions as cooks and cleaners in the elementary schools in each community (four jobs, all held by women), only a few scattered jobs in carpentry, construction, or (rarely) domestic work are available locally. Small furniture workshops operate in nearby hamlets, but with the exception of two bamboo-furniture shops just outside Santa Cruz, they are family-run businesses that do not provide employment for outsiders. In 1990, half a dozen young men and women from Santa Cruz boasted of their jobs in the bamboo-furniture workshops. Wages were good, the work was clean, and the shop was within walking distance of home. One shop was forced to close in early 1991, and it is unclear whether the other shop expanded and hired more workers. Most nonagricultural wage work is found in the market town of San Isidro. But distance and limited bus schedules make it difficult to commute daily to work in San Isidro. At the time of this study, only a handful of people living in Santa Cruz worked in San Isidro. No one in Palomas did, though I have since heard of one young Palomas woman who obtained domestic employment in the town, coming home on weekends to be with her parents.[5]

Microenterprises

The few shops in Palomas and Santa Cruz were owned and operated by nonfarming families, most of whom had come from outside the canton. The vast majority of farming households do not have the capital, the time, or the expertise to invest in nonagricultural businesses.[6] But with the low labor demands of coffee throughout most of the year, informal, part-time ventures are easily integrated with coffee production, and several households have developed what I term microenterprises as a way to supplement their incomes without abandoning years of investment in their coffee fields. These activities range from occasionally selling a few eggs, a liter of milk, or slices of cake through the kitchen window, to sewing or knitting clothes, cutting hair and manicuring nails, repairing shoes or furniture, transporting cargo by truck, or making and selling handicrafts. Unlike cottage industries found elsewhere in the world (see Chibnik 1996; Cook 1986; Meisch 1996; Wood 1996), in Santa Cruz and Palomas most services and products are marketed locally to friends, family, and neighbors, and production is small-scale and erratic. Nonetheless, although some activities generate only a few colónes, others make significant contributions to household incomes, and there are several cases in which those enterprises have the potential to grow into steady and profitable businesses.

For example, Beneficio Ubando and his wife, Lila, farm about 2.75 hectares of coffee. With only two daughters (who for cultural reasons the family prefers do not work in the fields), Ubando says he often finds himself short of help in the fields. He hires occasional laborers to help with the heavier work, but in 1989 he bought a gasoline-powered weed-cutter to help him clear weeds from his fields and around his home. At the time, such machines were rare in Pérez Zeledón, and he soon discovered that he could sell his weed-cutting services to other farmers in the community.

In another case, Elizabet Barrios and her two daughters spend most of their time cooking and cleaning house while her husband and her son care for the family's three hectares of coffee. But for the past ten years, Barrios has also been steadily producing stuffed animals, which she sells in her sister's shop in San Isidro. She estimates her profits at 20,000 colónes per year (approximately U.S.$220). In local terms, that is a considerable contribution to the family's income.

Then there is the case of Maria Vasquez and her knitting enterprise. With only one child at home, Vasquez found that outside of the harvest season (when she is busy picking her family's coffee) she could fulfill her domestic responsibilities and have time for other activities. Making or repairing clothes on home sewing machines is a popular way to earn extra money in both Santa Cruz and Palomas (I met eleven other men and women who did so), and Maria thought she could make a little extra cash in her spare time providing a similar service to her neighbors. When in early 1990 she saw an advertisement in a magazine for a knitting machine, she, her sister, and her sister-in-law (all living in separate households) together bought a knitting machine on credit. With that machine they took turns producing knitwear, which they sold at first to friends and neighbors but which their husbands now sell to several shops in San Isidro. With their earnings, they paid off the loan for the first machine and bought additional machines so that each woman now has her own.

Finding ways to earn cash is particularly difficult for women. Not only do their many household and child-care responsibilities keep them tethered to the home, but also the cultural code dictates that this is the proper place for them to be. Women and men agree that home and family should be a woman's priorities, but few have qualms about women's projects that will bring in additional income, provided that the women do not neglect their domestic duties and conduct these projects from inside the home. Handicraft production is particularly suited to rural women, because many handicrafts can be produced within the home, often with low capital investment, and are easily integrated with household work and child care (Sick 1991). Maria Vasquez and Elizabet Barrios have been able to build their small businesses because they meet these conditions.

Costa Ricans have a scant history of handicraft production: the baskets, textiles, pottery, and wood products found throughout much of Latin America are conspicuously absent in Costa Rica. The tourists who have flooded the country since the late 1980s, however, have created a tremendous market for crafts and souvenirs, and Costa Rican handicraft production is on the rise. Many women in Pérez Zeledón have become interested in tapping into this tourist market, but their distance from tourist centers has made it difficult for them to do so.

As noted in chapter 5, Coopeagri's Women's Group has been teaching rural women artisan skills as a way of improving household incomes. In 1989, the Swedish cooperative Cecoop (which provided financial support for other Coopeagri projects, such as the mobile supermarkets) began sending money specifically to support projects of the Women's Group. Since then, Coopeagri has provided training sessions in crafts such as macramé, cloth painting, and cornhusk doll and hat making.

Craft production at first appears to be a viable solution to the economic (and cultural) predicament of rural women in Costa Rica, but in 1991 Coopeagri's women were still a long way from earning real incomes from their efforts. The biggest problem was marketing. Though Coopeagri allowed these women to sell their macrame plant hangers, painted dish towels, and cornhusk dolls and hats on consignment in its supermarket, there was not much demand for such products in San Isidro (where tourists were few) or elsewhere. These handicrafts are attractive and involve a great deal of time and skill to make, but they did not sell well. Most Costa Ricans cannot afford to pay prices that would adequately compensate the women for their materials and labor, and tourists usually look for indigenous style.

Costa Rica has few visible native groups, and the rural women of Pérez Zeledón had not yet developed an artistic style that was distinctively their own. On the advice of a consultant from a craft cooperative in San José, Coopeagri's women began searching for less labor-intensive, more marketable souvenirs to produce. It remains to be seen whether they will eventually tap into the lucrative San José market; the shops and plaza stalls in the capital were already overflowing with every conceivable craft and souvenir—mostly inexpensive imports from Guatemala and Panama.

Although most of the Women's Group's projects have focused on training women in craft production, the group's leader, Marcelly Orozco, said she hopes they will eventually be able to put some of their energies into increasing economic opportunities for women outside the home. Already one local group had expanded its activities. After learning to make small souvenir dolls and hats from cornhusks, the women decided to purchase a *milpa* (cornfield) so that they would have their own raw material with which to work. They farmed the field collectively and sold the corn, the dolls, and the hats to the co-op. Despite their accomplishments, this group was an anomaly.

While I was doing my research, there had been no talk by Coopeagri of promoting such agricultural enterprises for other women, or even of specifically aiding women coffee farmers who could truly benefit from the cooperative's support. Orozco said that the co-op might eventually try to do so, but she admitted it had been a struggle to get Coopeagri's male-dominated administration even to support efforts to create employment for women inside the home. Promoting outside economic activities is a more radical idea and likely to meet with heavy opposition. Despite its limitations, Coopeagri's Women's Group has been applauded by national and international women's groups. Delegations from women's groups in Bolivia and Panama have met with the group for advice on organizing their own associations. In 1990, Marcelly Orozco was recognized by APROMUJER (the National Program for the Advising and Training of Women) for her outstanding work among rural women.

Moving Up and Moving Out: Education and Migration

Education. With land increasingly scarce and coffee revenues unpredictable, many individuals in farming households face a bleak future in agriculture—particularly daughters and younger sons who are not likely to inherit enough land to support themselves. For the most part, as we have seen, the alternative is low-paying and insecure wage work in agriculture. Education is one way to improve one's chances of finding better-paying employment. Though not without its problems, Costa Rica's education system is noted as one of the best in Latin America. Government investment in education has been steadily increasing since the 1940s, and rates of attendance for primary and secondary schools (for both girls and boys) are high (Biesanz, Biesanz, and Biesanz 1982:117). Sixty-two percent of all adults (over fourteen years old) in the sample households had completed six years of primary schooling (see table 14). At that level, few are adequately trained to move into the few better-paying (i.e., white-collar) jobs that might be found in the formal sector in San Isidro or other urban centers. Nevertheless, there is a growing awareness throughout Costa Rica of the link between formal education and good jobs, and some families in Palomas and Santa Cruz (particularly those unable to bequeath adequate farmland to all of their children) are providing for their children's future by investing more in education.

TABLE 14

Education Levels Attained in Palomas and Santa Cruz
(Adults Age 14 and Older)

Years of School Attended	Cumulative percent of Adult Population
12+	5.4
10–11	7.9
7–9	16.2
6	62.1
4–5	72.8
1–3	92.8

Source: Author's sample survey, 1990–1991.

For example, with seven daughters, four sons, and just over two hectares of land, Arnulfo Barboza and his wife, Haydee Picado, could easily see that there was not enough land to support all their children when they reach adulthood. Though Haydee received no formal education and Arnulfo had only three years as a child (he later took night classes to get his grade six diploma), they have been eager to ensure that their children have good educations. Last year, they took out an additional loan with one of the local coffee-processing factories so that they could send their daughter Nora to a university in San José. Two other daughters and one son had also attended university, and a fourth daughter was just completing grade eleven. Another couple, Sergio Monge and Aurea Rodriguez, who both left school after grade three, have four daughters and four sons. The 9.5 hectares of coffee and 3.5 hectares of sugar that Sergio works with three of his sons, each of whom has a grade six education, comfortably supports the family at the moment, but 13 hectares is not much to divide among eight children. Consequently, they have educated their youngest son and their youngest daughter through university; both are now school-teachers. Their three other daughters have married men with land.

Investing in education is not only for children with small inheritances. In several younger households, men and women are combining coffee farming with their own further schooling, anticipating the day when they might need to rely more on education than coffee. Miguel Arias, for example, knew that he could not possibly support himself and his future family (he and his wife, Fanni, as yet have no children) with the one manzana (.69 hectare) of land he inherited from his mother, so he returned to school and in 1991 received his *bachillerato* (secondary diploma). He is considering getting a university degree but hopes that his secondary education at least will allow him to find a well-paying job in San Isidro.

Migration. Despite the often creative efforts of farming families to improve their incomes locally, the bottom line is that currently there are few means other than coffee for making a living in rural Pérez Zeledón. At present, even those who are better educated frequently cannot find employment in the canton and ultimately go elsewhere. Some leave temporarily; others begin new lives elsewhere altogether. Pérez Zeledón, once the destination of thousands of landless families, is no longer an open agricultural frontier. By 1973, the net rate of im-migration into the canton had dropped to -8.6, down from 26.8 in 1963; by 1984, the rate was -2.5 (Locher n.d.). As for migrants else-where, the long-term strategies of migrants leaving Pérez Zeledón vary from one individual or household to another. Job scarcity, population pressure, and unemployment push people to emigrate, and opportunities for better employment, education, and other amenities pull them to new destinations. For large families, migration can alleviate pressures on household resources and provide additional income through remittances; for others, migration is "often a deliberate income expanding strategy" (Brown and Lawson 1985:416). As noted above, some join the vast seasonal migration of men, women, and entire families who follow the Costa Rican coffee harvest from zone to zone.

Although the national coffee harvest is one way for the underemployed of Pérez Zeledón to supplement their incomes (a method avidly encouraged by the government), many prefer better-paying or less strenuous work. An increasing number of young men and women are working in factories or on construction jobs in San José, in the banana plantations of Limón, or in various unskilled and semiskilled jobs in the United States. Many find such wage work elsewhere during the slack agricultural season, returning to help their families during the coffee harvest; others are gone for years at a time. In the spring of 1991, fourteen sample households in Palomas (35%) and eight in Santa Cruz (22%) had at least one member working long-term outside the canton and sending money home.

The United States is considered the ultimate destination: unskilled jobs are plentiful, wages are high, and an industrious and frugal worker can save, by Costa Rican standards, a lot of money. Everyone in Palomas and Santa Cruz has a relative, a friend, or a neighbor working in, recently returned from, or planning shortly to go to the United States. As elsewhere, social networks provide new migrants with crucial information and with economic and emotional support during their initial forays abroad.[7] Thus it happens that most migrants from Pérez Zeledón work in restaurants and hotels in New Jersey, or more recently in Connecticut, where employment opportunities and wages apparently are better. Some go with the blessings and support of their families; others do not. Many of the young migrants return with a nest egg that they use to buy land or build a house. Others return with memories of adventures abroad and perhaps a television set or CD player to show for their time away.

A son or a husband (less frequently a daughter) often goes to work for a specified length of time or until a specific amount of money has been saved: enough to pay a debt, build a new house, or buy a piece of land. In general, lengths of stay are brief (several months), but many young men, particularly those with little hope of inheriting adequate land to support themselves and their future families, emigrate for indefinite periods, though usually with the stated intention of returning in several years. For example, Luis and Adrian Montoya, like each of their five brothers, received from their father just over two hectares each, an average-size plot of land in Palomas but these days barely enough to support a growing family. Therefore, in 1989, Luis (age twenty-eight) went to the United States, leaving his wife and his two young children in Palomas. Twenty-five-year-old Adrian followed a year later, leaving behind a wife and a baby daughter. It is impossible to predict what they will ultimately do, but they are expected to return when they have saved enough money to buy more land.

Emigrant sons, daughters, and husbands are expected to send what they can to their families back home. Remittances received from family members who go to work outside the canton are an increasingly important share of household incomes for those who remain behind, but the amounts vary considerably. My data on remittances are not complete, but the following two cases illustrate the variation. Saidey Elizondo's eldest son, Jesus, left her home in 1986 to work in the banana plantations of Limón. Though she struggled alone with her one-half-hectare coffee field, her three young children, and her elderly mother, he sent her only two small sums in five years and rarely came home to visit.

Others fare better by emigrant relatives. In 1983, Jaime Delgado went to work in a New Jersey restaurant. His seventeen-year-old son, Randall, stayed behind to live with Petronila, Jaime's mother. Randall farms both Jaime's and Petronila's small coffee fields. Half a hectare of coffee is not much to live on, but he and Petronila manage to live quite comfortably because, as Petronila puts it, Jaime is *un buen hijo* (a good son), sending on average about one hundred dollars (U.S.) per month (a sizable income by village standards) and bringing her household appliances and electronic equipment on every trip home.

Since the 1940s, the open frontier of Pérez Zeledón has provided thousands of family farmers with the opportunity to participate in the coffee market. In today's rapidly changing national and global economies, farming households in Pérez Zeledón are feeling the multiple pressures of a monocrop export economy, increasing population density, and relative geographic isolation. Coffee production continues to dominate the local economy, but some are being forced to look elsewhere for their livelihoods. Farmers in Pérez Zeledón have constructed their strategies for survival and mobility to contend with international conditions and the internal dynamics of the household. Yet, the choices available to them, in large part, have been shaped by state policies mediating between the global and the local.

8

Family Farmers, Global Markets, and the State

State Policies and Small-Farm Options

For the past 150 years, farming households in highland Costa Rica have relied on the production and marketing of an international commodity. In the preceding chapters, I have examined the multifaceted strategies they have used to cope with the technical demands of coffee, the limitations of household resources, and local ecological, demographic, and political conditions. Using a commodity approach, I have focused my analysis of the survival strategies of farming households in Santa Cruz and Palomas on coffee production and marketing at the household, community, regional, national, and international levels. Although household strategies and the coffee market have been my main focus, broader "development" issues concerning standards of living, equitable access to resources, and empowerment have been underlying themes. In this chapter, I return to these issues briefly. Anthropologists have rightly been in the forefront of critics of top-down, state-oriented development policy. But as I have grappled with understanding the fate of household producers like these Costa Rican coffee farmers, I am constantly led back to the state and its potential as a mediator between households and wider economic and political arenas.

It is true that sociocultural norms and institutions, markets, and local environmental conditions shape household economic strategies, but the choices (or lack of choices) available to domestic producers are in large part also the result of national policies (which themselves are shaped by these factors on a broader scale). When the state withdraws agricultural subsidies, restructures credit institutions, or redefines land rights (as has happened recently in Mexico), farming households find they must make crucial decisions in a new and unfamiliar environment.

Since the early nineteenth century, by and large, powerful elites throughout Central America have perceived the state as a facilitator of export activities (Lindo-Fuentes 1995:73). But as noted earlier, the way in which Latin American states have done so and their relationships with small farmers have varied tremendously. In Costa Rica, cooperatives like Coopeagri have provided small and medium farmers with access to cheaper credit, technical assistance, organizational training, and larger markets (and hence better prices), thus enabling them to produce commercial crops more profitably. In contrast, in Peru, for example, the state likewise promotes coffee cooperatives, but there they "have served to exacerbate, rather than solve, the problems of isolation and poor market position faced by peasant producers" (Collins 1988:22). Coopeagri's achievements are due in large part to the efforts of the cooperative's leaders and members, but state policies toward cooperatives have also played an important role, for two main reasons. First, the ownership and democratic control of coops in Costa Rica remain with their members; cooperatives in Peru and many other countries are owned and controlled by paternalistic state or other outside agencies with little direct accountability to members.[1] Second, though the state has not been overly interfering, neither has it been hostile to cooperative enterprises. Some states, fearing unwanted political activity, put stringent controls on the autonomy of cooperatives. In Costa Rica, the state has encouraged and actively supported farmers' efforts to form cooperatives.

But state policies have not always favored the smallholder in Costa Rica, nor have they done so uniformly throughout the country. States funnel resources in various directions, supporting one group or institution over another, promoting some programs while abandoning others. Thus, in the coffee-producing highlands, where both the state and mercantile elites have benefitted from the persistence of small-scale coffee producers, the latter have enjoyed relatively secure land rights, have profited from state investments in infrastructure and processing facilities (including many cooperatives), and have been able to negotiate legislation guaranteeing their profit margins vis-à-vis processing and exporting companies. In contrast, in lowland regions such as Guanacaste Province, where cattle, rice, sugar, and cotton have variously been promoted, state policies have encouraged the persistence of large (and largely underproductive) landholdings; land for small-scale farmers is scarce and tenure insecure (Edelman 1992).[2]

In many ways, the Costa Rican government's obsession with coffee exports has reduced the number of options for farming families in the highlands. The social democrats who came to power after the 1948 civil war voiced concerns over the country's dependence on coffee (and the power of the coffee elite), but high coffee prices in the 1950s encouraged the state to continue its support for the coffee sector. Farmers were encouraged to increase production when "most of the rapidly expanding agricultural credit from the nationalized banking system was targeted toward investment in coffee" (González-Vega and Céspedes 1993:134).

In the early 1960s, following a period of declining coffee prices, Costa Rica began to implement import substitution policies, encouraging industrialization in order to reduce dependency on unstable agricultural exports and expensive, imported manufactured goods. Export agriculture, for political and economic reasons, continued to receive support in the form of production credit from the national bank (Bulmer-Thomas 1987:185), but the protectionist policies that accompanied import substitution (such as overvaluing currency in order to import industrial equipment at lower cost) "distorted relative commodity prices, turning the domestic terms of trade against agriculture" (González-Vega and Céspedes 1993:97). In other words, an overvalued domestic currency meant that foreign buyers were paying Costa Rican coffee farmers fewer colónes per bag of coffee, even if the international price remained stable in terms of U.S. dollars.

Production opportunities for the domestic market have not been much better. State policies regulating the prices of *granos básicos* (corn, beans, rice, and sorghum) were supposed to increase domestic production by guaranteeing minimum prices for those crops. But, as many farmers in Pérez Zeledón told me, the costs of production rose so quickly (particularly in poor soils requiring expensive fertilizers) that even with price guarantees, food crops became unprofitable. Because ceilings were set on consumer prices, the government was politically constrained from allowing food crop prices to rise, despite soaring production costs. As a result, grain production has plummeted, and Costa Rica now imports most of its basic grains.

Garden vegetables likewise have not provided much of an alternative for farmers in Pérez Zeledón. The lucrative San José market is too distant (and is supplied by farmers of the Meseta Central), whereas the local market in San Isidro is too small to accommodate more than a few farmers. Even worse, farmers in Pérez Zeledón who wished to supplement their incomes with vegetable and fruit production for the local market were constrained for many years by government policies compelling them to sell to licensed retail merchants; informal street markets such as those found throughout Latin America were illegal. The dampening effect of this policy became clear when it was finally lifted in 1991. Within six months, the one-street Friday market had expanded to cover two intersecting streets on both Fridays and Saturdays.

The effects of state policies are felt within households, as well, often affecting men and women in significantly different ways.[3] For example, agrarian reform programs throughout Latin America, including Costa Rica, have systematically targeted men rather than women. As Deere notes, "ideological norms governing the proper gender division of labor—that a woman's place is in the home while a man's is in the fields—often appear in the content of agrarian reform legislation" (1987:175). In a study of fifty governmental and nongovernmental development projects targeting rural women in Costa Rica, Madden (1985) found that, despite explicit goals of incorporating women into the economic development of the country, few addressed the real obstacles facing rural women and their lack of employment opportunities. Although these projects increased attention to the problems of women, they focused mainly on training women in activities such as cooking, sewing, and handicrafts. Thus, they not only did little to expand women's economic opportunities, they reinforced the cultural patterns and values that assume women's contributions to society are primarily domestic.

Other state policies reflect this same ideology—except when it conflicts with the needs of the state. Because women are expected to work in the home, government agricultural extension and credit programs are explicitly aimed at men, leaving female farmers with little support in a male-dominated cash-crop sector. Nevertheless, in the early 1990s, when the government feared an extreme shortage of harvest labor (which would have meant a large decrease in coffee exports and tax revenues), it rapidly invested in day-care centers so that more women could harvest coffee.

It is clear that state policy does have a dramatic impact on everyday lives. But it is equally clear that at the local level in particular, people use cultural norms and values to modify law, and customary practices often take precedence over state-formulated rules and regulations. This is especially evident with regard to inheritance, where by law Costa Rican daughters have equal rights to own and inherit property but in practice do not do so on par with their brothers.

Finally, state policies are influenced also by international economic and political forces. For example, during the oil crisis of the 1970s, farmers were hit hard by increased costs of fuel, transportation, and petroleum-based products (such as many fertilizers). The IMF-imposed restructuring of the economy following the debt crisis of the 1980s has included radical cutbacks in agricultural subsidies and drastic cuts in the social welfare system, changes that have greatly affected all Costa Ricans. Finally, we cannot overlook Costa Rica's importance to U.S. geopolitical interests. Because Costa Rica is a strategically important country in a region of turmoil, huge amounts of U.S. financial aid have been funneled into numerous development programs, private-sector organizations, and infrastructural improvements in Costa Rica. U.S. aid to Costa Rica has been so great that by the end of the 1980s, this vast network had come to be known as the "parallel state" (Shallat 1989).[4]

Smallholders versus the State

Costa Rican coffee producers have responded to the various national and international conditions affecting their lives primarily by negotiating with the state. Costa Ricans are noted in Central America for their democratic participation, lack of violent uprisings, and (despite their many cooperatives) low level of collective action in general. Some scholars blame the state for what they deplore as a lack of peasant political activity in Costa Rica, arguing that the state has co-opted "key segments of the rural population by giving them small concessions," thus effectively preempting other groups, such as the Catholic Church or labor unions, from organizing peasants (Shafer 1994:211–12; see also Donato and Rojas Bolaños 1989; Palma 1989).

There is some truth in the view that the state has acted to control labor movements and unionization by providing certain segments of adversarial groups with "concessions." But that argument fails to acknowledge the breadth of the concessions. Following the civil war in 1948, the reformist Costa Rican state created the kind of political and economic environment that small-scale farmers elsewhere in the region were fighting vigorously (against brutal state repression) to obtain. In Costa Rica, as Kincaid puts it, "the state got there first," greatly reducing the desire, ability, and, I would add, *need* for other actors to organize peasants for other purposes (1989:182, 184).

Costa Rica is by no means immune to poverty and injustice, but if we look at the situation through the eyes of the household producer, we find an economic environment in which small producers have been able to participate and at times prosper, where health care and education are among the best in Latin America, where the level of "human development" is ranked fifth among developing nations (United Nations Development Programme 1995:158), and where grassroots efforts such as farmer-managed cooperatives and citizen-run community development associations are encouraged and supported. What some call co-optation might better be described as accommodation by the state to smallholder interests and demands. It is not that Costa Ricans do not organize. We have seen that they do, in cooperatives and various kinds of local associations. But because the Costa Rican state has done much to accommodate peasant interests, their needs for organization have been different from those elsewhere in the region. For the most part, they have been able accomplish a great deal through negotiation (though at times quite heated negotiation), rather than violent confrontation, with the state.

Despite the relative scarcity of peasant unions and political militancy, small-scale farmers in Costa Rica do not passively accept all that the state dishes out. Fortunately, they have not often been forced to resort to violence. Instead, when their interests have been threatened, they have voiced their discontent, resisted unfavorable policies, and contributed to their changing society in more peaceful, yet effective, ways. Costa Rican peasants frequently participate in local community organizations and development projects, vote regularly in national elections, and sometimes even engage in illegal land occupations on a massive scale (Kincaid 1989:179; see also Edelman 1990). As we have seen, small-scale farmers in Santa Cruz and Palomas have enthusiastically used local associations to improve their communities. Rural Costa Ricans firmly believe that public resources are just that—public—and they persistently lobby and cultivate political connections to facilitate access to government (and other) resources.

Though many of their efforts to facilitate change are directed toward negotiation with the state, there are also times when small-scale farmers in Costa Rica have united to confront the state. When wealthy coffee processors and exporters began passing their losses on to producers in the 1920s and early 1930s, small and medium farmers were quick to form the Asociación Nacional de Cafetaleros (1929) and the Asociación Nacional de Productores de Café (1932) and successfully lobbied the state for protection (Williams 1994:259). Again in 1950, when the state proposed to hit farmers with a new tax on coffee, the Asociación de Pequeños Productores united with large-scale producers to successfully fight the new tax.

Deterioration of the country's social welfare programs since the economic crisis of the early 1980s has caused an increase in peasant mobilization. These efforts initially focused on the concerns of small-scale farmers (fuel and fertilizer prices, for example), but they have come to include the concerns of landless workers as well (Kincaid 1989:185). The alliance of Coopeagri with the UPIAV is one example of this type of mobilization. Through their united efforts, small-holders and landless agricultural workers have successfully lobbied for substantial infrastructural improvements in the canton. Their meeting in 1991 with then president Calderón Guardia—on their own turf in Pérez Zeledón—to discuss regional development plans and to petition for the distribution of state-owned lands to landless agricultural laborers demonstrates the force they have mustered in the national political arena.

One interesting example of resistance to state policies occurred while I was in Pérez Zeledón in 1991. During the Gulf War in the Middle East, the Costa Rican government decided to reduce oil imports and energy costs by implementing daylight saving time (a policy that had been attempted unsuccessfully once before, in the 1970s). As one who has spent her entire life moving clocks forward and backward each spring and fall, I was initially surprised at the reaction of Costa Rican farmers and their families to a time change of one hour: *they were outraged.* In a country that is still overwhelmingly rural and agrarian-based, people could not see where the savings in energy costs would occur. At a latitude of ten degrees north, the Costa Rican day varies little from season to season, the sun rising and setting at approximately 6:00 A.M. and 6:00 P.M. each day. Implementing daylight savings time simply changes sunrise to 7:00 A.M. and sunset to 7:00 P.M.

Although farmers could schedule their days according to sunrise and sunset, school children (whose schedules were fixed by government-run institutions) would have to leave for school, and wage-laborers for their jobs, in the government-imposed darkness before dawn. (At such low latitudes, twilight periods are virtually nonexistent; to natives of more northern latitudes, it appears that night becomes day there almost instantly.) Everywhere I went, people harshly criticized the government for playing God: "Solo Diós puede hacer cambios en el día" (only God can make changes in the day), they said. And many wearily speculated on how tired they would soon become by losing an hour's sleep each night.

There was much talk about "government time" and "real time," but people did more than complain. Throughout rural Costa Rica, angered parents decried the dangers of sending their children to school in the dark. Everyone I knew simply refused to operate on the new schedule. Priests said Mass at the "real" time; farmers left for work at the "real" time; even rural buses (until officially reprimanded) continued their schedules on "real" time. Finally, the government had to abandon the idea altogether and returned the time to its "rightful" place.

The Future for Household Producers

Despite the small scale and seeming simplicity of their operations, coffee-producing households in Costa Rica, through complex survival strategies, have dealt with the limitations of household resources, ever-changing household composition, a monocultural regional economy, shifting state policies, and the vagaries of the international coffee market in sophisticated ways. But what of their future and that of other household producers?

For the most part, coffee production has helped smallholders in highland Costa Rica to improve their lives and build better communities. But the collapse of the ICA in 1989, coupled with increasing population and land scarcity, has made it difficult for many farming families to continue to rely solely on coffee. Nonetheless, few farmers in Pérez Zeledón have expressed the intention of leaving coffee altogether.

Though some Pérez Zeledón farmers have experimented with alternative market crops, transportation and marketing problems, combined with large capital investments in a long-term tree crop, have made agricultural diversification difficult. State policies affect not only agricultural export production and marketing but also possibilities for other economic ventures: for example, they alter start-up costs for new businesses, costs of equipment and new materials, systems of credit, markets, and taxes. Import substitution policies led to support for some new industry in the Central Valley surrounding San José, but except for tourism the government has been slow to support small-scale enterprises in the more isolated regions of the country. This has been especially true in regions such as Pérez Zeledón, where coffee, still a vital component of the Costa Rican economy, grows well.

Coffee producers are used to the ups and downs of the coffee market, and most anticipate a revival. Indeed, improvement in the coffee market is not impossible. Coffee prices rose briefly in 1994 when the ACPC began to regulate supplies through retention programs, but competition among producer nations is keen, and prices fell sharply again in 1995. Specialized markets for high quality and organic coffees are growing, as is a trend among "politically aware" consumers in North America and Europe to support peasant producers with Fair Trade coffee.

Support for the consumption of "equitable" coffee comes from both the private sector and NGOs, such as Bridgehead Enterprises, which purports to return a higher percentage of the profits to the small coffee farmers from whom it buys. According to a recent news report, "sales of Fairtrade coffee are growing by about 40 percent a year"; even members of Britain's Parliament have begun to drink only "ethical" coffee ("Ethical Coffee," *Montréal Gazette*, 13 Nov. 1997). In Montreal, my home, several local restaurants and coffee shops now advertise that they serve only "equitable" coffees. Oxfam-Québec, in conjunction with A SEED (Action for Solidarity, Equity, Environment, and Development), has mounted a campaign to increase consumer awareness of the plight of the peasant producer and to promote the consumption of "equitable" coffees ("Cause Café," *Le Devoir* [Montreal], 2 Oct. 1997, 1). Coopeagri's current advertising pitch is aimed at this market, emphasizing the "Juan Valdez" image of its farmers: small-scale, peasant farmers who, with family labor, produce a fine product for the world at large. As consumer awareness and sympathy grows for the small, peasant producer, this marketing pitch is becoming more common among coffee growers worldwide.

Furthermore, worldwide demand for coffee may increase. Coffee drinking in Japan is on the increase (IATP 1995b), and if the Chinese should develop a taste for the brew, demand will skyrocket (though China is now experimenting with coffee production). The renewed popularity of coffee in North America and Europe is evidenced by the explosive increase in the number of gourmet coffee shops, trendy cafés, and Internet sites devoted to all aspects of coffee production and consumption. High-quality gourmet and specialty coffees account for a rapidly growing segment of today's coffee market. Like the European market of the late nineteenth and early twentieth centuries, the North American market of the 1990s is experiencing a renewed demand for estate brand coffees, based on specific coffee qualities. Changes in consumers' tastes have opened new, more lucrative niches for coffee producers. Such is the current state of the market, notes humorist Dave Barry (1997), that coffee berries that have passed through the digestive system of the luwak (a small mammal in Java) are among the world's most expensive, selling for three hundred dollars a pound.

In the absence of a good market for coffee, Costa Rican farmers will likely continue to experiment with alternative market crops. By 1997, most farmers in Pérez Zeledón had intercropped their coffee with citrus and tropical fruit trees; the domestic and international markets for these fruits apparently have greatly improved. In the meantime, small-scale farmers can only hope for disasters elsewhere (a frost in Brazil would be a big help) or else seek alternative work to supplement their dwindling coffee incomes. With few other options, most rural families have weathered the hard times by combining coffee production with agricultural wage labor. Some have improvised with household microenterprises; others have turned to temporary migration. Those who can afford to do so have invested in higher education for themselves and their children.

How these changes will affect social organization, gender relations, and cultural values remains to be seen. But the inclusion of nonfarm activities in the economic strategies of small-scale coffee farmers in Pérez Zeledón is not surprising, nor does it foreshadow the demise of the family farm in Costa Rica. Such flexibility has been documented among smallholders worldwide and noted as one of their greatest strengths (Netting 1993; Barlett 1993). As Netting noted, such strategies do not put smallholders out of business but rather allow them to continue farming (1993:191). Gladwin and Zabawa found in their study of Florida farmers that, though full-time farmers now have larger farms, their debt-to-asset ratios also doubled in seven years. Part-time farmers are, overall, much better off. "The transformation from full-time to part-time farmer has not been disastrous; indeed, it may even have been a blessing" (1987:224).

Historically, the Costa Rican state has done well in providing an environment in which household producers could survive and often prosper. What their future will look like depends in large part on what role the state plays as regional moderator between domestic and international spheres. How will it meet the challenges of "development" in the twenty-first century: how, in a rapidly globalizing and ever-changing economy, can it eliminate poverty, distribute resources and opportunities more equitably, empower people to determine the course of their lives, and maintain the productive capacity of the environment?

Though many policymakers and academics hailed the collapse of the former Soviet Union as a victory for free market policies, there is a great deal of evidence to suggest that the issues concerning the role of the state in national "development" have not been completely resolved.[5] Other models, such as the "governed markets" found in the dynamic economies of East Asia, suggest that the state, without becoming overly intrusive, can successfully promote economic growth and human development by providing support, incentives, and controls for selected sectors of the economy (Wade 1990). One of the key investments made by the East Asian governments has been in human capital, for example, by promoting universal primary and secondary education. Costa Rica likewise has invested heavily in human capital formation. Whether it can (or should) adopt other elements of the East Asian pattern of industrialization is unclear.

Many rural residents may not have (or want) a future in agriculture, but the survival of farming households in contemporary societies is not only a matter of academic or moral concern. Small-scale farmers have an important role to play in the health of developing societies. Intensive smallholder agriculture can absorb excess labor better than large, extensive operations. More important, a rural economy comprised of productive and successful smallholders can provide a strong base for dynamic regional and national economies (McGreevy 1972; Smith and Smith 1989). Even in such industrial societies as the United States, rural communities of family farmers have been shown to be more vibrant and pleasant places to live than those made up of absentee owners of large farms (Goldschmidt 1978).

The experiences of Costa Rican farmers have been shaped by a specific historical, political, and cultural context, but they may provide lessons for the millions of smallholders worldwide who are turning to commodity production as rising aspirations and standards of living make mere subsistence production less desirable. Given the opportunity to develop their human capital, and an environment in which they can pursue several economic options, household producers can use their skills and flexibility to move into the twenty-first century not as retrenched subsistence producers merely surviving, not as underpaid plantation and factory workers suffering from poor nutrition and ill health, not as perpetual migrants whose homes and families are disrupted by months or years of separation, but as the productive backbone of healthy societies.

9

Fair Trade—A Way Forward?

In July 2006, I stepped off a plane into the tourist-packed, franchise-filled Juan Santamaria Airport. The international coffee market had been in chaos since my visit to Costa Rica in 1993, and I had returned to see how family farmers were coping with this prolonged commodity crisis. In particular, I was curious as to whether the recent growth in Fair Trade (FT)—which had been just a "blip on the radar" when I had conducted my previous research—was helping them to do so. To try to understand the crisis and FT from a variety of perspectives, I planned to speak with farmers in Pérez Zeledón and with members of two FT cooperatives in the cantons of Sarapiqui, Herédia, and Montes de Oro, Puntarenas, in the north-central part of the country.

The expanded and newly renovated airport was but the first of many signs of the transformations that had been taking place. Tourism indeed had significantly increased, and throughout San José and the surrounding Central Valley dozens of North-American-style shopping malls and new housing developments had sprung up, and new-model cars clogged the streets. Much of this growth had come from the diversification of Costa Rica's economy. Tourism, already well-established in the early 1990s, is now burgeoning, as is the production of non-traditional exports—crops such as tropical fruits (especially pineapple) and industrial goods such as microchips (see, e.g., Hershberg et al. 2003; USBPA 2007).[1] In 1998, in partnership with a Costa Rican software company, Intel set up a microchip assembly plant in Herédia, which in 2000 accounted for 8 percent of Costa Rica's GDP and 40 percent of all export value (Luxner 2000). Coffee is no longer the country's number one export, yet the coffee industry remains a significant part of Costa Rica's economy and national identity. Over 78,000 farmers continue to rely on coffee as their economic mainstay, producing over 2.5 million quintals per year (ICAFE 2007).

Overall economic growth has been strong. Annual growth in GDP rose from 1.8 percent in 2000 to 5.9 percent in 2005 (World Bank 2007a). Yet while economic growth has been much stronger than expected and social indicators remained strong, incomes among the bottom 20 percent of the population have been deteriorating since 2000 (World Bank 2007b; see also UNDP 2006). Coffee-farming families in particular have been fighting for their livelihoods, as the coffee crisis of the early 1990s has continued to worsen. Coffee exports declined from U.S.$417 million in 1995 to U.S.$198 million in 2004 (World Bank 2006), due both to falling prices and to falling production. Like their counterparts throughout the world, Costa Rican coffee farmers have been contending with a fundamentally more competitive global market; supply has increased dramatically, in large part due to the entry of Vietnam into the market but also because of Brazil's recovery (and subsequent expansion) from frost damage during the mid-1990s (Varangis et al. 2003: 3).[2] The result has been one of the worst and most prolonged economic crises in coffee history.

Impacts of the crisis have been felt among producers worldwide. Coffee export revenues among Central American nations declined 44 percent when world prices dropped to U.S.$0.60/lb in 2001—a 100-year low when adjusted for inflation (ibid.: 11-15). Small- and medium-scale farmers have been hit particularly hard. With such low prices, the majority of small-scale coffee farmers are simply unable to cover even the costs of production. Coffee also provides a significant source of income for rural laborers; with falling prices, farmers are no longer able to hire agricultural workers, and rural unemployment is skyrocketing. According to Varangis et al., from 2000-2001, seasonal employment in the coffee sector in Central America declined 21 percent, and permanent agricultural employment declined 54 percent (2003: 17). Some studies indicate that rural workers have been able to find other employment, but small-scale farmers continue to suffer (Lewin, Giovannucci, and Varangis 2004: 12).

As discussed in earlier chapters, the booms and busts of the international commodity markets are not new, and Costa Rican coffee producers have long had to find creative ways to cope with fluctuating markets and price instability. But there are some signs that the nature of the current crisis is fundamentally different. According to Varangis et al., the current crisis is not just part of a cyclical phenomenon but "is also a direct consequence of the new structure of the market" (2003: 3). Not only has world supply increased, but the quality of unroasted "green" coffee has improved, particularly in Brazil, which is now using better washing techniques and quality control. Roasters have also developed new techniques to remove the bitter taste of lower-quality coffees, making *robustas* and other lower-quality coffees slightly more competitive with the higher-quality Extra Hard Bean (ibid.: 4). This particularly affects Central American producers who are among the largest producers of quality hard bean coffees.

This highly competitive market places new demands on producers, especially small-scale family farmers who, alone, have little influence in commodity markets. But while the international commodity market has been flooded with coffee since the collapse of the last ICA, as predicated by many analysts, there has simultaneously been a rapidly growing market for what are known as differentiated coffees. These include a wide variety of coffees, each bought and marketed according to specific characteristics related either to the taste qualities of the coffee bean itself and/or to how the coffee is grown. Some of these, such as high-quality gourmet and organic coffees, continue to be bought and sold through the conventional international coffee market. Others, often referred to as sustainable or ethical coffees, are part of a growing Alternative Trade (AT) movement that has been attempting to challenge the logic of conventional commodity trade by establishing new markets in which specific social and environmental concerns play a key role in determining the value of commodities. These coffees are certified as having been produced according to specific social and ecological values and are sold through Alternative Trade Organizations (ATOs), such as Fair Trade.

As consumers in the North become more aware of the plight of small-scale farmers and artisans, not only are increasing numbers of organizations adopting policies to sell fairly traded products to their members but many global corporations, such as Starbucks, are also heeding growing public demand for more ethically produced commodities. As one journalist quips: "Fair Trade is in vogue" (Karneef 2005). But while the good intentions of ethical consumers in the North are commendable, as I returned to Costa Rica, I wondered to what extent Fair Trade was making a difference in the lives of Costa Rican farming families trying to weather this ongoing coffee crisis.

The Changing Face of Pérez Zeledón

Driving south from San José toward Pérez Zeledón, the twisting road through the Talamancan cloud forest was much as I remembered. At first glance, the Valle del General appeared not to have changed much either: the Talamancan Mountains rising dramatically in the west, the Rio General snaking its way southward. Though overall production in the canton has been declining, Pérez Zeledón is the country's largest coffee-producing canton (Alvarado 2003), and small *cafetales* continue to dot the landscape. But as we descended into the valley and entered the town of San Isidro, it was clear that much had changed—and not quite as I had expected.

Over the years, Costa Rican friends had kept me apprised of how difficult life was becoming for coffee farmers, but they had not mentioned the hundreds of new marble-tiled houses, late-model cars, modern gas stations with mini-supermarkets, and—ultimate symbol of globalization—a brand new McDonald's with a PlayPlace. We drove through the car-filled streets of San Isidro surrounded by cell phone-toting pedestrians, bustling shops, and dusty construction sites. Search as I might, though, the familiar stucco building that had housed Coopeagri offices and its small *supermercado* could not be found. For ten frustrating minutes, I drove around and around the market area only to discover that the gleaming glass-and-concrete structure I had been circling *was* Coopeagri—or Corporación Coopeagri, R.L., as it is now known.

Coopeagri

For a coffee-processing cooperative in the midst of an international commodity crisis, Coopeagri is doing surprisingly well. On the ground floor of the new building, which covers half the block, are the cooperative's slick, modern supermarket, agricultural supply store, and international money transfer center; upstairs, computer-equipped offices and the new credit union are reached through automatic glass doors. In addition to its coffee-processing plant and its sugar refinery (it no longer runs the milk processing plant), Coopeagri now owns and operates the canton's largest chain of supermarkets, two modern gasoline stations with mini-supermarkets, and a thriving credit union. Though a factional dispute did lead to a split in which an ex-president and other members left Coopeagri to form a new processing association, membership at Coopeagri has steadily increased over the years, from approximately 5,000 producer and employee members in 1990 to 8,500 in 2006 (12,000 including those who are credit union

New Coopeagri building with co-op offices, supermarket, and credit union.

members only). In some respects the decline in coffee production has been good news for Coopeagri, as the decrease in overall coffee production in the canton has led to the closure of two private *beneficios* in Pérez Zeledón: El General and La Meseta. Though there are now a number of new, smaller processing companies and producer associations operating in the valley, Coopeagri has picked up many clients from El General and La Meseta and now processes 60–70 percent of the canton's coffee, up from 25 percent fifteen years ago.

Due to the expanding residential neighborhoods around its old *beneficio* in San Isidro, Coopeagri has recently built a new processing factory on a site several kilometers south of town. Like many throughout the country, Coopeagri's new *beneficio* incorporates a number of new technologies and techniques designed to reduce the impacts of coffee-processing on the environment. These include: a more energy-efficient factory; a large warehouse in which cherry husks are composted into organic fertilizer, which is then sold back to members at cost; and a series of wastewater filtration ponds in which the highly acidic runoff from the coffee-washing process is purified and neutralized before being returned to the nearby stream. Coopeagri is addressing environmental concerns in other ways as well. In addition to its ongoing reforestation projects, in 2003 Coopeagri entered into a partnership with York University's faculty of environmental studies to create an experimental sustainable coffee farm in Las Nubes Biological Reserve in the Talamancan Mountains. Here coffee is grown using minimal chemical inputs and techniques that help preserve forest cover and soil qualities.

Santa Cruz and Palomas

Though farming families in Palomas and Santa Cruz have long been tied to the larger world through the production of coffee for global markets, new phone lines and paved roads now allow villagers to connect to distant families, friends, and markets with greater ease. Jobs and shopping opportunities in San Isidro are just a smooth 15-minute bus or car ride away. While cell phones had been widely adopted by most households in the mid-1990s, they are expensive, and reception in this mountainous region is not reliable. During my visit, the arrival of landline phones—which are cheaper and more reliable—was the cause of much anticipation and excitement. However, as those who recently had landlines installed were quickly learning—with 6:00 a.m. phone calls from *suegras* (mothers-in-law), telemarketers, and scam artists—there is a downside to connectivity as well.

As elsewhere in the country, farmers in both villages have been dealing with the coffee crisis in a number of ways. One of the most dramatic and surprising responses has been the growing number of coffee farmers throughout the country who have cut down their coffee trees—an action that was unthinkable 15 years ago. While this trend is not as pronounced in Pérez Zeledón as elsewhere, many farmers here have begun to tear out their coffee to grow pineapple or sugar or raise dairy cattle. The most obvious example is the former Finca Santa Fe (now owned by the Pindeco Company of Buenos Aires), where thousands of hectares of coffee have been replaced with pineapple to take advantage of new markets in North America.

While many *cafetales* in Palomas and Santa Cruz show signs of neglect or abandonment (more so in the former than in the latter), for the most part coffee-producing households in both villages have continued to try to ride out the current downturn, waiting for a rebound in prices.[3] In the meantime, farming families continue to rely on various forms of diversification, micro-enterprises, and especially migration for wage labor in order to weather the current crisis. Several farmers with whom I spoke have been raising herds of 5–10 pigs, which they fatten and then sell during the holiday seasons. Others have not given up on coffee altogether but have cut a portion of their coffee to create pasture for a few dairy cows to supplement their incomes.

The question of whether it is time to cut the coffee or to hold on is a common topic of family conversations these days. One father and son with whom I spoke were in heated disagreement about what to do. Jorge, the son, wants to cut a *manzana* of coffee and buy a couple of cows. He feels that it is time to have some alternative to coffee. His wife's aunt has gradually built a small herd of dairy cattle and does quite well from the sale of milk and cheese to families in the area. As Celia, Jorge's wife, explained: ". . . at least we would have the milk to use or to sell."

Jorge's father, Roberto, thinks his son would be foolish to tear out any of their coffee. "People aren't thinking clearly," he says. "One *manzana* is not enough pasture to keep cattle. And a few cows are not going to make a big difference. If they just keep the coffee, in the end they will be much better off." Roberto's comments reflect his understanding of the long-term cyclical nature of the international coffee market. He has seen these ups and downs before and believes in the long run that they should protect their investments in coffee. But the younger Jorge has seen very little of the good times in his 10 years as a coffee farmer. He believes there has been a fundamental change in the structure of the world economy and feels it is necessary to begin to look for alternative ways to support his family.

To survive, most families in Pérez Zeledón have been relying heavily on remittances from household or family members working in urban centers in Costa Rica and/or the United States.[4] According to several farmers with whom I spoke, the money that is clearly pouring into San Isidro comes from family remittances from this migratory labor, which explains how a regional economy that is so intricately linked to the dismal international coffee market could be showing such marked signs of diversification and economic growth. As noted in Chapter 7, in the late 1980s and early 1990s, most Costa Ricans who migrated to the United States did so temporarily, with the intention of earning enough money to bring home and invest in land, houses, or businesses. This seems to be what is currently happening as well. According to local farmers, one downside of this infusion of money from abroad is a growing lack of harvest labor. As rural workers can now find employment in construction and service industries, they no longer need to accept lower-paying harvest work. With coffee prices so low, farmers cannot afford to entice labor with higher wages.

Just as the decision to tear out years' worth of investment in coffee is not easy, neither is the decision to migrate for wage labor, even on a temporary basis. As Pedro Vasquez, a young farmer in Santa Cruz told me:

Coffee prices have been so bad that we can no longer support ourselves. I don't want to divide my family by going away to the US to work. Maybe it is time to tear out my coffee and get dairy cattle like so many others are doing. But would raising dairy cattle be any better? I am a coffee farmer; that is what I know and love to do. We don't need a lot, if I could just be sure of a certain income each year, that would be enough. It is this insecurity, not knowing, that is intolerable.

Fair Trade: An Alternative Market

With roots dating back to the 1950s, Fair Trade is perhaps the oldest and best known of a growing number of Alternative Trade Organizations (ATOs) that buy and sell what are known as ethical or sustainable coffees. There is a great deal of variation among ATOs in the type of "value added" that they emphasize, but the basic goal is to produce coffee under conditions that are environmentally, socially, and/or economically sustainable. For example, sustainable coffees certified by the Rainforest Alliance or the Smithsonian Institution (e.g., Bird Friendly coffee) emphasize the ecological aspects of coffee production, with social and economic sustainability playing a visible, but lesser, role.

Fair Trade, on the other hand, has focused primarily on the social side of production by attempting to address the problems of market inequities and uncertainties facing small-scale artisans and farmers, like Pedro Vasquez (discussed above). While increasing efforts are made to address the environmental aspects of coffee production, Fair Trade's main concern has been to create a market in which socially conscious consumers pay premium prices for commodities in order to help small-scale and disadvantaged producers earn higher and more reliable incomes from commodity production (see, e.g., FTF 2003). While all sustainable coffees tend to fetch higher prices than conventionally produced coffee, Fair Trade is also the only organization that pays a guaranteed minimum price for its certified coffees.

The Fair Trade Mandate

With its emphasis on the well-being of small-scale coffee producers, FT has been particularly influential in calling consumer attention to the plight of coffee-farming families. As Paul notes, Fair Trade "is at once a social movement, an alternative form of trade, and a development intervention" intended to change international trading practices, raise consumer awareness, and ultimately improve economic, social, and environmental conditions for marginal and disadvantaged producers (2005: 134; see also Brown 1993; Hudson and Hudson 2004). Fair Trade standards have been evolving over the years, but, in general, FTOs must meet four criteria in order to be certified by international organizations such as the FT Labelling Organizations (FLO) (see, e.g., Transfair 2006). The first is a commitment to return a larger proportion of the retail value of the product to producers, thus providing a living income for small-scale producers and a fair living wage for workers. For coffee, FT organizations offer a guaranteed minimum price of U.S.$1.26/pound for washed *arabicas* when world prices are low and a guaranteed premium above the world price when it rises above this minimum. In March 2007, the FLO raised this premium from U.S.$0.05/pound to U.S.$0.10/pound (FLO 2007a). Though environmentally friendly production practices are not, per se, a *requirement* of FT, organic farming and other environmentally sustainable practices are increasingly encouraged, and FTOs pay additional premiums for certified organic coffee. This premium was also raised in 2007 from U.S.$0.15/pound to U.S.$0.20/pound.

Second, FTOs must also commit to longer partnerships with coffee producers so as to provide a more stable market and lower transaction costs for producers. Though earlier FLO guidelines suggested a minimum two-year contract with producers, current FLO guidelines mandate only that FTOs strive for mutually beneficial long term relationships (FLO 2007b); no minimum length of contract is specified. FTOs are also obligated, when possible, to provide technical support and services and to facilitate access to reasonable credit (up to 60% of contracted harvest earnings) so as to help farmers avoid excessive debt with private lenders.

Third, though the FLO is now working with larger plantations to establish better conditions for plantation workers, most FT efforts are aimed at providing farmers of small- and medium-sized coffee farms with a better market for their coffee. FTOs are required to deal with democratically organized cooperatives and producer associations rather than individual farmers. As with other development initiatives discussed in earlier chapters, FTOs see cooperatives as a means to provide small-scale producers with economies of scale and a stronger, collective voice in the marketplace. By working primarily with cooperatives, FTOs hope to encourage the participation of more marginal producers, including women. To stimulate local development, FTOs mandate that the U.S.$0.05 "social premium" be allocated to a fund for use on social programs and development projects voted upon by members of these cooperatives—much as Coopeagri has long done with its social capital fund.

Fourth, the Fair Trade movement is committed to consumer education. By raising consumer awareness of the conditions under which small-scale farmers operate, the FT movement hopes to increase demand for FT products. To raise consumer confidence, FTOs regulate and monitor FT production and provide certification and labelling through programs such as those run by the FLO.[5]

While accounting for a still relatively small share of world trade, sales of FT products—most notably coffee—are rapidly rising. Sales worldwide in 2005 reached over U.S.$1.5 billion, up 37 percent from 2004 (FLO 2006). This growth is the result of increasing awareness on the part of consumers and the growing social chic of FT products. But what have been the impacts of FT on coffee-farming families?

By drawing social concerns into the global marketplace, FT has created a space in which small-scale producers finally hold an advantage over larger producers and multi-national corporations, thus providing new opportunities for family farmers. For Pedro Vasquez and the many thousands of family farmers worldwide still struggling to earn a living from coffee production, FT offers the hope of sustainable livelihoods. Nevertheless, assessing the impacts of FT on family farmers is not a straightforward matter.

Fair Trade seems to have made some significant contributions toward improving the lives of small coffee farmers and their families. Recent research indicates that FT has increased incomes, reduced vulnerability for many small-scale producers (Bacon 2005; Nigh 1997), helped small-scale producers build organizational skills and other forms of human and social capital (Bray et al. 2002; Raynolds, Murray, and Taylor 2004; Rice 2001), and initiated new forms of governance in commodity production and marketing (Taylor et al. 2005). On the other hand, a number of studies of FT and other ethical trade initiatives have begun to raise questions regarding the sustainability, economic effectiveness, and equity of Alternative Trade initiatives in general (see, e.g., Bisaillon et al. 2005; Blowfield 1999; Levi and Linton 2003; Meacham 2002; Murray et al. 2006; Utting-Chamorro 2005). Of particular concern are the stringent certification requirements that many producers are finding unduly burdensome given the modest price premiums they are paid (see, e.g., Moberg 2005; Muradian and Pelupessy 2005).[6]

Farmers and Fair Trade in Costa Rica

Compared to other coffee-producing countries like Peru, Mexico, or Nicaragua, to date Fair Trade has accounted for a relatively small portion (about 1%) of overall coffee production in Costa Rica.[7] Most of Costa Rica's Fair Trade–certified coffee is produced by the approximately 3,500 farmers who belong to Coocafé, a consortium of nine small coffee-producing cooperatives, most of which are located in the northern part of the country (Coocafé 2006). At the time of my research, none of the producer associations in Pérez Zeledón belonged to Coocafé, but Coopeagri did receive FT certification in 2005 for the coffee produced on its experimental farm in the Las Nubes Biological Corridor, as well as for its sugar. Rather than sell this FT coffee through Coocafé, Coopeagri—following its past strategy of bypassing middlemen—sells this coffee directly to its partner, York University, and to Timothy's World Coffee. Though Ronchi (2002), in her study of Coocafé, concluded that farmers were benefiting both financially and organizationally from their involvement in Fair Trade, my discussions with cooperative leaders, employees, and farmers in Pérez Zeledón, Sarapiqui, and Montes de Oro (these latter two are long-term Fair Trade producers belonging to Coocafé) revealed a number of problems that farmers and cooperatives are facing in their efforts to reap the potential benefits of Fair Trade.[8]

Demand Issues

One of the biggest problems facing farmers wishing to produce for FT markets is low global demand. As noted earlier, despite overall growth in the last decade, the market for FT coffee is still quite small. While FT pays farmers a consistent minimum above the conventional world market price, demand for FT coffee remains well below production from certified FT producers. Cale and Wise found in their study of organic and Fair Trade markets in Mexico that FT premiums for organic coffee made the effort highly remunerative— *"for those able to sell their coffee in that market"* (2005: 8, emphasis added). Not everyone is able to access this alternative market, and even with FT partnership agreements, producer associations still must sell a portion (sometimes a large portion) of their coffee on the conventional market.

Low demand undoubtedly plays a significant role in limiting the ability of FTOs to create a viable alternative market for small-scale coffee producers, and for this reason the FT movement focuses heavily on improving demand through consumer education. But low demand is not the only concern that farmers have with producing for FTOs. A number of structural factors are also affecting farmers' perceptions of FT and hence its role in both their collective and individual production and marketing strategies.

Certification Costs

The most common concern echoed by representatives of Coopeagri, CoopeSarapiqui, and Coope Montes de Oro were the costs of certification and marketing through FTOs. Certification requirements and procedures vary among ATOs, but for coffee producers in Costa Rica, FT certification costs include U.S.$2.00 per quintal charged by FLO for its seal of certification and U.S.$1.00 for each FLO coffee sack. Members of Coocafé also pay U.S.$1.65 per quintal for operating expenses of the consortium.

In addition to these direct costs, farmers' organizations wishing to become FT certified must meet the basic production requirements as outlined in the FLO's 24-page Generic Fairtrade Standards for Small Farmers' Organizations (FLO 2007c). These include: the creation of non-discriminatory, democratically elected producer associations; formal plans outlining the transparent use of FT social premiums for democratically agreed-upon community development projects; protection against child labor; and commitments toward eliminating chemical inputs and implementing more environmentally friendly production practices. In Mexico the government has created an internationally recognized certifying organization, Certimex, which helps keep the costs of sustainable certification low (Cale and Wise 2005: 24); in Costa Rica there is no such national organization, and FT cooperatives themselves must bear all the costs related to meeting these requirements. They must also bear the ongoing financial and transaction costs of monitoring farmers' fields to ensure that the environmental and social conditions of FT production continue to be met as well as sanctioning those who "defect" (i.e., break the rules). As one co-op leader commented, sanctioning non-compliers (e.g., those who pull their children out of school to help with farm chores) is particularly difficult in smaller communities where nearly everyone is related by both consanguineal and affinal kin ties.

Environmental Concerns

Growing concerns on the part of northern consumers about the environmental impacts of coffee production are spurring demand for more ecologically friendly coffee. Though the FLO does not require FT coffee to be organically produced, following the lead of the more eco-oriented ATOs, FT now also requires its partner cooperatives to show signs of progress in implementing environmentally sound production practices. As opposed to certified *organic* production in which no chemical inputs are allowed, with certified *sustainable* coffee, chemical fertilizers are allowed in limited amounts, herbicides are prohibited, and organic pest control and shade production are encouraged. In order to be certified, sustainable coffee, like organic coffee, must be processed separately from conventionally produced coffee.

Demand for sustainable coffee is growing not just among ATOs but among conventional corporate buyers such as Starbucks, Kraft, and Van Houte. As a result, prices for certified sustainably produced coffees are higher than for most conventionally produced coffee, for which there are few restrictions on chemical inputs. Nevertheless, producing more environmentally friendly coffee has a number of added costs in terms of additional labor, processing, and certification. Furthermore, yields are considerably lower than with conventional coffee production (see Table 15). Many farmers in Costa Rica expressed doubts that the benefits of producing more socially beneficial and/or environmentally friendly coffees would outweigh the costs. Some farmers with whom I spoke complained that once all certification and marketing costs were deducted, despite higher FT minimum prices, they were receiving not much more than they would selling to the conventional market. (Cale and Wise 2005 found a similar situation in Mexico.)

One matter that has received little attention is the question of regional variations in the day-to-day costs of labor and inputs that farmers must bear. In Costa Rica, where the costs of living and farm labor are relatively high—and inflation in 2005–06 was running at 14.1 percent (UN 2006)—farmers receive the same price for their FT coffee as their counterparts in other coffee-producing countries where costs of living and labor are lower.[9] Because demand in all types of alternative markets (Fair Trade, Rainforest Alliance, etc.) is insufficient to absorb production, markets are limited, and many farmers feel that the efforts put into meeting social and environmental requirements are not fully compensated.

Furthermore, though FT guarantees a minimum price above average world market prices, this is not necessarily the *best* price available at any given time. In today's competitive global coffee market, quality coffees are increasingly in demand. Buyers representing global firms roam the countryside offering higher prices to farmers producing better-quality coffees (i.e. those from higher altitudes). Contrary to agreements with their producer cooperatives and FTOs, many farmers opt to sell their better-quality coffee to independent buyers at higher prices. The remainder of their crop is sold to local private or cooperative processors for sale to their partner FTOs and/or on the conventional market.[10]

The complexity of the relationship between alternative markets and the conventional international coffee market is evident in the varied

TABLE 15

Comparison of Price and Yields by Type
of Coffee Production and Market

Eco-conditions of production	Approx. yields (q./ha.)	Average Prices by Market* (U.S.$/q.)	
		Conventional	Fair Trade
Conventional	60+	$106	$126
"Sustainable"	30–40	$131–$136	
Organic	15–20	$141	$156

Source: author's interviews with cooperative leaders 2006.
* For July 2006.

strategies that farmers in Sarapiqui, Montes de Oro, and Pérez Zeledón have developed to survive the current crisis. As noted above, at an individual level, farming families are reacting to the prolonged depression in prices in a number of ways, ranging from complete withdrawal from coffee production to increased reliance on alternative sources of income. On a collective level, responses of producer cooperatives in these three regions to current conditions are indicative of both the potential and limitations of FT in helping small-scale coffee farmers negotiate the continuing challenges of export commodity production.

For example, despite the fact that in 2005 Coope Montes de Oro was able to sell just 40 percent of its members' coffee via FT, co-op leaders continue to see their FT partnership as an opportunity to produce for the more lucrative organic and "sustainable production" markets. While only 20 percent of current production among farmer members is certified organic, another 30 percent is certified sustainably produced, and the hope is that coffee produced in these fields will soon be certified organic as well. As noted above, the FT organic market is among the most lucrative, and this co-op is hoping to be able to take advantage of that niche.

Coope Montes de Oro is also developing ways both to cut operating costs and to stand out as an environmentally innovative cooperative. While wastewater purification tanks and coffee-husk composting are becoming standard features of coffee processors throughout

Costa Rica, this co-op, through a partnership with a U.S.-based solar company, has built one of the first solar-powered coffee-drying factories.[11] It is also working to develop ways to convert methane gas (a by-product of processing) into electricity to power its processing factory and offices. In addition to helping maintain a healthier environment, such innovations are likely to make their coffee more desirable among environmentally conscious consumers.

Farmers in Sarapiqui see FT quite differently. Despite nearly 30 years producing for Coocafé, many of CoopeSarapiqui's 380 member farmers have become disillusioned with FT. Farmers with whom I spoke expressed their perspective like this: "Fair Trade has not brought us a better income. It is still the same: those who really make money from our coffee are those who sell it cup-by-cup in the coffee shops in the North. That is where the profit is. We don't see it here."

Though many in Sarapiqui have already converted their *cafetales* in the lower elevations to pastures for dairy cattle, many wish to continue to produce coffee but not for export—neither for FT nor for the conventional market. They plan, instead, to focus on the domestic market by selling their coffee by the cup directly to visiting tourists from the North. As Sarapiqui is along a major tourist route, the hope is that income from tourist-oriented coffee shops and tours of coffee plantations will provide a better income than coffee exporting and will allow farmers more control over the marketing process.

In Pérez Zeledón, Coopeagri has long been committed to many of the ideals of social and economic justice that are also the foundations of Fair Trade. Its organizational structure, commitment to paying farmers higher prices, and its 5 percent social capital fund for community development seem to make it an ideal partner for FTOs. Yet FT has not played a large role in Coopeagri's production and marketing strategies. Coopeagri representatives say that they are happy with the production and sale of FT coffee from the Las Nubes experimental farm. They are currently exploring the possibility of certifying member farmers who produce coffee in and around Las Nubes Biological Corridor (though outside the experimental farm), but they are reluctant to expand the program because of the high costs of certification. When pressed, one co-op representative explained that they might eventually try to certify the other producer members throughout the valley, but the high costs of certifying thousands of producers, coupled with the low quantity of coffee that FTOs would actually buy (he estimated it would be only about 5 percent of Coopeagri production) make it unlikely to happen anytime in the near future.

Coopeagri continues to deal with the ups and downs of export commodity production through diversification and pursuing multiple strategies aimed at securing the highest price possible for farmers' coffee. For example, in order to take advantage of the growing diversification of niche markets, Coopeagri now classifies its coffee into four brand-name types based on quality of the beans and, in the case of its Las Nubes brand, environmental criteria as well. In marketing all these coffees, Coopeagri continues to follow a strategy of eliminating intermediaries in the commodity chain and establishing direct relationships with buyers in North America and Europe. Even in marketing its FT-certified coffee, Coopeagri has chosen to bypass Coocafé and sell directly to its northern partners in Canada. According to one official, Coopeagri now has 19 direct partnerships worldwide and continues to work on creating others. At the moment, Coopeagri leaders are doing what they have done before: weighing the pros and cons of FT and other sustainable coffee markets in terms of a set of diverse strategies needed to survive in today's increasingly differentiated and highly competitive markets.[12]

New Markets, New Hopes, Old Problems?

The twenty-first century has brought changes, both welcome and unwelcome, to farming families throughout Costa Rica. Like many countries, Costa Rica recently has been implementing more neoliberal, free-market economic policies. Such policies can help reduce excessive government expenditures, facilitate access to larger world markets, and increase foreign investment—and have contributed to the rapid diversification of Costa Rica's economy. While the liberalization of the economy can also increase environmental degradation and social inequalities, deregulation at the national level has benefited small-scale coffee producers at least in some respects. For example, cooperatives are no longer required to export their coffee through the state-run Fedecoop agency but can now sell directly—either to FTOs or to buyers such as Starbucks in the conventional market—as they choose. (As noted in chapter 5, Coopeagri had earlier received special dispensation to bypass Fedecoop, but now this option is available to all.) While this helps cooperatives bypass middlemen in the export processes, they nevertheless must confront a world market that, despite the elimination of the old quota system, is not entirely deregulated. For example, the European Union continues to impose tariffs on imports of roasted (though not green) coffee (FTF 2002: 27). Such policies limit the ability of coffee producers in developing countries to capture much of the extra value added in the coffee trade.

In Pérez Zeledón, as elsewhere in Costa Rica, the future of coffee farming remains uncertain. As evidenced throughout this case study, the Costa Rican state historically supported small family farmers by encouraging the creation of producer cooperatives and providing access to credit on reasonable terms—two criteria now also central to the FT mandate. While many producer cooperatives have foundered, some, like Coopeagri, have made a significant difference in obtaining relatively better prices for their members, in promoting community development through a social capital fund, and in establishing environmental conservation programs.

While these policies have helped family farmers in Costa Rica, the adverse impacts of a glutted international market remain severe. Despite the creation of the National Fund for Coffee Stabilization (FONECAFE) to provide assistance to coffee farmers during the current crisis (Varangis et al. 2003: 25), many farmers have made the difficult decision to tear out their coffee trees. Many more have temporarily abandoned coffee and turned to wage labor in San José or, more typically, the United States in order to survive and, in some cases, prosper. Indeed, one might ask if the international coffee crisis has been indirectly responsible for much of the economic prosperity so evident in Pérez Zeledón today. Remittances sent home by workers in the United States seem to have provided capital for investments in land, cars, and businesses, stimulating economic growth in the canton. Yet it might be difficult to argue that remittances from insecure migrant jobs thousands of miles from home could be considered a sustainable or desirable means of rural development.

For many social activists, scholars, and ethically minded consumers, FT (and AT in general) provides a socially, economically, and environmentally appealing alternative to the "ecologically and socially destructive practices" that characterize conventional, corporate-dominated world markets (Murray and Raynolds 2000: 66; see also Simpson and Rapone 2000; Renard 1999). For the thousands of farming families who constitute the backbone of the rural Costa Rican economy, FT offers hope that they can survive in international commodity markets.

But FT is no magic bullet. Insufficient demand for sustainable coffees remains a significant problem, and farmers find certification a double-edged sword. In today's glutted global market, competition is keen not just among growers trying to sell their beans but among sellers at the other end of the commodity chain who, in their efforts to attract more consumers, are searching for ways to make their coffees stand out. An increasing number of today's coffee traders are searching for gourmet and sustainable coffees that will attract cus-tomers. While gourmet and even organic coffee can be produced by large-scale corporate operations, in the production of most sustain-able coffees, small-scale producers hold the advantage because, by definition, "sustainable" coffee is produced by small growers. Therefore, for family farmers, the production of sustainable and other specialty coffees for differentiated markets is perhaps the key to survival. Certification, then, becomes a "reputation" tool that provides farmers with a "preferred supplier" status and facilitates ac-cess to potentially more secure and lucrative niche markets (Mura-dian and Pelupessy 2005: 2039).

On the other hand, meeting certification criteria is costly in many ways. Farmers and producer organizations often find guidelines con-fusing or production criteria inappropriate for local social and/or eco-logical conditions. Some analysts argue that the certification for alter-native markets is based on "northern" norms of production that are incongruent with tropical agriculture and that the certification process is further complicated by inappropriate language and record-keeping requirements and inspectors' lack of experience with tropical systems (Gómez Tovar et al. 1999, cited in Cale and Wise 2005: 28).

Other analysts argue that while FT and other voluntary certifica-tion systems have been setting standards "for excluding the worst so-cial and environmental practices from the coffee industry," these stan-dards are also imposing on farmers a number of restrictions that are becoming "*de facto* market requirements" yet are not always compen-sated with price premiums (Muradian and Pelupessy 2005: 2039–40).[13] In this respect, "ethical" consumer demands are placing additional burdens on small-scale producers, who may or may not see their addi-tional efforts financially rewarded. One might argue that the regula-tory void left by the breakdown of the International Coffee Agree-ment has been filled by a burgeoning number of ATOs, which themselves are creating an increasingly regulated market. While this regulated market brings new opportunities, it also places additional burdens on small-scale farmers for uncertain gains.

The question of financial compensation is a central concern for farmers. FTOs do at least pay a guaranteed minimum price for certi-fied coffee, but not all ATOs do so. And with low demand for all sus-tainable coffees, overall profits for farmers do not always outweigh the costs of certification. Furthermore, sustainable coffee markets do not reward farmers financially according to coffee quality the way the con-ventional market does. Though FT ostensibly operates outside the logic of conventional commodity markets, both production and con-sumption decisions about FT coffee are highly influenced by conditions in the conventional global coffee market. The conventional market continues to provide farmers with an opportunity to earn premium prices (above sustainable and even guaranteed FT prices) for better-quality and estate-branded coffees. From this perspective, the rigid FT marketing structure—one global price for conventional coffee and one global organic price, rather than a price differential also based on taste qualities—works to the disadvantage of FTOs when farmers sell their better coffee to non-FT buyers.

Conclusions

While many family farmers have benefited from FT, the hopes that such new market possibilities bring are tempered by the same concerns that shaped the strategies of coffee farmers producing for conventional markets 15 years ago. Farmers and producer associations today face a highly competitive and complex global marketplace in which neither conventional prices nor the benefits of sustainable coffee markets are stable, or even evident. In addition, as the varied responses of farmers in Montes de Oro, Sarapiqui, and Pérez Zeledón suggest, local conditions also play a role in how farmers and producer associations gauge the benefits of production for FT. These include: local ecological conditions (soils, altitudes, etc.), infrastructure (roads, electricity, etc.), distance from markets, available alternatives, and the size of the cooperative (larger co-ops will have higher certification costs). Consequently farmers evaluate production for FT and other sustainable coffee markets just as they have always evaluated production for the conventional market: in terms of the perceived costs, risks, and benefits stemming from both global and local factors. As Parrish et al. (2005) found in a comparative study of coffee farmers in Tanzania, those working with FTOs do not always fare significantly better than those working with free-market organizations. Depending on specific market conditions, the two approaches can be complementary.

The significant headway that the Fair Trade movement has made in bringing social and environmental concerns to the international coffee market is an example of the considerable influence that civil society organizations can have on reshaping global economic systems. Yet conventional commodity markets and national economic policies continue to play a large role in shaping the opportunities and constraints that family farmers face in producing international commodities. For example, worried about growing economic and social instability among its coffee-producing "friends and neighbors" in 2004, the United States rejoined the ICO and is working to "ensure that sustainable development is at the forefront of the coffee trade agenda" (Wayne 2004). Such support from the world's largest consumer nation may significantly improve conditions for small-scale producers in the coffee market.

The relationship between Fair Trade and free trade raises some basic questions as to the respective roles of markets, civil society, nation-states, and international trade policies in promoting equitable and sustainable development. For family farmers, survival is not merely a question of Fair Trade or free trade but of the availability of a variety of options that allow them to take advantage of opportunities in diversifying markets. Whether these forces can strike a regulatory balance allowing small-scale commodity, producers such as Costa Rica's coffee-farming families, to flourish remains to be seen. *Ojala, si*—hopefully, yes.

Glossary

agua dulce   traditional drink made with *dulce,* unrefined brown sugar, hot water and milk

ama de casa   mistress of the house; housewife

arabica   *Coffea arbica* L., a mild type of coffee

asociaciónes de desarrollo comunal   community development associations

bachillerato   secondary school diploma

benami   practice in which land title is nominally transferred from one person to another to avoid taxation or land ceiling laws, but in the original owner maintains control

beneficio   coffee processing plant

buen hijo   a good son; one who fulfills his duties to and cares for his parents

café generaleño   coffee from the *Valle del General* (General Valley) of Pérez Zeledón

café en oro   term used to designate coffee beans that have been processed and dried to final pre-roasting stage in preparation for sale on the world market

cafetal(es)   coffee field. In Costa Rica, refers to both small and large plots

cafeteros   coffee farmers

cajuela   a standard-sized basket used for the collection and measurement of coffee; equal to one decaliter. Twenty *cajuelas* equals one *fanega (see below),* or about 256 kilograms.

canasta basica   the basic basket; refers to minimum food requirements

canephora   *Coffea canephora* L., a type of coffee referred to as *robusta*

caña de india   cane-like ornamental plant

colón(es)   currency of Costa Rica. In 1990-91 $1 U.S. = approximately 100 *colones*

colono   tenant farmer

conjunto   together. Living *conjunto* refers to common-law marriage.

cooperativismo   principle pertaining to belief in cooperative ideals

copa   drink (alcoholic)

dulce   crude brown sugar processed in domestic cane crushers

encomienda   colonial estates granted by the Spanish Crown; included rights over both land and labor or indigenous peoples

fanega   unit of measurement equal to 4 hectoliters or approximately 256 kilograms

gallo pinto   spotted rooster; typical breakfast dish of rice and beans mixed

granilla   refers to the few ripe coffee cherries ready for picking at the beginning of the harvest season

grano de oro   the golden bean (lit. grain); common term for commercial coffee. According to some the term the term refers to the golden color of the washed and dried bean; others attribute the term to the wealth the crop has brought.

granos básicos   basic grains such as corn, wheat, and rice

gringa   gringo (fem.); in Costa Rica refers primarily to Americans. Usually not used in a pejorative manner.

ingenio (de azúcar)   sugar processing factory

jornalero   day laborer

ladinos   Latin Americans of mixed heritage who associate with Spanish culture rather than indigenous cultures. Spanish-speaking ladinos dominate national affairs and often consider themselves superior to indigenous peoples.

manzana   standard unit of land measurement in Costa Rica. 1 manzana = 0.69 hectares, or 1.7 acres.

maquinista   machinist. In Venezuela, term used to refer to those who hull coffee in small hulling machines.

milpa   corn field

muy coopertavista   very cooperative-minded; adhering to and promoting cooperative ideals

oficios domesticos   domestic duties

peones   in Costa Rica, refers to full-time, permanent farm workers

politiqueros   petty politician; those who avidly follow politics

poro   a fast-growing, fruitless, deciduous tree with large, broad leaves; commonly used as a shade tree for coffee and noted as a good nitrogen supplier

potrero   pasture; grazing land

pulpería   small, family-run corner store

recibidor(es)   receiving station; collection stations for raw coffee; established throughout countryside by processing factories

repela   refers to the few remaining ripe coffee cherries on the trees at the end of the harvest season

robusta   descriptive reference to *Coffea canephora* L.

sindicalismo   principle, doctrine pertaining to the support and promotion of worker unions and worker rights
sindicatos   syndicates; unions
soda   in Costa Rica, refers to snack bars/soda fountains
solidadismo   term coined in Costa Rica to refer to the principle, doctrine pertaining to the support and promotion of cooperative
ideals; *solidadismo* promotes worker-manager cooperation, as opposed to *sindicalismo* (*see* above), the union movement, which
sees the two as primarily in opposition to one another
supermercado   supermarket
supermobil   supermarket on wheels; refers to large vans purchased by
Coopeagri which, equipped with a variety of foodstuffs, travel
weekly to rural communities; priced to be competitive with rural
corner stores
tierra libre   unoccupied land available for homesteading
trapiche   small domestic cane crusher powered by oxen or small
diesel engines
union libre   common-law marriage
veranillo   little summer; refers to a short two to three week period
of dry weather in late June which follows the early wet season
rains begun in May

Notes

1: The Fate of the Family Farmer

1. Much of the work pertaining to the nature of domestic producers and their place in modern capitalist societies is rooted in Chayanov (e.g., 1966), Lenin (e.g., 1956), and Marx (e.g., 1967). See also Gudeman 1978; Gudeman and Rivera 1990; Smith and Wallerstein 1978; Smith, Wallerstein, and Evers 1984; McClelland 1961; Rogers 1969; Rostow 1960; Vakil and Brahmanand 1963.

2. This is where Lloyd's of London got its start.

3. The decline may have been due to health concerns, but "poor quality and inadequate grading standards and controls" have also been identified as factors (Mwandha, Nicholls, and Sargent 1985:14).

4. For historical discussions of the rise of coffee economies throughout Latin America see Bergard 1983 and Wolf 1956 on Puerto Rico; Berquist 1978, Machado 1977, and Palacios 1980 on Colombia; Cambranes 1985 on Guatemala; North 1981 on El Salvador; Gudmundson 1986, 1995a, Hall 1982, 1985, and Samper 1990, 1995 on Costa Rica; and Roseberry 1983 on Venezuela.

5. The rank of coffee in primary commodity trade varies with market conditions; but over the last fifty years, it has generally placed second, petroleum ranking first.

6. New varieties of coffee are constantly being developed. The most important arabica varieties introduced in recent years have been *bourbon, caturra,* and *catuai,* noted for their high yields on small, easy-to-harvest trees. These new varieties require more fertilizers and pesticides, though, resulting in greater costs for the farmer.

7. For a good discussion of export commodity markets, see Adams and Behrman 1982.

8. It is generally believed that the United States signed the agreement because it feared the political instability that might have resulted from the collapse of Latin American economies dependent on coffee production.

9. The rumor of rising coffee prices must have been considered fairly reliable, for some farmers in Pérez Zeledón actually were considering expanding production in anticipation of a price recovery.

10. The trend in flavored coffees may be a ploy to convert the "soft drink generation" into coffee drinkers (Roseberry 1996:769), but I suspect that large suppliers have also been promoting flavorful additives as a way to cover the taste of stale coffee.

11. My discussion of the household is based largely on the works of Netting (1993), Wilk (1989, 1991), and Wilk and Netting (1984). See also Collins 1986, Friedman 1980, Harris 1984, Sen 1990, and Schmink 1984.

12. See also Chayanov 1966, Goody 1958, and Shah 1988 for discussions on the family cycle.

13. See, for example, Ortiz 1973 on Colombian coffee farmers or Acheson 1985 on Maine lobster fishermen.

2: Coffee and the Farming Household

1. See also Bulmer-Thomas 1987, Cancian 1987, de Janvry 1981, de Janvry and Vandeman 1987, Gudeman 1978, Seligson 1980, and Sheahan 1987.

2. I suspect that the insecurity of living in a land plagued by frequent earthquakes and volcanic eruptions also discouraged many from settling in Costa Rica.

3. The extreme poverty of colonial Costa Rica was most evident during the seventeenth-century depression: coined money was so scarce that by 1709 cacao had become the official currency (Blutstein et al. 1970:16; Seligson 1980:9).

4. According to Seligson, the church attempted to concentrate settlers into towns, but it had neither the power nor the economic resources to do so (1980:6–7).

5. From the 1570s to the 1630s, indigenous populations throughout the New World were decimated by widespread epidemics introduced from the Old World. Estimates of the numbers killed range from hundreds of thousands to many millions.

6. Seligson disagrees. He argues that high agricultural wages were one cause for the concentration of land and the "massive proletarianization of the Costa Rican peasantry" (1980:21–23), reasoning that small landowners gave up farming entirely for rural wage work. Although there is little evidence to support Seligson's argument, it is true that a large number of Costa Rican coffee farms were (and still

are) too small (less than 3.45 ha) to support a family, forcing house-holds to supplement their incomes with wage work (Paige 1987:158).

7. See also Brockett 1990, Cardoso 1977, Hall 1985, and Weeks 1985.

8. Even today, most *Ticos*, as Costa Ricans refer to themselves, make a point of claiming Spanish, as opposed to indigenous, ancestors.

9. As an additional concession to all coffee interests, the new law stated that no tax would be paid if the export price of coffee fell below forty dollars per quintal.

10. For an excellent comparative analysis of cooperative perfor-mance, see Attwood and Baviskar 1988 and Baviskar and Attwood 1995.

11. Others (e.g., Acheson 1985; Coase 1952) describe this same advantage in terms of vertical integration, that is, the incorpora-tion of intermediary processes into a single firm.

12. The Communist Party was notably anticooperative. Accord-ing to the Communist Party, in light of the economic and social problems facing the country, the promotion of cooperatives was mere charlatanism (Cazanga 1987:49). Tension between the cooperative movement and the syndicate movement of the Communist Party is still apparent today.

3: *Los Cafeteros* of Pérez Zeledón

1. According to several sources (e.g., Altenburg, Hein, and Weller 1990:240; the Consejo Nacional de Producion 1982), Pérez Zeledón had the highest coffee production of any canton in 1981, producing 13.3 percent of the country's coffee. It is unclear whether this continues to hold true. According to ICAFE production figures for 1984–1985, the canton's percentage of national production was 6.4; by 1988–1989, it was approximately 8.2 (ICAFE 1989). Though production in Pérez Zeledón has increased more than 20 percent from 1981 to 1989, it appears that elsewhere production has in-creased even more.

2. Most coffee in Pérez Zeledón is of medium quality (medium-hard bean, MHB), though at higher altitudes around Mount Chirripo, some higher quality coffee (strictly hard bean, SHB) is grown.

3. These are pseudonyms.

4. Not included in the averages are those who were residents for less than one year, because they tended to be migrant laborers.

5. Until 1990, La Meseta had a recibidor in Palomas, but a dwindling clientele forced them to remove that station.

6. In Palomas, an evangelical Protestant sect built a small wooden church, but only two families in the village proper profess being evangelicals; the rest of the small congregation comes from surrounding communities. In Santa Cruz proper, only one family is Protestant, and there is no church building for services.

7. For a discussion of the political system and powers of representatives see Biesanz, Biesanz, and Biesanz 1982:177–95.

8. The larger number of landless households in Palomas is interesting, but the causes are as yet unclear. Sound answers require longitudinal data and must await further research.

9. Several households had to be reclassified as new information came to light; two had to be dropped altogether. Most of my analysis is based primarily on data from seventy-six households. Because of the disproportionate number of "employer" farmers in the sample, I weighted the sample data, but the effect of weighting was so slight that, for simplicity and ease of reading, I present only unweighted figures in my discussions.

10. Villagers consider size of landholdings a sensitive subject to discuss with outsiders; many feared tax increases, but I was able to double-check the reliability of their responses in separate interviews several months apart, often with different members of the household. Figures reported were remarkably similar. Later, when coffee yields were reported, I was able to check reported landholdings in coffee against reported yields and was satisfied with the reporting of landholding figures.

4: The Political Economy of Coffee-Farming Households

1. Hoodfar also notes how personal skills at negotiating can help (1997:211–14).

2. Most farmers broadcast their fertilizer rather than using the labor-intensive method of depositing it in small holes near the base of the plant, as advocated by the Ministry of Agriculture. Much fertilizer is washed away by rains. As the price of chemical fertilizers continues to rise, farmers may change their methods.

3. I know of only one woman from either community who drove. (She frequently drove coffee from the family's farm to the pickup station and also was taught by her father how to maintain the vehicle.) Many people expressed a desire to learn, but few own cars or trucks, so the opportunities for either men or women to learn to drive are limited.

4. Likewise, Wadley found in India that a woman's frugality, cleverness, and other housekeeping skills contribute to the prosperity of the household (1994:38–40).

5. The question also arises whether women avoid work in coffee fields because they are vulnerable to sexual assault. Certainly the danger is low if they work alongside their husbands or adult sons; even among single women, I heard no mention of this as a reason for not working in the fields.

6. In 1991, a new law was passed that allows students who leave school to pick coffee to take a tutorial during this last trimester ("School Schedule Studied," *Tico Times*, San José, 5 April 1991, 20). It is unclear how this is accomplished or how many families participate.

7. For good discussions of women and land claims in India, see Agarwal 1989 and 1994.

8. See Lamar (1994) on partible inheritance among Chilean merchant families.

9. Other forces, such as coercion and manipulation, might also be used to gain control of resources but were not readily evident in Palomas and Santa Cruz. This is not to say they were not used; discussion of these factors will require further study.

10. De facto ownership is not easily identifiable or measurable, particularly for the outside observer. Yet the process of transferring title from one owner to another is a lengthy and costly undertaking in Costa Rica, especially if lands are being subdivided and each parcel must be surveyed. In such cases, where the acquisition of legal title lags well behind on-the-ground processes, de jure title to land, as evidenced in land records, is also problematic. The only solution is long-term acquaintance with the situation and data from a variety of sources.

5: Against the Wind

1. *Beneficiando* Pérez Zeledón (actually the slogan of the La Meseta beneficio) plays on the double meaning of the verb *beneficiar*, which means both to process (e.g., to process coffee) and to benefit.

2. It is interesting that this fear of cooperatives as "communist" institutions was, and still is to some extent, widespread, despite the fact that cooperatives were being widely promoted by the United States in an effort to prevent communist uprisings, such as those that had occurred in Cuba.

3. This amount was voted to be raised to 6 percent at the 1991

General Assembly. The additional 1 percent will be used to provide working capital for the new Savings and Credit Department.

4. It was then that the Cooperativa Caficultura de Pérez Zeledón changed its name to the Cooperativa Agrícola Industrial El General, R.L. (Coopeagri).

5. One might question whether the great reluctance of the co-op's leaders to close the refinery was due to personal interests they may have had as cane producers themselves. The answer is not clear, though the information I was able to gather concerning the leaders' agricultural interests indicates that this was probably not the case.

6. Because I was attending the meeting in Palomas, I was unable to attend the one in Santa Cruz. I was told about the latter meeting in detail by a volunteer community development worker who had been living in Santa Cruz that year and had attended the meeting.

7. During my stay in Palomas, I was approached by several people who hoped I had contacts with USAID, CIDA (the Canadian International Development Agency), or any other aid program and could help them to get funding for road, school, and health center projects. Having no such connections, I was unable to help; I found, furthermore, that the local community leaders knew infinitely more ways of obtaining aid moneys than I did.

6: To Market, To Market

1. The newly arrived Peters company (which has no beneficio in the canton) has been paying more than Coopeagri. In the first two years it bought coffee in Pérez Zeledón, Peters paid more than five thousand colónes/fanega. Both farmers and managers of the other beneficios were well aware of the high prices, yet all agreed that new companies paid such extraordinarily high prices in order to attract new clients. Once the company was established, prices would fall into line with those of the other beneficios. Apparently, El Aguila offered similar prices when it first started operations in the canton.

2. In this discussion of marketing by "farmers" and "households," the reader is reminded that although some marketing decisions are made unilaterally by the person (or persons) most active in farming, others are reached through consultation with various "stakeholders" in the household.

3. Nor did political ideology correlate with membership in the cooperative. The proportion of farmers identifying themselves with

the National Liberation Party (PLN) versus the Christian Social Party (USC) was nearly identical in all factories: approximately 75 percent PLN and 25 percent USC. These proportions held true in the general populations of Palomas and Santa Cruz, also.

4. According to the manager of one private beneficio, one advantage Coopeagri has over the private factories, in terms of credit, is that it receives financing in colónes through Fedecoop. Though private beneficios can receive credit through Costa Rica's national banks, most private beneficios are foreign-owned and are financed from abroad with U.S. dollars. With the devaluation of the colón in the late 1980s and early 1990s, companies that invested dollars but were repaid by farmers in devalued colónes lost through this devaluation and so had to charge their clients more.

5. The greater proportion in Palomas is most likely because at that time all five factories serviced Palomas, whereas only three had recibidores in Santa Cruz.

6. Ortiz found that Paéz coffee farmers in Colombia also tried to "develop personal trading relations with a trader in the hope of receiving important fringe benefits, such as credit" (1973:6).

7: When Coffee Is Not Enough

1. Fedecoop estimated costs in 1990–1991 at 4,552 colónes per fanega ("Preocupa acaparamiento de tierras," *La Nación*, San José, 19 July 1990, 5A). My estimates are based on detailed data from only three households, but I believe they are reliable for this region. Farmers in Pérez Zeledón are on average smaller producers who usually do not make all of the recommended applications of fertilizers and pesticides and do not hire much harvest labor (all of which are included in Fedecoop's cost estimates).

2. Three farmers in Palomas were receiving small pensions from the Atlantic banana plantations, which closed in the 1980s.

3. This figure is based on payments of 4,500 colónes per fanega, the average price paid by beneficios in 1990–1991; expenses of 560 colónes per fanega; and a median household yield of twenty fanegas of coffee.

4. Two farmers who tried to grow fruit or vegetables for home consumption in the mountains said those lands are too far from the homesite for household members to provide the necessary labor on a daily basis. And with few inhabitants in the remote regions, there is little local labor available for hire.

5. I heard rumors in Palomas that several women worked as prostitutes in San Isidro. Though this is likely, I have no confirmation that it was true.

6. Three households have combined nonagricultural business ventures with farming. In Palomas, Beneficio Cifuentes rents several houses, though the others he provides rent-free to families in return for guaranteed harvest labor. In Santa Cruz, Maria Mondragon runs the village's only soda/cantina, and Jorge Contreras owns and operates, with his two sons, an agricultural supply and hardware store in San Isidro.

7. See, for example, Bentley 1992, Dandekar 1986, Lobo 1988, Lomnitz 1976, and Hirabayashi 1993 for discussion of migration networks elsewhere.

8: Family Farmers, Global Markets, and the State

1. For further discussion on this topic, see Attwood 1992, Baviskar and Attwood 1995, Esman and Uphoff 1984, Hyden 1988, and Mathers 1969.

2. A similar situation is found in the Atlantic lowlands, where foreign-owned banana plantations dominate.

3. The literature pertaining to state policies and rural women is quite large, see, for example, Boserup 1970, Bossen 1984, Deere and León 1987, and Morvaridi 1995.

4. Wade points out that the United States also "invited" Taiwan, Korea, and Japan to become economically strong because of their location on the West's defense perimeter (1990:346).

5. Mexico is a case in point; the effects of recent neoliberal reforms have been varied.

9: Fair Trade: A Way Forward?

1. Pineapple production has now surpassed coffee production to become the number two agricultural export (bananas are number one) (US Bureau of Public Affairs 2007).

2. Vietnam is now the world's second largest coffee producer, though the quality of its coffee is notably poor.

3. I was told by one *beneficio* employee in Puntarenas that the International Development Bank had given thousands of new seedlings to farmers in the country's northern provinces who had previously ripped out their coffee; these seedlings have been planted at higher elevations (at whose suggestion is unclear) in order to take advantage in 4–5 years of the current rapid growth of the quality-coffee niche markets.

4. Post 9/11 security measures in the United States have made entry and exit for temporary work much more difficult.

5. Other "ethically based" labeling organizations include Rainforest Alliance and Utz Kapeh.

6. One organic extension agent goes so far as to suggest stringent certification is another form of neo-colonialism (cited in Mutersbaugh 2002: 106).

7. Precise figures are not available. Estimate is based on Transfair (2007) and ICO (2006) data on FT and total production by country.

8. The 380 member CoopeSarapiqui in Herédia has been a member of the Coocafé FT consortium since 1969; in northern Puntarenas, Coope Montes de Oro (550 members) has been a member since 1983.

9. This issue was raised by Latin American FTOs in 2004. At that time, the FLO voted not to increase FT minimum prices and premiums, but to conduct a more extensive review in 2007 (TransFair 2004).

10. This problem plagues all coffee processors: private, cooperative; FT and non-FT.

11. This is an actual factory, as opposed to the simple sun-drying used by coffee producers in Colombia, for example.

12. Coopeagri's sugar recently received FT certification.

13. Not all commodity certification programs provide price premiums. For example, buyers are not required to pay extra for forest products that meet environmental standards and have been certified by the Forest Stewardship Council.

References Cited

Acheson, James
   1985   Social Organization of the Maine Lobster Market. In *Markets and Marketing,* Monographs in Economic Anthropology, no. 4, ed. Stuart Plattner, 105–30. Lanham, Md.: University Press of America.
Acuña Ortega, Victor H.
   1986   Patrones del conflicto social en la economia cafetalera costarricense (1900–1948). *Ciencias Sociales* 31: 113–22.
Adams, Gerard F., and Jere R. Behrman
   1982   *Commodity Exports and Economic Development.* Toronto: Lexington Books.
Agarwal, Bina
   1989   Women, Land and Ideology in India. In *Women, Poverty and Ideology in Asia: Contradictory Pressures, Uneasy Resolutions,* ed. Haleh Afshar and Bina Agarwal, 70–98. London: Macmillan.
   1992   Gender Relations and Food Security: Coping with Seasonality, Drought, and Famine in South Asia. In *Unequal Burden: Economic Crisis, Persistent Poverty and Women's Work,* ed. Lourdes Benerie and Shelley Feldman, 181–218. Boulder: Westview Press.
   1994a   Gender, Resistance, and Land: Interlinked Struggles Over Resources and Meanings in South Asia. *The Journal of Peasant Studies* 22 (1): 81–125.
   1994b   *A Field of One's Own: Gender and Land Rights in South Asia.* Cambridge: Cambridge University Press.
Alderson-Smith, Gavin
   1976   Peasant Response to Cooperativization under Agrarian Reform in the Communities of the Peruvian Sierra. In Nash, Dandler, and Hopkins, 113–55.
Alfaro, Luis Carlos
   1982   Interrelaciones entre la renta y el espacio en San Isidro de El General. In *Regiones periféricas y ciudades intermedias en*

Costa Rica, ed. Miguel Morales and Gerhard Sandner, 105–53. San José, Costa Rica: Escuela de Ciencias Geographicas de la Universidad Nacional and the Departmento de Geografia Economica Universidad de Hamburgo.

Almy, Susan
1988   Vertical Societies and Co-operative Structures: Problems of Fit in North-eastern Brazil. In Attwood and Baviskar, 46–68.

Altenburg, Tilman, Wolfgang Hein, and Jurgen Weller
1990   *El desafío económico de Costa Rica: Desarrollo agroindustrial autocentrado como alternativa.* San José, Costa Rica: Editorial Departamento Ecumenico de Investigaciones.

Alvarado Salas, Ronulfo
2003   Cantones Productores de Café: Formación y Desafios Actuales. Dirrección de gestion municipal sección de investigación y desarrollo. Serie Cantones de Costa Rica: No. 5. San Jose: IFAM.

Annis, Sheldon, and Peter Hakim, eds.
1988   *Direct to the Poor: Grassroots Development in Latin America.* Boulder: Lynne Rienner.

Appadurai, Arjun
1986   Introduction: Commodities and the Politics of Value. In *The Social Life of Things: Commodities in Cultural Perspective,* ed. Arjun Appadurai, 3–63. Cambridge: Cambridge University Press.

Apthorpe, Raymond
1971   Some Evaluation Problems for Cooperative Studies, with Special Reference to Primary Cooperatives in Highland Kenya. In *Two Blades of Grass,* ed. Peter Worsley, 67–82. Manchester: Manchester University Press.

Attwood, Donald W.
1985   Peasants versus Capitalists in the Indian Sugar Industry: The Impact of the Irrigation Frontier. *Journal of Asian Studies* 45 (1): 59–80.
1992   *Raising Cane: The Political Economy of Sugar in Western India.* Boulder: Westview Press.

Attwood, Donald W., and B. S. Baviskar, eds.
1988   *Who Shares? Co-operatives and Rural Development.* Delhi: Oxford University Press.

Bacon, Christopher
2005   Confronting the Coffee Crisis: Can Fair Trade, Organic, and Specialty Coffees Reduce Small-Scale Farmer Vulnerability in Northern Nicaragua? *World Development* 33 (3): 497–511.

Balassa, Bela
  1989 *Comparative Advantage, Trade Policy, and Economic Development*. New York: New York University Press.
Bandyopadhyay, Suraj, and Donald Von Eschen
  1988 Villager Failure to Co-operate: Some Evidence From West Bengal, India. In Attwood and Baviskar, 112–45.
Barlett, Peggy
  1976 Labor Efficiency and the Mechanism of Agricultural Evolution. *Journal of Anthropological Research* 32: 124–40.
  1982 *Agricultural Choice and Change*. New Brunswick, N.J.: Rutgers University Press.
  1993 *American Dreams, Rural Realities: Family Farms in Crisis*. Chapel Hill: University of North Carolina Press.
Barry, Dave
  1997 Please, Just a Plain Old Cup of Coffee. *Montréal Gazette*, 9 November, D6.
Barry, Tom
  1987 *Roots of Rebellion: Land and Hunger in Central America*. Boston: South End Press.
Baviskar, B. S.
  1971 Cooperatives and Caste in Maharashtra: A Case Study. In *Two Blades of Grass*, ed. Peter Worsley, 275–92. Manchester: Manchester University Press.
  1980 *The Politics of Development: Sugar Co-operatives in Rural Maharashtra*. Delhi: Oxford University Press.
  1988 Dairy Co-operatives and Rural Development in Gujarat. In Attwood and Baviskar, 345–61.
  1995 Leadership, Democracy and Development: Cooperatives in Kolhapur District. In Baviskar and Attwood, 157–75.
Baviskar, B. S., and Donald W. Attwood
  1995 *Finding the Middle Path: The Political Economy of Cooperation in Rural India*. Boulder: Westview Press.
Bennett, John W.
  1983 Agricultural Cooperatives in the Development Process: Perspectives from Social Science. *Studies in Comparative International Development* 18 (1–2): 3–68.
Bentley, Jeffery
  1992 *Today There Is No Misery*. Tucson: University of Arizona Press.
Bergad, Laird W.
  1983 *Coffee and the Growth of Agrarian Capitalism in Nineteenth-Century Puerto Rico*. Princeton, N.J.: Princeton University Press.

Berger, Peter, and Richard John Neuhaus
  1984   To Empower People. In Korten and Klauss, 250–61.
Berquist, Charles W.
  1978   *Coffee and Conflict in Colombia, 1886–1910*. Durham, N.C.: Duke University Press.
Berry, Sara S.
  1975   *Cocoa, Custom, and Socio-Economic Change in Rural Western Nigeria*. Oxford: Clarendon Press.
Bhowmik, Sharit
  1988   Producers' Co-operatives in the Indian Tea Industry. In Attwood and Baviskar, 172–87.
Biesanz, Richard, Karen Z. Biesanz, and Mavis H. Biesanz
  1982   *The Costa Ricans*. Prospect Heights, Ill.: Waveland Press.
Bisaillon, Véronique, C. Gendron, & M. Turcott
  2005   Commerce Équitable Comme Vecteur de Développement Durable? *Nouvelles Pratiques Sociales* 18 (1): 73–89.
Blowfield, Mick
  1999   Ethical Trade: A Review of Developments and Issues. *Third World Quarterly* 20 (4): 753–70.
Blutstein, Howard I., Lynne Anderson, Elinor Betters, John Dombrowski, and Charles Townsend
  1970   *Area Handbook for Costa Rica*. Washington, D.C.: U.S. Government Printing Office.
Booth, John A., and Thomas W. Walker
  1989   *Understanding Central America*. Boulder: Westview Press.
Boserup, Ester
  1970   *Woman's Role in Economic Development*. New York: St. Martin's Press.
  1990   Economic Change and the Roles of Women. In *Persistent Inequalities: Women and World Development,* ed. Irene Tinker, 14–24. New York: Oxford University Press.
Bossen, Laurel
  1984   *The Redivision of Labor: Women and Economic Choice in Four Guatemalan Communities*. Albany: State University of New York.
  1991a Changing Land Tenure Systems in China: Common Problem, Uncommon Solution. *Sociological Bulletin* 40 (1–2): 47–67.
  1991b Gender and Systems of Inheritance. Revised version of a paper presented at the American Anthropological Association meetings, Chicago, 25 November.
  1995   All Words and No Deeds: Rural Women's Property Rights in Reform China. Paper presented at the Northeastern Anthropology Association meeting, Lake Placid, N.Y., 3 April.

Bray, David B., Jose L.P. Sanchez, and Ellen C. Murphy
2002 Social Dimensions of Organic Coffee Production in Mexico: Lessons for Eco-Labelling Initiatives. *Society and Natural Resources* 15: 429–46.
Brockett, Charles D.
1990 *Land, Power, and Poverty: Agrarian Transformation and Political Conflict in Central America.* Boston: Unwin Hyman.
Brown, Lawrence A., and Victoria A. Lawson
1985 Rural-Destined Migration in Third World Settings: A Neglected Phenomenon? *Regional Studies* 19 (5): 415–32.
Brown, Michael Barratt
1993 *Fair Trade: Reform and Realities in the International Trading System.* London: Zed Books.
Browning, David
1983 Agrarian Reform in El Salvador. *Journal of Latin American Studies* 15: 399–426.
Buechler, Hans C., and Judith-Maria Buechler
1992 *Manufacturing against the Odds: Small-Scale Producers in an Andean City.* Boulder: Westview Press.
Bulmer-Thomas, Victor
1987 *The Political Economy of Central America since 1920.* Cambridge: Cambridge University Press.
Cale, Muriel, and Timothy Wise
2005 Revaluing Peasant Coffee Production: Organic and Fair Trade Markets in Mexico. Report from the Global Development and Environment Institute. Medford, MA: Tufts University.
Cambranes, J. C.
1985 *Coffee and Peasants in Guatemala.* San Carlos: University of San Carlos, Guatemala.
Cancian, Frank
1980 Risk and Uncertainty in Agricultural Decision Making. In *Agricultural Decision Making,* ed. Peggy Barlett, 161–76. New York: Academic Press.
1987 Proletarianization in Zinacantan, 1960–1983. In *Household Economies and Their Transformations,* ed. Morgan D. Maclachlan, 131–42. Lanham, Md.: University Press of America.
Cardoso, Ciro F. S.
1977 The Formation of the Coffee Estate in Nineteenth-Century Costa Rica. In *Land and Labour in Latin America,* ed. Malcolm Deas, Clifford T. Smith, and John Street, 165–202. Cambridge: Cambridge University Press.

Carroll, Thomas F.
1971   Peasant Cooperation in Latin America. In *Two Blades of Grass*, ed. Peter Worsley, 199–249. Manchester: Manchester University Press.

Castillo, Carlos Manuel
1988   The Costa Rican Experience with the International Debt Crisis. In *Development and External Debt in Latin America*, ed. Richard Feinberg and Ricardo Ffrench-Davis, 210–31. Notre Dame, Ind.: University of Notre Dame Press.

Cazanga S., Jose D.
1987   *Las cooperativas de caficultores en Costa Rica*. San José: University of Costa Rica.

Cernea, Michael M.
1988   Entrance Points for Sociological Knowledge in Planned Rural Development. *Research in Rural Sociology and Development* 3: 1–25.

Chambers, Robert
1983   *Rural Development: Putting the Last First*. New York: Longman Scientific and Technical; New York: John Wiley.

Chayanov, A. V.
1966   *The Theory of Peasant Economy*. Translated. ed. Daniel Thorner, R. E. F. Smith, and Basile Kerblay. Homewood, Ill.: Irwin.

Chibnik, Michael
1996   Labor Organization in Oaxacan Wood Carving Workshops. Paper presented at the ninety-fifth annual meeting of the American Anthropological Association, San Francisco, 20–24 November.

Coase, R. H.
1952   The Nature of the Firm. In *Readings in Price Theory*, ed. George Stigler and Kenneth Boulding, 331–51. Chicago: Richard D. Irwin.

Collins, Jane
1986   The Household and Relations of Production in Southern Peru. *Comparative Studies in Society and History* 28: 651–71.

1988   *Unseasonal Migrations: The Effects of Rural Labor Scarcity in Peru*. Princeton, N.J.: Princeton University Press.

Consejo Nacional de Producion
1982   Boletin sobre districtos productos. San José, Costa Rica.

Coocafé
2006   Coocafé. <http://www.coocafe.com/home.htm>. Accessed 7 June 2007.

Cook, Scott
  1986 The "Managerial" vs. the "Labor" Function, Capital Accumulation and the Dynamics of Simple Commodity Production in Rural Oaxaca, Mexico. In *Entrepreneurship and Social Change*, ed. Sidney M. Greenfield and Arnold Strickon, 54–95. Lanham, Md.: University Press of America.
Cook, Scott, and Leigh Binford
  1990 *Obliging Need: Rural Petty Industry in Mexican Capitalism.* Austin: University of Texas Press.
Coopeagri
  1989 Resumen y conclusiones del informe del Consejo de Administracion y Gerencia a la Asamblea General. No. 47, 26 March, San Isidro de El General, Costa Rica.
  1990 Informe gerencia a la Asamblea General de Delegados. No. 50, 31 March, San Isidro de El General, Costa Rica.
  1991 Informe del Consejo de Administración a la Asamblea General de Delegados. No. 51, 23 March, San Isidro de El General, Costa Rica.
Dandekar, Hemalata C.
  1986 *Men to Bombay, Women at Home.* Ann Arbor: Center for South and Southeast Asian Studies, University of Michigan.
de Andrade, Moretzsohn
  1966 Decadência do campesinato costariquenho. *Revista Geographica* (Brazil) 66 (June): 135–51.
Deere, Carmen Diana
  1982 A Comparative Analysis of Agrarian Reform in El Salvador and Nicaragua 1979–81. *Development and Change* (winter): 1–41.
  1987 The Latin American Agrarian Reform Experience. In Deere and León, 165–90.
Deere, Carmen Diana, and Magdalena León, eds.
  1987 *Rural Women and State Policy: Feminist Perspectives on Latin American Agricultural Development.* Boulder: Westview Press.
de Janvry, Alain
  1981 *The Agrarian Question and Reformism in Latin America.* Baltimore: Johns Hopkins University Press.
  1987 Peasants, Capitalism and the State in Latin American Culture. In *Peasants and Peasant Societies,* 2nd ed., ed. Teodor Shanin, 391–404. Basil Blackwell.
de Janvry, Alain, and Ann Vandeman
  1987 Patterns of Proletarianization in Agriculture: An International Comparison. In *Household Economies and Their Transformations,* ed. Morgan D. Maclachlan, 28–73. Lanham, Md.: University Press of America.

Donato, Elisa M., and Manuel Rojas Bolaños
  1989   Problems and Prospects of the Costa Rican Trade Unions.
          In *The Costa Rica Reader*, ed. Marc Edelman and Joanne
          Kenen, 152–57. New York: Grove Weidenfeld.
Dore, Ronald F.
  1971   Modern Cooperatives in Traditional Communities. In *Two
          Blades of Grass*, ed. Peter Worsley, 43–60. Manchester:
          Manchester University Press.
Eckstein, Shlomo
  1970   Collective Farming in Mexico: The Case of the Laguna. In
          Agrarian Problems and Peasant Movements in Latin America,
          ed. Rodolfo Stavenhagen, 271–99. Garden City, N.Y.: Double-
          day.
Eckstein, Shlomo, and Thomas F. Carroll
  1976   Peasant Cooperation in Land-Reform Programs: Some
          Latin American Experiences. In Nash, Dandler, and Hop-
          kins, 233–64.
Edelman, Marc
  1983   Recent Literature on Costa Rica's Economic Crisis. *Latin
          American Research Review* 18 (2): 166–89.
  1989   Rethinking the Hamburger Debate. Paper presented at the
          American Anthropological Association meeting, Washing-
          ton, D.C., 15–19 November.
  1990   When They Took the "Muni": Political Culture and Anti-
          Austerity Protest in Rural Northwestern Costa Rica. *Amer-
          ican Ethnologist* 17 (4): 736–57.
  1992   *The Logic of the Latifundio: The Large Estates of Northwest-
          ern Costa Rica since the Late Nineteenth Century*. Stanford,
          Calif.: Stanford University Press.
EIU (Economist Intelligence Unit)
  1995   *Costa Rica: Country Profile*. London: EIU.
Esman, Milton J., and Norman T. Uphoff
  1984   *Local Organizations: Intermediaries in Rural Development*.
          Ithaca, N.Y.: Cornell University Press.
Estrella del Sur (San Isidro, Pérez Zeledón, Costa Rica), 15 January–
          15 April 1991.
Evans, Peter
  1979   *Dependent Development: The Alliance of Multinational,
          State, and Local Capital in Brazil*. Princeton, N.J.: Prince-
          ton University Press.
Evans, Peter, Dietrich Rueschemeyer, and Evelyne Huber Stephens, eds.
  1985   Introduction to *States versus Markets in the World-System*.
          Beverly Hills, Calif.: Sage.

Eversole, Robyn
n.d.   Why Small?: A Bibliographic Essay on Micro-Entrepreneurs
        and Household-Based Production. Department of Anthro-
        pology, McGill University, Montreal. Typescript.
Facio, Rodrigo
1943   Ventajas sociales y economicas de las cooperativas. *Revista
        Surco* 31: 19–26.
Fair Trade Federation (FTF)
2002   Spilling the Beans on the Coffee Trade. London.
        <http://www.fairtrade.org.uk>.
2003   Report on Fair Trade Trends in US, Canada & the Pacific
        Rim. <http://www.fairtradefederation.org>.
Fairtrade Labelling Organizations (FLO)
2006   Building Trust. Annual Report 2005/06. Bonn.
        <http://www.fairtrade.net>.
2007a   FLO announces increase in Fairtrade Premium and Organic
        Differential for Coffee. <http://www.fairtrade.net/
        news.html>. Accessed 25 April.
2007b   Explanatory Document: Introducing Fairtrade and Its Or-
        ganizations. <http://www.fairtrade.net/info_sheets0.html>.
        Accessed 30 August.
2007c   Generic Fairtrade Standards for Small Farmers' Organiza-
        tions. <http://www.fairtrade.net/generic_standards.html>.
Fals-Borda, Orlando, Raymond Apthorpe, and Inayatullah
1976   The Crisis of Rural Cooperatives: Problems in Africa, Asia,
        and Latin America. In Nash, Dandler, and Hopkins,
        439–56.
Flanders, Nicholas E.
1989   The Alaska Native Corporation as Conglomerate: The
        Problem of Profitability. *Human Organization* 48 (4):
        299–312.
Flores, Edmundo
1970   The Economics of Land Reform. In *Agrarian Problems
        and Peasant Movements in Latin America,* ed. Rodolfo
        Stavenhagen, 139–58. Garden City, N.Y.: Doubleday.
Folbre, Nancy
1984   Household Production in the Philippines: A Non-
        Neoclassical Approach. *Economic Development and Cul-
        tural Change* 32: 303–30.
1988   The Black Four of Hearts: Toward a New Paradigm of
        Household Economics. In *A Home Divided: Women and
        Income in the Third World,* ed. Daisy Dwyer and Judith
        Bruce. Stanford, Calif.: Stanford University Press.

Freed, Stanley A., and Ruth S. Freed
  1983   The Domestic Cycle in India: Natural History of a Will-o'-
         the-Wisp. *American Ethnologist* 10: 312–27.
Friedmann, Harriet
  1980   Household Production and the National Economy: Con-
         cepts for the Analysis of Agrarian Formations. *Journal of
         Peasant Studies* 7 (2): 158–83.
Furtado, Celso
  1965   *The Economic Growth of Brazil.* Berkeley: University of Cali-
         fornia Press.
Gagnon, Gabriel
  1976   Cooperatives, Participation, and Development: Three Fail-
         ures. In Nash, Dandler, and Hopkins, 365–80.
Gladwin, Christina H., and Robert Zabawa
  1987   Transformations of Full-Time Family Farms in the U.S.:
         Can They Survive? In *Household Economies and Their
         Transformations,* ed. Morgan D. Maclachlan, 212–27. Lan-
         ham, Md.: University Press of America.
Godoy, Ricardo, and Christopher Bennett
  1989   Diversification among Coffee Smallholders in the High-
         lands of South Sumatra, Indonesia. *Human Ecology* 16 (4):
         397–420.
Goldschmidt, Walter
  1978   *As You Sow: Three Studies in the Social Consequences of Agribusi-
         ness.* 1947. Reprint, Montclair, N.J.: Allanheld, Osmun.
Gómez Tovar, L., M. Gómez Cruz, and R. Schwentesius Rinderman
  1999   *Desafíos de la agricultura orgánica en México: commercial-
         ización y certificación.* Chapingo, México.
González-Vega, Claudio, and Victor Hugo Céspedes
  1993   Part I: Costa Rica. In Rottenberg, 3–183.
Goodman, Jordan
  1995   Excitantia: Or, How Enlightenment Europe Took to Soft
         Drugs. In *Consuming Habits: Drugs in History and Anthro-
         pology,* ed. Jordan Goodman, Paul E. Lovejoy, and Andrew
         Sherratt. London: Routledge.
Goody, Jack
  1958   *The Development Cycle in Domestic Groups.* Cambridge:
         Cambridge University Press.
  1976   *Production and Reproduction: A Comparative Study of the
         Domestic Domain.* Cambridge: Cambridge University Press.
Gordon, Alec
  1990   The Future of Commodity Agreements. *Multinational
         Business* 1: 28–31.

Granovetter, Mark
  1985 Economic Action and Social Structure: The Problem of
        Embeddedness. *American Journal of Sociology* 91: 481–510.
Gudeman, Stephen
  1978 *The Demise of a Rural Economy*. London: Routledge and
        Kegan Paul.
Gudeman, Stephen, and Alberto Rivera
  1990 *Conversations in Colombia*. Cambridge: Cambridge Univer-
        sity Press.
Gudmundson, Lowell
  1983 Costa Rica before Coffee: Occupational Distribution,
        Wealth Inequality, and Elite Society in the Village Economy
        of the 1840s. *Journal of Latin American Studies* 15:
        427–52.
  1986 *Costa Rica before Coffee: Society and Economy on the Eve of
        the Export Boom*. Baton Rouge: Louisiana State University
        Press.
  1995a Peasant, Farmer, Proletarian: Class Formation in a Small-
        holder Coffee Economy, 1850–1950. In Roseberry, Gud-
        mundson, and Kutschbach, 112–50.
  1995b Society and Politics in Central America, 1821–1871. In
        Gudmundson and Lindo-Fuentes, 79–132.
Gudmundson, Lowell, and Héctor Lindo-Fuentes
  1995 *Central America, 1821–1871: Liberalism before Liberal Re-
        form*. Tuscaloosa: University of Alabama Press.
Guillet, David
  1981 Surplus Extraction, Risk Management, and Economic
        Change among Peruvian Peasants. *Journal of Development
        Studies* 18 (1): 3–24.
Hall, Carolyn
  1982 *El café y el desarrollo histórico-geográfico de Costa Rica*. San
        José: Editorial Costa Rica.
  1985 *Costa Rica: A Geographical Interpretation in Historical Per-
        spective*. Dellplain Latin American Studies, no. 17. Boulder:
        Westview Press.
Hammel, E. A.
  1984 On the *** of Studying Household Form and Function. In
        *Households: Comparative and Historical Studies of the Do-
        mestic Group*, ed. Robert McC. Netting, Richard R. Wilk,
        and Eric J. Arnould, 29–43. Berkeley: University of Califor-
        nia Press.
Harris, Marvin
  1964 *Patterns of Race in the Americas*. New York: Walker.

Harris, Michael S.
  1989   Land, Inheritance, and Economic Mobility: An Example
         from Bangladesh. *Urban Anthropology* 18 (3–4): 329–46.
Harris, Olivia
  1984   Households as Natural Units. In *Of Marriage and the Mar-
         ket,* ed. Kate Young, Carol Wolkowitz, and Roslyn McCul-
         lagh, 136–55. London: Routledge and Kegan Paul.
Helm, Franz C.
  1968   *The Economics of Co-operative Enterprise.* London: Univer-
         sity of London Press.
Herbst, Jeffrey
  1993   *The Politics of Reform in Ghana, 1982–1991.* Berkeley: Uni-
         versity of California Press.
Hershberg, Eric, Jorge Monge, and Juan Pablo Pérez, eds.
  2003   *From Coffee to Semi-Conductors: Costa Rica's Strategy for
         Industrial Upgrading and Equity.* FLAACSO: Costa Rica.
Hill, Polly
  1970   *Studies in Rural Capitalism in West Africa.* Cambridge:
         Cambridge University Press.
Hirabayashi, Lane Ryo
  1993   *Cultural Capital: Mountain Zapotec Migrant Associations
         in Mexico City.* Tucson: University of Arizona Press.
Holloway, Thomas
  1977   The Coffee Colono of Sao Paulo, Brazil: Migration and
         Mobility, 1880–1930. In *Land and Labour in Latin Amer-
         ica,* ed. Malcolm Deas, Clifford T. Smith, and John Street,
         301–22. Cambridge: Cambridge University Press.
Hoodfar, Homa
  1997   *Between Marriage and the Market: Intimate Politics and
         Survival in Cairo.* Berkeley: University of California Press.
Hopkins, Nicholas S.
  1988   Co-operatives and the Non-Cooperative Sector in Tunisia
         and Egypt. In Attwood and Baviskar, 211–30.
Hudson, Mark, and Ian Hudson
  2004   Justice, Sustainability, and the Fair Trade Movement: A
         Case Study of Coffee Production in Chiapas. *Social Justice*
         31 (3): 130–46.
Hyden, Goran
  1970   Co-operatives and their Socio-Political Environment. In
         Cooperatives and Rural Development in East Africa, ed.
         Carl Gosta Widstrand, 61–88. New York: Africana.
  1988   Approaches to Co-operative Development: Blueprint versus
         Greenhouse. In Attwood and Baviskar, 149–71.

IATP (Institute for Agriculture and Trade Policy)
  1995a Coffee Producers Restrict Exports. *NAFTA and Inter-American Trade Monitor* 2, no. 23.
  1995b Coffee Up, Coffee Down. *NAFTA and Inter-American Trade Monitor* 2, no. 30.
  1996a Coffee Prices Fall, Producers Meet. *NAFTA and Inter-American Trade Monitor* 3, no. 3.
  1996b Coffee Prices, Production Uncertain. *NAFTA and Inter-American Trade Monitor* 3, no. 8.
ICAFE (Instituto del Café)
  1989 Total de café declarado por los beneficiadores. Annual Reports of the Departamento de Liquidaciones. Mimeograph. San José, Costa Rica.
  1979–1989 Liquidaciones Final. Annual Reports of the Departmento de Liquidaciones. Mimeograph. San José, Costa Rica.
  2007 Costa Rican Coffee, The Coffee of Peace. <http://www.icafe.go.cr/homepage.nsf>.
ICO (International Coffee Organization)
  2006 Letter from the Director: Coffee Market Report. London: ICO.
International Labour Organisation
  1962 Current Information: Land and Settlement Act in Costa Rica. *International Labour Review* 85: 390–94.
Irvin, George
  1988 ECLAC and the Political Economy of the Central American Common Market. *Latin American Research Review* 23 (3): 7–29.
Jaquette, Jane S.
  1990 Gender and Justice in Economic Development. In *Persistent Inequalities: Women and World Development,* ed. Irene Tinker, 54–69. New York: Oxford University Press.
Johnson, Allen W.
  1971 Security and Risk-Taking among Poor Peasants: A Brazilian Case. In *Studies in Economic Anthropology,* ed. Paul J. Bohannan, 144–51. Washington, D.C.: American Anthropological Association.
Jones, Jeffrey R., and Norman Price
  1985 Agroforestry: An Application of the Farming Systems Approach to Forestry. *Human Organization* 44 (4): 322–31.
Joy, Leonard
  1971 The Analysis of Existing Social Factors Favourable to Successful Modern Cooperatives. In *Two Blades of Grass,* ed. Peter Worsley, 61–88. Manchester: Manchester University Press.

Karneef, Natalie
2005   Ethical Chic. *The Gazette*. Montreal. 26 May, page D1.

Kincaid, A. Douglas
1989   Costa Rican Peasants and the Politics of Quiescence. In *The Costa Rica Reader*, ed. Marc Edelman and Joanne Kenen, 178–86. New York: Grove Weidenfeld.

Korten, David, and Rudi Klauss, eds.
1984   *People-Centered Development*. West Hartford, Conn.: Kumarian Press.

Kummer, Corby
1990   Before the First Sip: How to Start a Good Cup of Coffee. *Atlantic*, May, 117–23.

Lamar, Marti
1994   "Choosing" Partible Inheritance: Chilean Merchant Families, 1795–1825. *Journal of Social History* 28 (1): 125–45.

La Nación (San José, Costa Rica) 5 April 1989, 23 May–14 December 1990, 23 January 1991.

Le Devoir (Montreal), 2 October 1997.

Lenin, Vladimir I.
1956   *The Development of Capitalism in Russia: The Process of the Formation of a Home Market for Large-Scale Industry*. Moscow: Foreign Languages.

Leon, Jorge
1948   Land Utilization in Costa Rica. *Geographical Review* 38 (3): 444–56.

Leonard, H. Jeffrey
1987   *Natural Resources and Economic Development in Central America*. International Institute for Environment and Development. New Brunswick, N.J.: Transaction Books.

Levi, Margaret, and A. Linton
2003   Fair Trade: A Cup at a Time? *Politics & Society* 31 (3): 407–32.

Levin, Michael D.
1988   Accountability and Legitimacy in Traditional Co-operation in Nigeria. In Attwood and Baviskar, 330–42.

Lewin, Bryan, Danielle Giovannucci, and Paul Varangis
2004   Coffee Markets: New Paradigms in Global Supply and Demand. Agriculture and Rural Development Discussion Paper 3. Washington, D.C.: World Bank.

Lindo-Fuentes, Héctor
1995   The Economy of Central America: From Bourbon Reforms to Liberal Reforms. In Gudmundson and Lindo-Fuentes, 13–78.

Littrell, Mary A., and Marsha A. Dickson
  1997 Alternative Trading Organizations: Shifting Paradigm in a Culture of Social Responsibility. *Human Organization* 56 (3): 344–52.
Lobo, Susan
  1988 *A House of My Own: Social Organization in the Squatter Settlements of Lima, Peru.* Tucson: University of Arizona Press.
Locher, Uli
  n.d. Migraciones y cambios medioambientales en Costa Rica desde 1927. Unpublished paper. Department of Sociology, McGill University.
Lockwood, Victoria S.
  1989 Tubuai Women Potato Planters and the Political Economy of Intra-Household Gender Relations. In Wilk, 197–220.
Lomnitz, Larrisa
  1976 Migration and Network in Latin America. In *Current Perspectives in Latin American Urban Research,* ed. Alejandro Portes and Harley Brownings, 133–50. Austin: Institute of Latin American Studies, University of Texas.
Loomis, Charles P., Julio O. Morales, Roy A. Clifford, Olen E. Leonard, eds.
  1953 *Turrialba: Social Systems and the Introduction of Change.* Glencoe, Ill.: Free Press.
Luxner, Larry
  2000 Microchips With Macro Power. *Americas* 52 (6): 3–5.
Machado, Absalon C.
  1977 *El café: De la aparceria al capitalismo.* Bogota, Colombia: Punta de Lanza.
MacLeod, Murdo J.
  1973 *Spanish Central America: A Socioeconomic History, 1520–1720.* Berkeley: University of California Press.
Madden A, Lidiethe
  1985 El agro costarricense y la situacion de la mujer campesina: Recomendaciones de politica, programas y proyectos de accion institucional. Paper presented at the symposium Las politicas de desarrollo agrario en America Latina y su impacto sobre la mujer rural, forty-fifth Congreso Internacional de Americanistas, Bogota, Colombia, 1–7 July.
Marcus, George E.
  1995 Ethnography in/of the World System: The Emergence of Multi-Sited Ethnography. *Annual Review of Anthropology* 24: 95–117.

Marx, Karl
   1967   *Capital: A Critique of Political Economy.* 3 vols. New York:
           International.
Mather, Loys L.
   1969   The Principles, Functions, and Benefits of Cooperation: The
           Traditional Model. In *Agricultural Cooperatives and Markets in
           Developing Countries,* ed. Kurt R. Anschel, Russell H. Brannon,
           and Eldon D. Smith, 13–27. New York: Frederick A. Praeger.
McClelland, David
   1961   *The Achieving Society.* New York: Free Press.
McClintock, Cynthia
   1981   *Peasant Cooperatives and Political Change in Peru.* Prince-
           ton, N.J.: Princeton University Press.
McGreevy, William
   1972   *An Economic History of Colombia, 1845–1930.* Cambridge:
           Cambridge University Press.
Meacham, Bradley
   2002   How Fair Is Fair Trade Coffee? *Seattle Times.* 11 September.
Meisch, Lynn A.
   1996   Two Amoebas Dancing the Lambada: Artesanias Produc-
           tion, Wealth and Fluid Identities in Otavalo, Ecuador. Pa-
           per presented at the ninety-fifth annual meeting of the
           American Anthropological Association, San Francisco,
           20–24 November.
Melmed-Sanjak, Jolyne, Carlos E. Santiago, and Alvin Magid, eds.
   1993   *Recovery or Relapse in the Global Economy: Comparative Perspec-
           tives on Restructuring in Central America.* Westport, Conn.:
           Praeger.
Miller, Barbara
   1982   Female Labor Participation and Female Seclusion in Rural
           India: A Regional View. *Economic Development and Cul-
           tural Change* 30: 777–94.
Ministerio de agricultura y ganaderia
   1989   Executive Decree no. 19302. San José, Costa Rica.
Mintz, Sidney W.
   1985   *Sweetness and Power: The Place of Sugar in Modern History.*
           New York: Viking Penguin.
Moberg, Mark
   2005   Fair Trade and Eastern Caribbean Banana Farmers:
           Rhetoric and Reality in the Anti-Globalization Movement.
           Human Organization 64 (1): 4–15.
Montréal Gazette.
   1997   Ethical Coffee. 13 November.

Mora Zuñiga, Bienvenido
1987   Puntos historicos [de] Coopeagri El General, R.L. (journal written by B. Mora Zuñiga for Coopeagri). Notebook in Coopeagri archives. San Isidro Pérez Zeledón, Costa Rica.
Morvaridi, Behrooz
1995   Macroeconomic Policies and Gender Relations: The Study of Farming Households in Two Turkish Villages. In *EnGENDERing Wealth and Well-Being,* ed. Rae Lesser Blumberg, Cathy A. Rakowski, Irene Tinker, and Michael Monteón, 135–52. Boulder: Westview Press.
Muradian, Roldan, and Wim Pelupessy
2005   Governing the Coffee Chain: The Role of Voluntary Regulatory Systems. *World Development* 33 (12): 2029–44.
Murray, Douglas L., and L. T. Raynolds
2000   Alternative Trade in Bananas: Obstacles and Opportunities for Progressive Social Change in the Global Economy. *Agriculture and Human Values* 17: 65–74.
Murray, Douglas, L. T. Raynolds, and P. L. Taylor
2003   *One Cup at a Time: Poverty Alleviation and Fair Trade Coffee in Latin America.* New York: The Ford Foundation.
2006   The Future of Fair Trade Coffee: Dilemmas Facing Latin America's Small-Scale Producers. *Development in Practice* 16 (2): 179–92.
Mutersbaugh, Tad
2002   Ethical Trade and Certified Organic Coffee: Implications of Rules-Based Agricultural Product Certification for Mexican Producer Households and Villages. *Transnational Law and Contemporary Problems* 12: 88–107.
Mwandha, James, John Nicholls, and Malcolm Sargent
1985   *Coffee: The International Commodity Agreements.* Brookfield, Vt.: Gower.
Nash, June
1979   *We Eat the Mines and the Mines Eat Us.* New York: Columbia University Press.
Nash, June, Jorge Dandler, and Nicholas S. Hopkins, eds.
1976   *Popular Participation in Social Change.* The Hague: Mouton.
Nash, June, and Nicholas S. Hopkins
1976   Anthropological Approaches to the Study of Cooperatives, Collectives, and Self-Management. In Nash, Dandler, and Hopkins, 3–32.
Netting, Robert McC.
1981   *Balancing on an Alp: Ecological Change and Continuity in a Swiss Mountain Community.* Cambridge: Cambridge University Press.

1993   *Smallholders, Householders: Farm Families and the Ecology of Intensive, Sustainable Agriculture*. Stanford, Calif.: Stanford University Press.

Nigh, Ronald
1997   Organic Agriculture and Globalization: A Maya Associative Corporation in Chiapas, Mexico. *Human Organization* 56 (40): 427–36.

Norris, Thomas L.
1953   A *Colono* System and Its Relation to Seasonal Labor Problems on a Costa Rican Hacienda. *Rural Sociology* 18: 376–78.

North, Liisa
1981   *Bitter Grounds: Roots of Revolt in El Salvador*. Toronto: Between the Lines.

Olwig, Karen Fog
1985   *Cultural Adaptation and Resistance on St. John: Three Centuries of Afro-Caribbean Life*. Gainesville: University of Florida Press.

Ortiz, Sutti
1973   *Uncertainties in Peasant Farming: A Colombian Case*. New York: Humanities Press.

1990   Uncertainty Reducing Strategies and Unsteady States: Labor Contracts in Coffee Agriculture. In *Risk and Uncertainty in Tribal and Peasant Economies*, ed. Elizabeth Cashdan, 303–17. Boulder: Westview Press.

Ortner, Sherry B.
1984   Theory in Anthropology since the Sixties. *Comparative Studies in Society and History* 26: 126–66.

Paige, Jeffery
1975   *Agrarian Revolution*. New York: Free Press.

1987   Coffee and Politics in Central America. In *Crises in the Caribbean Basin*, ed. Richard Tardanico, 141–89. Beverly Hills, Calif.: Sage.

Palacios, Marco
1980   *Coffee in Colombia, 1850–1970: An Economic, Social, and Political History*. Cambridge: Cambridge University Press.

Palma, Diego
1989   The State and Social Co-optation in Costa Rica. In *The Costa Rica Reader*, ed. Marc Edelman and Joanne Kenen, 128–31. New York: Grove Weidenfeld.

Parrish, Bradley, V. Luzadis, and W. Bentley
2005   What Tanzania's Coffee Farmers Can Teach the World: A Performance-Based Look at the Fair Trade–Free Trade Debate. *Sustainable Development* 13: 177–89.

Paul, Elisabeth
2005   Evaluating Fair Trade as a Development Project: Methodologi-
        cal Considerations. *Development in Practice* 15 (2): 134–50.
Pérez Brignoli, Héctor
1989   Reckoning with the Central American Past: Economic
        Growth and Political Regimes. In *The Costa Rica Reader*,
        ed. Marc Edelman and Joanne Kenen, 35–40. New York:
        Grove Weidenfeld.
Peterson, Stephen B.
1982   Government, Cooperatives, and the Private Sector in Peas-
        ant Agriculture. In *Institutions of Rural Development for the
        Poor*, ed. David K. Leonard and Dale Rogers Marshall,
        73–124. Research Series no. 49. Berkeley: Institute of In-
        ternational Studies, University of California.
Platteau, Jean-Philippe
1989   The Dynamics of Fisheries Development in Developing
        Countries: A General Overview. *Development and Change*
        20: 565–97.
Plattner, Stuart
1985   Equilibrating Market Relationships. In *Markets and Mar-
        keting*, ed. Stuart Plattner, 133–52. Monographs in Eco-
        nomic Anthropology, no. 4. Lanham, Md.: University Press
        of America.
1989   Economic Behavior in Markets. In *Economic Anthropology*,
        ed. Stuart Plattner, 209–21. Stanford, Calif.: Stanford Uni-
        versity Press.
Raynolds, Laura, D. Murray, and P. L. Taylor
2004   Fair Trade Coffee: Building Producer Capacity via Global
        Networks. *Journal of International Development* 16:
        1109–21.
Reinhardt, Nola
1988   *Our Daily Bread: The Peasant Question and Family Farm-
        ing in the Colombian Andes.* Berkeley: University of Califor-
        nia Press.
Renard, Marie-Christine
1999   The Interstices of Globalization: The Example of Fair Cof-
        fee. *Sociologia Ruralis* 39 (4): 484–500.
Rice, Robert A.
2001   Noble Goals and Challenging Terrain: Organic and Fair
        Trade Coffee Movements in the Global Marketplace.
        Journal of Agricultural and Environmental Ethics 14:
        39–66.

Rodriguez, Ennio
  1988   Comments. In *Development and External Debt in Latin America*, ed. Richard E. Feinberg and Ricardo Ffrench-Davis, 232–36. Notre Dame, Ind.: University of Notre Dame Press.
Rogers, Everett
  1969   *Modernization among Peasants*. New York: Holt, Rinehart, and Winston.
Rojas Vargas, Aracelley, et al.
  1978   *El café en el cantón de Pérez Zeledón años 1973–1977*. San Isidro de El General, Costa Rica: Universidad Nacional Sección Regional de Pérez Zeledón, Area de Humanidades.
Ronchi, Loraine
  2002   The Impact of Fair Trade on Producers and Their Organisations: A Case Study with Coocafé in Costa Rica. PRUS Working Paper No. 11. Poverty Research Unit at Sussex: University of Sussex.
Roseberry, William
  1983   *Coffee and Capitalism in the Venezuelan Andes*. Austin: University of Texas Press.
  1996   The Rise of Yuppie Coffees and the Reimagination of Class in the United States. *American Anthropologist* 98 (4): 762–75.
Roseberry, William, Lowell Gudmundson, and Mario Samper Kutschbach, eds.
  1995   *Coffee, Society, and Power in Latin America*. Baltimore: Johns Hopkins University Press.
Rostow, Walt Whitman
  1960   *The Stages of Economic Growth*. Cambridge: Cambridge University Press.
Rottenberg, Simon, ed.
  1993   *The Political Economy of Poverty, Equity, and Growth: Costa Rica and Uruguay*. World Bank Comparative Study. Oxford: Oxford University Press.
Rowe, John Wikenson Foster
  1963   *The World's Coffee: A Study of the Economics and Politics of the Coffee Industries of Certain Countries and of the International Problem*. London: Her Majesty's Stationery Office.
Samper, Mario
  1990   *Generations of Settlers: Rural Households and Markets on the Costa Rican Frontier, 1850–1935*. Boulder: Westview Press.
  1995   In Difficult Times: Colombian and Costa Rican Coffee Growers from Prosperity to Crisis, 1920–1936. In Roseberry, Gudmundson, and Kutschbach, 151–80.

Sanchez Salas, Porfirio
1986   Estimado de los costos de produccion de cafe en Costa
        Rica. Cosecha 1985–86. Instituto del Cafe de Costa Rica,
        Boletin Tecnico 37. San José, Costa Rica.
Schivelbusch, Wolfgang
1992   *Tastes of Paradise: A Social History of Spices, Stimulants, and In-
        toxicants.* Trans. David Jacobson. New York: Vintage Books.
Schmink, Marianne
1984   Household Economic Strategies. *Latin American Research
        Review* 19 (3): 87–101.
Scott, J. T., and Lehman B. Fletcher
1969   Cooperatives as Instruments of Market Reform: The Econo-
        mist's View. In *Agricultural Cooperatives and Markets in De-
        veloping Countries,* ed. Kurt R. Anschel, Russel H. Brannon,
        and Eldon D. Smith, 213–26. New York: Frederick A. Praeger.
Scott, James C.
1985   *Weapons of the Weak: Everyday Forms of Peasant Resistance.*
        New Haven, Conn.: Yale University Press.
Seligson, Mitchell
1980   *Peasants of Costa Rica and the Development of Agrarian
        Capitalism.* Madison: University of Wisconsin Press.
Sen, Amartya K.
1990   Gender and Cooperative Conflicts. In *Persistent Inequali-
        ties: Women and World Development,* ed. Irene Tinker,
        123–49. New York: Oxford University Press.
Shafer, D. Michael
1994   *Winners and Losers: How Sectors Shape the Developmental
        Prospects of States.* Ithaca, N.Y.: Cornell University Press.
Shah, A. M.
1988   The Phase of Dispersal in the Indian Family Process. *Socio-
        logical Bulletin* 37 (1): 33–47.
Shallat, Lezak
1989   AID and the Secret Parallel State. In *The Costa Rica
        Reader,* ed. Marc Edelman and Joanne Kenen, 221–27.
        New York: Grove Weidenfeld.
Sharpe, Kenneth
1977   *Peasant Politics: Struggle in a Dominican Village.* Baltimore:
        Johns Hopkins University Press.
Sheahan, John
1987   *Patterns of Development in Latin America: Poverty, Repres-
        sion, and Economic Strategy.* Princeton, N.J.: Princeton Uni-
        versity Press.

Sheridan, Thomas
  1988   *Where the Dove Calls.* Tucson: University of Arizona Press.
Shreck, Aimee
  2005   Resistance, Redistribution, and Power in the Fair Trade Banana Initiative. *Agriculture and Human Values* 22: 17–29.
Sick, Deborah
  1991   Preliminary Research in the Development Process: Reexamining a Case Study among the San Juan Southern Paiute. *Human Organization* 50 (4): 358–68.
Simpson, Charles, and A. Rapone
  2000   Community Development from the Ground Up: Social-Justice Coffee. *Human Ecology Review* 7 (1): 46–57..
Singh, Shamsher, Jos de Vries, John C. L. Hulley, and Patrick Yeung
  1977   *Coffee, Tea, and Cocoa: Market Prospects and Development Lending.* Baltimore: Johns Hopkins University Press.
Smith, Carol
  1984   Local History in Global Context: Social and Economic Transitions in Western Guatemala. *Comparative Studies in Sociology and History* 26: 193–228.
Smith, Gavin
  1989   *Livelihood and Resistance: Peasants and the Politics of Land in Peru.* Berkeley: University of California Press.
Smith, Joan, and Immanuel Wallerstein, eds.
  1978   *Creating and Transforming Households: The Constraints of the World-Economy.* Paris: Cambridge University Press.
Smith, Joan, Immanuel Wallerstein, and Hans-Dieter Evers, eds.
  1984   *Households and the World-Economy.* Beverly Hills, Calif.: Sage.
Smith, Sheldon, and Richard Smith
  1989   Horizontal and Vertical Linkages in Highland Antioquia, Colombia: The Architecture of the Landscape. In *Human Systems Ecology: Studies in the Integration of Political Economy, Adaptation, and Socionatural Regions,* ed. Sheldon Smith and Ed Reeves, 170–201. Boulder: Westview Press.
Spencer, C. C.
  1967   World Situation and Outlook for Coffee. In *Agricultural Producers and Their Markets,* ed. T. K. Warley. Oxford: Basil Blackwell.
Stone, Samuel
  1975   *La dinastía de los conquistadores: La crisis del poder en la Costa Rica contemporánea.* San José, Costa Rica: Editorial Universitaria Centroamericana.

1983   Production and Politics in Central America's Convulsions. *Journal of Latin American Studies* 15 (2): 453–69.

Stull, Donald, and Jean Schensul, eds.
1987   *Collaborative Research and Social Change.* Boulder: Westview Press.

Suarez, Luis A.
1953   Cooperatives in Puerto Rico: History, Problems, and Research. *Rural Sociology* 18 (1–4): 226–33.

Talbot, John M.
2004   *Grounds for Agreement: The Political Economy of the Coffee Commodity Chain.* Lanham, Md: Rowman & Littlefield.

Taylor, Peter L.
2005   In the Market But Not of It: Fair Trade Coffee and Forest Stewardship Council Certification as Market-Based Social Change. *World Development* 33 (1): 129–47.

Taylor, Peter L., D. Murray, and L. Raynolds
2005   Keeping Trade Fair: Governance Challenges in the Fair Trade Coffee Initiative. *Sustainable Development* 13: 199–208.

Tendler, Judith, with Kevin Healy and Carol O'Laughlin
1988   What to Think about Cooperatives: A Guide from Bolivia. In Annis and Hakim, 85–116.

Tice, Karin E.
1995   *Kuna Crafts, Gender, and the Global Economy.* Austin: University of Texas Press.

Tico Times (San José, Costa Rica) 5 April–22 November 1991, 8 May 1992.

Torres Rivas, Edelberto
1978   *Elementos para la caracterización de la estructura agrária de Costa Rica.* San José: Instituto de Investigaciones Sociales, University of Costa Rica.

1985   The Nature of the Central American Crisis. In *Towards an Alternative for Central America and the Caribbean,* ed. George Irvin and Xabier Gorostiaga, 38–53. London: George Allen and Unwin.

Transfair USA
2004   Fair Trade Coffee Price Review: The Way Forward. Transfair USA Press Release. <http://transfairusa.org/content/about/ppr_070123.php>. Accessed 25 April 2007.

2006   About Fair Trade. <http://www.transfair.ca/en/fairtrade>. Accessed 25 April 2007.

2007   Fair Trade Social Premium and Organic Differential for Coffee to Increase. Transfair USA Press Release. <http://transfairusa.org/content/about/pr_070321.php>. Accessed 25 April 2007.

United Nations
2006   Economic Survey of Latin America and the Caribbean 2005/06. ECLAC Publication. <http://www.eclac.cl/publicaciones/default.asp?idioma=IN>. Accessed 4 May 2007.

United Nations Development Programme (UNDP)
1991   *Human Development Report 1991*. New York: Oxford University Press.
1992   *Human Development Report 1992*. New York: Oxford University Press.
1995   *Human Development Report 1995*. New York: Oxford University Press.
2003   *Human Development Report 2003*. New York: United Nations Development Programme
2005   *Human Development Report 2005*. New York: United Nations Development Programme
2006   *Human Development Report 2006*. New York: United Nations Development Programme.

United States Bureau of Public Affairs (USBPA)
2007   Background Note: Costa Rica. Bureau of Western Hemisphere Affairs. <http://www.state.gov/r/pa/ei/bgn/2019.htm>. Accessed 5 May.

Utting-Chamorro, Karla
2005   Does Fair Trade Make a Difference? The Case of Small Coffee Producers in Nicaragua. *Development in Practice* 15 (3&4): 584–600.

Vakil, C. N., and P. R. Brahmanand
1963   Technical Knowledge and Managerial Capacity as Limiting Factors on Industrial Expansion in Under-Developed Countries. In *Social Change and Economic Development*, ed. Jean Meynaud, 164–69. Leiden: Sijthoff.

Van den Berghe, Pierre L., and Karl Peters
1988   Hutterites and Kibbutzniks: A Tale of Nepotistic Communism. *Man* 23 (3): 522–39.

Varangis, Panos, Paul Siegel, Danielle Giovannucci, and Bryan Lewin
2003   Dealing with the Coffee Crisis in Central America: Impacts and Strategies. Policy Research Working Paper 2993. World Bank Development Research Group. Washington, D.C.: World Bank.

Villasuso Etomba, Juan
1989   The Impact of the Economic Crisis on Income Distribution. In *The Costa Rica Reader*, ed. Marc Edelman and Joanne Kenen, 197–203. New York: Grove Weidenfeld.

Wade, Robert
1990 *Governing the Market: Economic Theory and the Role of Government in East Asian Industrialization.* Princeton, N.J.: Princeton University Press.
Wadley, Susan S.
1994 *Struggling with Destiny in Karimpur, 1925–1984.* Berkeley: University of California Press.
Wallerstein, Immanuel
1979 *The Capitalist World-Economy.* Cambridge: Cambridge University Press.
Wayne, Anthony
2004 U.S. Determined to Aid Sustainable World Coffee Production. Op-ed by U.S. Assistant Secretary of State. <http://usinfo.state.gov/xarchives/display.html>. Accessed 20 June 2007.
Weeks, John
1985 *The Economies of Central America.* New York: Homes and Meier.
Wharton, Clifton, Jr.
1971 Risk and the Subsistence Farmer. In *Studies in Economic Anthropology,* ed. Paul J. Bohannan, 152–79. Washington, D.C.: American Anthropological Association.
White, Sarah C.
1992 *Arguing with the Crocodile: Gender and Class in Bangladesh.* London: Zed Books.
Wilk, Richard R.
1989 Decision Making and Resource Flows within the Household: Beyond the Black Box. In Wilk, ed., 23–52.
1991 *Household Ecology: Economic Change and Domestic Life among the Kekchi Maya in Belize.* Tucson: University of Arizona Press.
Wilk, Richard R., ed.
1989 *The Household Economy: Reconsidering the Domestic Mode of Production.* Boulder: Westview Press.
Wilk, Richard, and Robert McC. Netting
1984 Households: Changing Form and Function. In *Households: Comparative and Historical Studies of the Domestic Group,* ed. Robert McC. Netting, Richard R. Wilk, and Eric J. Arnould, 1–28. Berkeley: University of California Press.
Williams, Robert G.
1994 *States and Social Evolution: Coffee and the Rise of National Governments in Central America.* Chapel Hill: University of North Carolina Press.

Williamson, Oliver E.
1975   *Markets and Hierarchies: Analysis and Antitrust Implications.* New York: Free Press.
Winson, Anthony
1984   Confronting the Coffee Oligarchy: The Roots of Costa Rica's "Middle Road." *Canadian Journal of Latin American and Caribbean Studies* 9 (17): 33–50.
1989   *Coffee and Democracy in Modern Costa Rica.* Toronto: Between the Lines.
Wolf, Eric R.
1956   San José: Subcultures of a "Traditional" Coffee Municipality. In *The People of Puerto Rico,* Julian Steward, Robert Manners, Eric Wolf, Elena Podilla Seda, Sidney Mintz, and Raymond Scheele, 171–264. Urbana: University of Illinois Press.
Wood, William Warner
1996   Teotitlan del Valle: A Maquiladora in Oaxaca, Mexico. Paper presented at the ninety-fifth annual meeting of the American Anthropological Association, San Francisco, 20–24 November.
Woodward, Ralph Lee
1987   Central America. In *Spanish America after Independence c.1820–c.1870,* ed. Leslie Bethell, 171–206. Cambridge: Cambridge University Press.
World Bank
1978   *World Development Report, 1978.* Washington, D.C.: World Bank.
1990   Policy Responses to the Collapse of World Coffee Prices: The Cases of Costa Rica, Mexico and El Salvador. World Bank Report no. 8311-LAC. Washington, D.C.
2006   Costa Rica at a Glance. <http://devdata.worldbank.org/AAG/cri_aag.pdf>. Accessed 30 April 2007.
2007a   Costa Rica Data Profile. Key Development Data and Statistics. <http://devdata.worldbank.org>. Accessed 25 April.
2007b   Costa Rica Country Brief. <http://devdata.worldbank.org>. Accessed 25 April.
Worsley, Peter
1971   Introduction to *Two Blades of Grass,* ed. Peter Worsley, 1–42. Manchester: Manchester University Press.

Index

Alliance for Progress, 31
Alternative trade (AT), 134, 139
Alternative Trade Organizations (ATOs). *See* Alternative trade
Appadurai, Arjun, 9
ACPC (Association of Coffee Producing Countries), 16, 128

Beneficios (coffee-processing factories), 26–27; control of, 27–28; and credit, 97–98; competition among, 90, 92; in Pérez Zeledón, 37, 39, 90; relations with farmers, 26, 30, 76, 100–102, 126. *See also* Coffee: prices, farmer
Brazil, 7, 12, 14, 134

Cacao, 22
Catholicism. *See* Religion
Cattle, 111–12
Cazanga S., Jose, 32
Central America. *See names of individual countries;* Export agriculture, in Central America
Central American Common Market, 8
CEPN, 30
Coffee: consumption, 8–10, 129; historical development in Central America, 23–24; prices, farmer, 26, 28, 92, 97; prices, international, 15, 90–91, 105, 107, 128, 133, 145; quality of, 11, 29, 90–91, 129; sustainable, 143–47; taxation of in Costa Rica, 27, 28, 126; varieties of, 11, 14. *See also* Coffee, international market; Coffee processing; Coffee production
Coffee cooperatives. *See* Cooperatives
Coffee international market, xiv, 12–16, 90, 128–29; crisis in, xiv, xv–xvi, 132, 133–34, 148; differentiation in, 134, 145, 148–49
Coffee processing, 11, 26, 90. *See also Beneficios*
Coffee production, 10–11; costs of, 105–6, 113; harvesting, 57–59; labor requirements in, 52–53; organic, 106–7; organization of, 67–69; technical requirements of, 10, 26–27, 59, 107
Colombia, 13, 26, 61, 108
Commodity markets. *See* Export agriculture; Markets, commodity
Community development organizations, 41, 75, 84–88, 126
Coope Montes de Oro, xxi, 142, 145–46

Lightning Source UK Ltd.
Milton Keynes UK
UKHW041036031019
350630UK00042B/134/P